Bringing History to Life

Lucy Calkins and Anna Gratz Cockerille

Photography by Peter Cunningham

HEINEMANN ◆ PORTSMOUTH, NH

This book is dedicated to Michael and Cheryl, who began my history, and to James, who completes it. —Anna

This book is dedicated to Molly Feeney, teacher extraordinaire, who shows us what's possible. —Lucy

DEDICATED TO TEACHERS™

*first*hand
An imprint of Heinemann
361 Hanover Street
Portsmouth, NH 03801–3912
www.heinemann.com

Offices and agents throughout the world

© 2013 by Lucy Calkins and Anna Gratz Cockerille

The authors and publisher wish to thank those who have generously given permission to reprint borrowed material:

Excerpts from *The Revolutionary War* by Josh Gregory, Children's Press, 2011. Copyright © 2012 Scholastic Inc. All rights reserved. Used by permission of Children's Press an imprint of Scholastic Library Publishing, Inc.

Cataloging-in-Publication data is on file with the Library of Congress.

ISBN-13: 978-0-325-04738-6
ISBN-10: 0-325-04738-3

Production: Elizabeth Valway, David Stirling, and Abigail Heim
Cover and interior designs: Jenny Jensen Greenleaf
Series includes photographs by Peter Cunningham, Nadine Baldasare, and Elizabeth Dunford
Composition: Publishers' Design and Production Services, Inc.
Manufacturing: Steve Bernier

Printed in the United States of America on acid-free paper
17 16 15 14 13 VP 2 3 4 5

Acknowledgments

THIS BOOK BROKE NEW GROUND in many ways. We are grateful to the architects of the Common Core, because their leadership made it especially imperative that we wrestle with the content that we bring to you in this book. We're grateful for their effort to rally teachers and school leaders to think seriously about content literacy and to prioritize writing instruction.

The new thinking that led to this book would not have been possible without the thought leadership of several people at the Reading and Writing Project, including Mary Ehrenworth and Kathleen Tolan. When it was clear that one of the first iterations of the book needed to be rethought, Mary stepped in as a sounding board and advisor, she helped us imagine a new approach. Kathleen has led the Project's content literacy work and, for the past several years, has been one of the lead people helping us develop a branch of our curriculum that embeds our best literacy practices into the content areas. Many of the ideas in this book stem from the work of think tanks that Kathleen has led.

Hareem Atif Kahn stepped in toward the later stages of the process and was instrumental in helping us think through the final bend. It was she who helped us make sure that the unit supported fourth-graders to grow deep interpretations of the stories of history. Jasmine Junsay was an enormous help to the unit—conducting research, helping with Getting Ready sections, and in general lending her excellent organizational skills and attention to detail. Colleen Cruz has been instrumental in supporting the Project's advancing work in informational writing in the upper grades. She offered ideas and insights that enriched several parts of this unit, contributing especially to sessions in the first and second bends.

We are grateful for the work of Felicia O'Brien, our content editor. She helped us cross our *t*'s and dot our *i*'s and made many wise suggestions that helped bring the unit to the best version of itself.

Kate Montgomery, the lead editor and coleader of the entire series, has been invaluable to this book. She acted as an advisor, a writer, a cheerleader, a coach, and an editor. Her unending wisdom and support of every step of our process has made the work possible.

We owe a debt of gratitude to the teachers who have helped us develop our thinking about information writing and research. Those teachers work in a diverse range of communities, and have all contributed in important ways to this work. Most of all, we are thankful to Molly Feeney Wood and her fourth-grade class at PS 199 in Manhattan. We were awed by Molly and her students' generosity and willingness to try anything and everything we threw at them. The work of those students and Molly's insights are deeply imprinted in this book. Additionally, we'd like to thank the fourth-grade teachers at PS 107 in Brooklyn and the upper-grade team at Leschi Elementary in Seattle, including Sereatha Brooks, Rina Kido, Tamikya St. Clair, and Katy Pence. Thanks as well to Liz Dunford and the kids at PS 189 in the Bronx for their willingness to lend a hand in the book's final moments.

Finally, there has been a whole team of people at Heinemann who have made the book into a reality. Teva Blair, lead editor, has devoted every waking minute to this project for eighteen months, and her leadership has been especially critical. We're grateful, too, for the extraordinary efforts and leadership that Charles McQuillen and Buzz Rhodes will play in bringing this book and the others into the world.

The class described in this unit is a composite class, gleaned from classrooms in very different contexts. We wrote the units this way to bring you both a wide array of wonderful, quirky, various children and also to illustrate for you the predictable (and unpredictable) situations and responses this unit has created in classrooms across the nation and world.

Contents

Acknowledgments • iii

Welcome to the Unit • vi

Bend I Informational Books: Making a Conglomerate of Forms

1. Getting the Sense of Informational Books • 2

In this session, you'll teach students that writers imagine the text they are going to make. They think about the parts and the whole and then come up with a plan for their writing project.

2. Planning the Structure of Writing • 14

In this session, you'll teach students that writers of information texts make a plan for the structure of their writing and then use this structure to organize research and note-taking.

3. Planning and Writing with Greater Independence • 22

In this session, you'll remind students that writers take strategies they've learned in the past and apply them to new situations, working with more independence and skill each time.

4. Teaching as a Way to Rehearse for Information Writing • 30

In this session, you'll teach students that when writing to teach, it helps writers to do some actual teaching about their topic.

5. Elaboration: The Details that Let People Picture What Happened Long Ago and Far Away • 38

In this session, you'll teach students that writers improve their writing by adding details. History writers often try to include details that help readers picture what happened long ago.

6. Bringing Information Alive: Stories inside Nonfiction Texts • 47

In this session, you'll teach students that writers who are writing a story about a time in history think about the three most important elements in any story: character, setting, and conflict.

7. Essays within Information Texts • 56

In this session, you'll teach students that when writers are writing essays about historical topics, they think about all they know about essay writing: the structure, the thesis, and the supports. They also need to do research to find facts to develop and support their idea.

8. Taking Stock and Setting Goals: A Letter to Teachers • 67

In this session, you could teach students that writers step back from their writing to reflect on how they are doing, asking themselves, "What have I accomplished as a writer and what do I still need to work on?"

Bend II Writing with Greater Independence

9. Writers Plan for Their Research • 76

In this session, you'll remind students that when tackling a new piece of informational writing, nonfiction writers come up with a research plan.

10. The Intense Mind-Work of Note-Taking • 87

In this session, you'll teach students that note-taking is not the easy part of research writing. When writers take notes, they need to understand what they are writing well enough that they are able to explain their notes to someone else.

11. Drafting Is Like Tobogganing: First the Preparation, the Positioning . . . Then the Whooosh! • 97

In this session, you could remind students that writers draw on all they know as information writers to draft new information books.

12. Developing a Logical Structure Using Introductions and Transitions • 102

In this session, you'll remind students that when writing an informational text, writers need to organize information. In an introduction, writers let readers in on their organizational plan.

13. Text Features: Popping Out the Important Information • 113

In this session, you'll teach students that writers think about the most important information and ideas that they're trying to convey in a chapter or a section, and they use text features to highlight that information.

14. Quotations Accentuate Importance: Voices Chime In to Make a Point • 124

In this session, you'll teach students that history writers add quotations to their writing to accentuate a central idea.

15. Using All We Know to Craft Essay and Narrative Sections • 135

In this session, you could teach students that writers often draw on what they know about other genres, including narrative, essay, and how-to writing, to craft chapters for their information books in the style and form of those genres.

16. The Other Side of the Story • 140

In this session, you'll teach students that history writers need to remember and address more than one side of a story.

17. Self-Assessment and Goal Setting: Taking on New Challenges • 151

In this session, you could remind students that writers reflect on how much they have grown as writers, especially when they are about to take on new and challenging work, so they can set new goals for this upcoming work.

BEND III   Building Ideas in Informational Writing

18. Information Writing Gives Way to Idea Writing • 156

In this session, you'll teach students that history writers write and develop their own ideas about the information that they find as they research.

19. Digging Deeper: Interpreting the Life Lessons that History Teaches • 164

In this session, you'll teach students that history writing is not just made from facts but also from ideas. History writers convey larger ideas about a people, a nation, and a time. As they write they ask themselves, "What life lessons might this be teaching?" and write about them.

20. Using Confusions to Guide Research • 172

In this session, you'll teach students that nonfiction writers don't always start out as experts on the topic they're writing about, but instead work to become short-term experts on their topic. They start with their musings, then turn these into research questions, and then see what they can learn.

21. Questions without a Ready Answer • 183

In this session, you'll teach students that historians don't always find answers to every question they have. But they can use all of their research and knowledge to create possible answers to questions for which people can't find ready-made answers.

22. Editing • 192

In this session, you could remind students that writers edit their writing to make sure it is ready for readers.

23. A Final Celebration: An Expert Fair • 197

In this session, you could teach students that information writers share their writing with an audience, teaching their audience all they have learned about their topic.

Welcome to the Unit

JEROME BRUNER ONCE SAID, "Experience over the past decade points to the fact that our schools may be wasting precious years by postponing the teaching of many important subjects on the grounds that they are too difficult . . . The foundations of any subject may be taught to anybody at any age in some form." (*The Process of Education* 1976, 76.)

In this unit, you bring your fourth-graders squarely into the rigors of academic life. You help them dive deep into the project of writing research reports, writing not one but two reports during the unit. The students write about the American Revolution in the unit, but the curriculum is designed so that it can be adapted to apply to other history-based units as well. As part of their research, they wrestle with citations, primary documents, conflicting views on a subject, and with the challenge of incorporating and synthesizing information of all sorts into logically structured chapters. That is, you teach the foundations of research report writing to your students.

You could decide to fend off academic pressures for as long as possible, showing your fourth-graders small ways to ramp up their third-grade work, but in this unit, you do the opposite. You bring students headlong into this invigorating work. And, most importantly, you explicitly teach students, step by step, what they need to know to rise to this challenge. Before long, students will be assigned to write research reports and sent off to the library and to their homes. Their teachers will signal, "It's up to you. Sink or swim." You instead get into the deep water with your kids and give them a hand. You stay involved at every step along the way, demonstrating, scaffolding, and guiding. You help students succeed first with text-based information writing that is fairly accessible, and then you ratchet things up a notch. This time you remind them to draw on what they already know, and you help with the especially new and demanding aspects of the work. In that way, you move students along, step by step, toward proficiency.

Most units begin with you providing lots of scaffolding and in the end have you remove the scaffolds and say to kids, "Go to it! Proceed with more independence." This unit, instead, keeps the scaffolds in place and brings students to more and more challenging work. It will be your job, after the unit is over, to teach a second cycle of this work, bringing all that students did to write these research reports to a new topic, this time saying to youngsters, "Go to it! You know how to organize a research report. You know how to incorporate citations, to build a logical structure, to use text features to highlight your central idea, to . . . go to it!"

OVERVIEW OF THE UNIT

At the start of the unit, you'll remind students of what they know about writing a basic, boxes-and-bullets information text, and then they'll draw on this to write two information chapters, starting with one on the more accessible and general topic, "all about the American Revolution," and then progressing to one on a more focused topic. The expectation is that students will be bringing with them all they know about information writing from previous years and that their work in this portion of the unit will meet the big requirements of the third-grade Common Core State Standards (CCSS). For example, they should be able to introduce a topic and group related information (W.3.2a) and then develop the topic, elaborating with some facts, definitions, and details (W.3.2b).

Students will select those more focused topics, but one of the ways that you scaffold them in this work is to strongly encourage them to select topics the class has studied together. This is a writing unit, and most of the class time is spent writing, rather than researching, so this makes it especially important for students to rely on research they have already done, when possible.

Students tend to select topics such as the Boston Tea Party and the Boston Massacre. As students write all about these topics, you'll help them to transfer and apply all they learned in third grade. You'll also help by providing them with a mentor text that is not one written by an adult author but, instead, is one written by a student from a previous year.

All in all, this means that just as earlier in the year, fourth-graders began their essay work with a spirited boot camp in which the whole class worked together to compose an essay in defense of ice cream, your students will now be given lots of help writing first an overview about the American Revolution. As they write these overviews, you will immediately begin to steer them toward some of the new work they are expected to do as fourth-grade information writers according to the CCSS. You will teach them more sophisticated ways to organize their writing, such as including formatting such as headings and subheadings (W.4.2a), and to include information that is rich, detailed, and concrete (W.4.2b).

You'll also help them learn that information texts are often conglomerates, containing a lot of other kinds of texts. This means that a research report on the American Revolution might contain a few all-about chapters, a how-to chapter (maybe "How to Protect Your Home from the British"), and an essay (perhaps "The American Revolution Has Shaped American History"). Such a nonfiction book could contain stories as well (maybe "The Day of the First Shot Fired"). The first bend in the road of the unit ends with students completing a small book in which each chapter is written as a different genre.

In the second bend of the unit, students will narrow in on a subtopic of their choice—with some students continuing to research their original topic. Fourth grade is the first level in the Common Core in which students are expected to draw evidence from texts to support analysis, reflection, and research (W.4.9). This bend in the unit provides an opportunity for students to do just that, in a way that is carefully scaffolded and guided. Again, students will learn to choose a logical structure for their books. In this portion of the unit, because students are working on subtopics of their own choosing, they'll rely on their knowledge and their research. They'll continue to be explicitly taught the skills of effective research writing. They'll learn to use increasingly sophisticated transition words and phrases in a purposeful way (W.4.2c) and to clarify and bring out the structure in their writing (W.4.2a). They'll move toward the challenging expectations of the Common Core regarding elaboration in fourth grade as they learn how to present important information through the use of historical details, text features, and quotations. A

main thread that weaves throughout this bend is highlighting importance. Students will learn to make logical choices about structure to help readers to understand the most important information in their pieces. In doing so, they'll begin to move toward the fifth-grade expectations of the Common Core regarding structure (W.5.2a). They'll also learn that text features, when created thoughtfully, can help to underscore the main message of a piece of writing, as can a writer's thoughtful decisions about the kinds of vocabulary words to include (W.4.2d and W.5.2d).

Bend III takes this work to an entirely new level as students move from organizing information to developing their own ideas about the information. This bend is all about historical interpretation, very heady work for fourth-graders, but work for which they have been aptly prepared throughout not only this unit of study but the entire school year. Their research will take on a new bent as they generate life lessons from their topics, generate questions, and then hypothesize and research answers to those questions. This work is directly in line with the Common Core's expectation that fourth- and fifth-grade writers embark on investigations of a topic (W.4.7 and W.5.7) and is carefully scaffolded in such a way that it feels approachable for students trying it for perhaps the first time. Of course, as students take on this work, they are reaching not only for the Common Core State Standards in *writing*, but in *reading* as well. They are considering themes and lessons, (R.L4.2), considering different points of view (R.I4.6), and integrating information from texts in a way that feels purposeful and organic (R.I4.9). As always, students will spend time editing their writing before publication, this time with a focus on the unique way that historical writers use punctuation. The unit will culminate with an expert fair, at which students will be given the opportunity to teach others all they have learned about their topic.

ASSESSMENT

Our expectation is that at the start of the year, you will have assessed your students as information writers, and we assume their information writing has grown stronger since then, because work in one type of writing enriches what students can do in other types of writing. Also, presumably your students will have done some writing and a lot of reading of information texts outside of writing workshop in the content areas. If you did conduct an assessment at the start of the year, you'll be able to track the progress students have made from then until now in information writing.

In any case, we recommend that just before launching this unit, you spend one class period conducting another on-demand information writing assessment. Ideally, you will use the same prompt and same conditions as before, and the same as other teachers, so that the products your writers produce will be comparable. On the day before the assessment, you can let your students know that you will be conducting the assessment so that they can be prepared. Say to them:

> "Think of a topic that you've studied or that you know a lot about. Tomorrow, you will have forty-five minutes to write an informational (or all-about) text that teaches others interesting and important information and ideas about that topic. If you want to find and use information from a book or another outside source to help you with this writing, you may bring that with you tomorrow. Please keep in mind that you'll have only forty-five minutes to complete this. You will have only this one period, so you'll need to plan, draft, revise, and edit in one sitting. Write in a way that shows all that you know about information writing."

Of course, you'll say this again, right before the assessment, and then you'll provide forty-five minutes for writing. Don't worry if your students do not bring source information. They do not need to do so to be at standard for fourth grade. This clause (and some others like it) is part of the prompt simply because the prompt needs to be consistent for K–8 students, and some portions of the prompt become important for middle school students. When students actually do the on-demand writing, you will want to add:

"In your writing, make sure you:
- Write an introduction
- Elaborate with a variety of information
- Organize your writing
- Use transition words
- Write a conclusion"

Once your students have completed this task, you'll want to use the information writing checklists to study their work. By this point in the year, you will expect to see that most of your students demonstrate that they have mastered most of the big work of the third-grade expectations outlined by the checklists and the third-grade Common Core State Standards and some of the fourth-grade standards as well. That is, you may find that many of your students already introduce their topic, group related information together, and provide some elaboration, which means some will already be doing much of the work of the fourth-grade standards. This assessment, however, comes at the start of this unit, so if your students are performing solidly at the third-grade level, that should not be a cause for concern.

If your students are, for the most part, doing work that is more closely aligned to the second-grade standards, level 2 of the Information Writing Learning Progression, you may want to teach another information writing unit prior to embarking on this one. If one of your colleagues in the school has *The Art of Information Writing,* the third-grade book from this series, and is not using it at this point, you could borrow that book and teach a variation of that unit. The *If . . . Then . . . Curriculum* book provides other options.

Most teachers who have done the on-demand assessment have been pleasantly surprised by how much students bring into this unit of study and by the volume of writing students are able to produce in just one day's writing workshop. The work that students produce in the on-demand situation becomes the baseline, and you can increase expectations as the unit progresses.

Early on, we recommend that you introduce your class to the checklists that they will use to study their work throughout the unit. From the other units of study, your fourth-graders will already be familiar with how to use these checklists. By providing this opportunity to preview what will be expected of them, you allow your students to begin to visualize final products and to reach for lofty goals right from the start. You may even take some class time for your students to study their on-demand writing with the checklist in hand and to set a few preliminary goals for their work. Throughout the unit, you will channel students to study their work, thus providing them the opportunity to celebrate their progress and set new goals to ensure they are continually outgrowing themselves as writers.

GETTING READY

Because this unit has a research component, you will need to spend some time beforehand collecting engaging, appropriately leveled materials on the topic you are studying. On the CD-ROM, you will find a bibliography of online and print sources at various reading levels that you can use to support the work of this unit if you go along with our choice of topic, the American Revolution.

This unit has been designed so that it follows a social studies unit. That is, if your students are going to use the writing workshop to write about the

Revolutionary War, they need to have already studied that topic during social studies time. If you want to teach this unit, and your students do not have that prior knowledge base, one of your options is to take a different social studies unit and to infuse it into this unit. That is, the students could be writing about Ancient Egypt instead of the American Revolution. A switch like that will increase the amount of work you need to do because you'll need to find your own articles, write your own examples, and so forth, but this is all entirely possible. The other option is to teach this social studies unit, at least for a week, prior to embarking on this unit, and then during the unit to allow there to be double periods for English and social studies.

The unit is designed so that you need not have taught a stellar unit on the American Revolution prior to this work. However, there is no question but that the more your students know about the topic, the richer their learning and their writing will be. So yes, ideally, leading up to the launch of the unit, you will teach your children a lot about the topic of study so they'll begin on Day One with lots and lots to say. If you can flood your children with images and stories about the time period, their writing will be much richer. You might want to set up each child with a social studies folder and have them decorate the covers with a picture of themselves as a historian or person of the time period. Alternatively, perhaps kids will collect their learning in a tabbed section in their already-established social studies notebook or writer's notebook. In any case, the more information your students are able to collect beforehand, the better equipped they'll be to stock their reports with rich elaboration without having to constantly interrupt writing to seek out information. As they become experts, they'll be eager to share what they've learned and the ideas they have about all the new information.

Most teachers find that mentor texts can be powerful coteachers in any writing unit. This is especially true in information writing, when clear examples of structure, elaboration, and other hallmarks of the genre will be key. For this unit, we recommend *The Revolutionary War* by Josh Gregory, the book that comes in the trade book pack that is sold alongside this series, and we provide tips for how best to use this text throughout the unit.

Examples of particularly helpful kinds of sources you'll find on the CD-ROM are:

- A list of trade books on the American Revolution—especially *Liberty! How the Revolutionary War Began* by Lucille Recht Penner, *The Eve of the Revolution* by Barbara Burt, and books by Jean Fritz, such as *What's the Big Idea, Ben Franklin?* and *Can't You Make Them Behave, King George?*

- Internet sites for video resources related to the American Revolution

- Primary sources related to the American Revolution

- Bookmarked kid-friendly Internet search engines

Meanwhile, we hope you have colleagues who will be teaching this unit alongside you and that you set up a schedule of times to share. There will be lots to talk about!

Getting the Sense of Informational Books

IN THIS SESSION, you'll teach students that writers imagine the text they are going to make. They think about the parts and the whole and then come up with a plan for their writing project.

GETTING READY

✔ A list of topics your children know well related to the class topic of focus. The topic we use is the Revolutionary War (see Connection).

✔ Copies of a mentor historical information book, written by a fourth-grader, one copy for you and enough copies for students to study in groups of two to four (see Teaching and Active Engagement) ⊛

✔ A piece of chart paper with a list of questions to guide students in studying a mentor text (see Teaching and Active Engagement)

✔ Post-it notes and paper clips (see Link)

✔ Your own writer's notebook, set up for note-taking (see Link)

✔ "Possible Sections of an Informational Book" chart (see Mid-Workshop Teaching)

✔ "Getting Ready to Write an Informational Book" chart (see Mid-Workshop Teaching)

COMMON CORE STATE STANDARDS: W.4.2, W.4.4, W.4.5, W.4.8, RI.4.3, RI.4.5, SL.4.1, SL.4.2, SL.4.3, SL.4.4, L.4.1, L.4.2, L.4.3, L.4.6

I F YOU'VE EVER PICKED UP A CLUSTER-LIKE ROCK from a riverbed or from a turbulent shore, you may have noticed its conglomerate structure. This kind of rock is made of a variety of pebbles—of quartz perhaps, or chert or maybe limestone—bound together in a matrix of sand and clay. The one single rock is made up of distinct mineral parts, each tumbled into rounded clasts and then melded together through compaction or chemical processes. This structure—differently structured parts bound into one whole—is also the structure of many informational texts.

Look at informational writing within your reach right now, perhaps a website or a feature article or a nonfiction picture book. With only a few samples, you will see parts of the text structured like a story, parts structured like lists of reasons or consequences, parts structured like a summary or a synthesis of complicated events. You will see captions, labels, and subheadings, as well as fictionalizations of events. Information writing is not one kind of mineral through and through; it's a conglomerate form of text. Building these quirky texts full of a variety of forms is the work of this bright new unit.

Your children come to this unit having written both narratives, in the first unit of the year, and essays, in the second unit. Now they'll take these forms, and you will teach them some new structures of writing that are even more particular to informational texts. Then, perhaps most importantly, you'll teach children ways to bind these forms together sensibly, under the force of their topic. In the forming of a conglomerate rock, the clubbing of the various types of rocks may occur quite rapidly, depending on the conditions. The filling of the interstitial spaces between these casts, however, may take years. So too, the filling of the interstitial spaces in informational writing, the binding of the pieces of writing together for one coherent purpose, will take time, and care.

In this session, you will start on this process by helping children choose a writing topic, quickly, from a subject they have studied in Social Studies. We've chosen the Revolutionary War as that subject, but tried to write the unit so that you could apply it to another topic the children have studied. Then, you'll teach children ways writers prepare to write in a new genre: by studying texts like those they will write, by preparing the tools they'll use to catch their early ideas and notes, and by talking aloud with partners about what they are planning to do and about how the writing may go. By the end of the session, children will have an idea of how to get started writing what might be their first historical information book.

"Information writing is . . . a conglomerate form of text. Building these quirky texts full of a variety of forms is the work of this unit."

Notice that each day of this unit, you give students a homework assignment. Chances are good that by this time in fourth grade, your students are ready to do significant amounts of homework, but if you prefer to give them time outside the writing workshop during the school day to do this work, that is your decision. Some of the homework is essential to the upcoming lesson; some of it is not. We've starred the homework that we think is especially significant. You should also make sure that your writing center is fully stocked with Post-it notes, paper clips, note cards, and any other materials that your students have come to know as useful tools for research. It will also be important that your students come to the minilesson each day with their writer's notebooks, notes, and a writing tool.

Getting the Sense of Informational Books

CONNECTION

Explain that to create anything, people often begin by imagining the end. It will be important for the students to imagine the historical information books they're going to write.

"The great American poet, Lucille Clifton, once gave me some advice. She said, 'We cannot create what we cannot imagine. Nurture your image of what's possible.' And I do think it helps to be able to imagine whatever it is you want to create. Athletes know this. You imagine the ball spiraling, just as you want it to go, before you throw the pass. It is the same for writers.

"Today, we start a unit on writing historical information books, and we're going to write a book during each of the first two bends of this unit. That's a lot of writing! It will help if you start the unit by imagining the sort of thing you're going to write."

Coach children into choosing a topic quickly by advising them to follow their interests. Offer parameters (so that the teaching you plan will work for the topics they choose).

"To start imagining the book you will write, you need to have your topic in mind. I know you have been thinking about the topic and that you know we'll be writing out of the unit we have just completed on the Revolutionary War. I'm going to ask you to make your final choice in just a minute so that you can get started writing that book.

"Here is the thing about choosing the topic. It is easy to do. Your topic, really, chooses you. Your topic is the thing you know about and the thing you can tell others about. It interests you enough that you want to learn more about it. In your writing, you are going to make history come alive, so your topic might be a person (like Thomas Jefferson or Paul Revere) or a group of people (like the patriots, or Continental soldiers) and an event, combined. So your topic could be George Washington and the troops' experience at Valley Forge. Or Paul Revere and his historic ride. Or it could be simply an event, like the Boston Massacre. Right now, call to mind a few possible topics."

The connection in this minilesson carries a greater workload than most connections. You'll soon move on toward helping students choose a topic for their first research project. The reason we are doing this in the connection is that in a few minutes, students will be thinking about the form of the books they are going to be writing—and that sort of thinking will be vastly more helpful to them if they are marrying a sense of form with their anticipated topic. In any case, because we decided to channel students to choose their topic during the connection, the initial drumroll for the unit needs to be a bit abbreviated.

You can alter the content focus of this unit and still follow most of it without much trouble. That is, your students could be writing about the settling of America or the colonies, or the Civil War rather than the Revolutionary War and the battle for independence. In the next bend of the unit, some students write about The Making of a New Nation, so you will see that topic is given some attention in this unit.

The truth is that choosing a topic is not always so easy to do. But in an instance like this, the youngsters don't have endless choices. They need to choose a topic about which they know enough history that they can focus on some of the writing challenges.

I left a moment of silence. "Choose something that you have read about and talked about, so you have something to say," I coached, and again let the room grow silent. "There are probably only a handful of topics that most of you, in this class, know well, so many of you will be probably be choosing":

Ask children to discuss their initial topic choice with a partner. Model weighing one topic against another, then ask children to discuss their topic choice with a partner again.

"Turn and talk with your partner. What are you thinking?"

I listened as the children talked, and soon recognized some had other topics in mind. "I'm hearing topics other than the ones on our list," I said, and soon the list had grown:

- The Delegates and the Continental Congress
- The Surrender at Yorktown
- The Battles of Lexington and Concord

"I'm trying to decide between the Boston Massacre, the midnight ride, and George Washington and Valley Forge," I said. "I know the Boston Massacre would be great to write about because we have read and talked so much about it, and we even have a film about it. Knowing all that will *really* help me write with detail, like telling about the ways the colonists were taunting the soldiers. And if I wrote about the midnight ride, I'd get to tell the whole story, that it wasn't just Paul Revere who risked his life to warn the patriots that the British were coming. But I am also interested in George Washington at Valley Forge. I think he tried to help his army stay determined, even though they were freezing and starving. Also, we've talked about that as one of the war's turning points, so that makes it interesting. What about you? Are some of you having a hard time deciding too?"

Milo said, "I'm thinking about the Boston Tea Party. Could I put in the reasons they were mad at the British—like, the stuff leading up to the Tea Party?"

"Absolutely. You know things about that, right? It is wise to think about what you know, and what you could learn quickly—like if there is a book you like on the topic, and you are thinking you could take it home tonight, that might make for a good topic. You also want to choose something that is interesting to you. For example, I know a few of you have been talking about the way Washington led his army—you were putting some heart into your ideas about that topic, and that makes it a powerful topic.

The Revolutionary War: Possible Topics

- The Boston Tea Party
- The Boston Massacre
- Paul Revere and Midnight Ride
- Betsy Ross and First Flag
- TJ and Declaration of Indep.
- GW and major event in war (Valley Forge, Crossing Delaware, Trenton, etc.)
- Delegates and Continental Congress
- Surrender at Yorktown
- Battles of Lexington & Concord

The reason for doing this—brooding over several possible topics, aloud—is that this helps students to consider those topics. This is a subtle form of scaffolding, and I've chosen some of the most popular topics for the kids because I'm intending for my writing to support their writing. You may decide your kids know the topic well enough that they don't need this scaffolding. We've tried to write this book so that it will help students who may have gone through a fairly typical three-week-long, not the most intensive, history unit. Although, of course, the more they know about the topic the more ready they will be for this unit.

"Okay, turn and tell your partner what you are choosing. Put your thumb up once you have made a choice. I'm hoping some of you get onto one of the topics I'm considering!"

The room buzzed, with many children touting topics. Some seemed unsure, which I noted but didn't address.

Remind children that to create anything, people often begin by imagining the end.

"Great! Now you all have your topics. Writers, earlier I quoted Lucille Clifton who said, 'You cannot create what you cannot imagine.' I told you that athletes know that. A quarterback imagines the ball spiraling to the receiver in the end zone before it leaves his fingertips. The architect knows this as well. She creates the new building first on paper, thinking about the dimensions of each room, the way the parts will fit into the whole, before anyone begins carting in the lumber."

Name the teaching point.

"Today I want to remind you that writers, like other creators, imagine the text they're going to make before they get started. They imagine the parts and the whole, and they think about the work they're going to need to do to write each of those parts. This helps them get started; it gives them a plan for the project."

TEACHING

Tell the class that you find it helps to study texts that match your vision for the sort of text you want to make, and share a text written another year by a student just their age.

"Whenever I'm asked to write a report or a curriculum or any other sort of informational writing—and teachers are asked to do this sort of writing all the time—I always say, 'I need to see an example of the sort of thing I'm going to make!' I know you already realize that writers often study the work of other authors to get an image of the sort of things they're planning to write. But that is especially important when a writer is trying to write a report about a giant and complicated topic—like the Revolutionary War—because you can't put everything about that topic into a book. You will need to make some choices. So it helps to have an image for what you *will* do—*and* for what you *won't* do.

"I thought we could start by studying a book that a writer just your age wrote. Like you, Naomi was trying to bring the Revolutionary War to life for kids who don't know anything about that important part of American history. And a lot of grown-ups thought her writing was pretty good for a fourth-grader—so you can use her writing as a goal, almost, and aim for your first book to be something like this. Then you can use what you learned while making your first book to make your second book even better."

Whenever you channel the whole class to do some intellectual work, there will be children who aren't able to do that work on the spot. It is good to notice this, and sometimes you'll decide that there are enough strugglers that you want to adapt your teaching to support them. For example, if many children seem unclear right now, you might say, "I'm hearing some wonderful topics. Who's thinking of writing about Paul Revere and that exciting ride he made to notify people the British were coming? Who's thinking of writing about . . . ?" In such a way, you provide an added scaffold. But it is also entirely likely that you notice a few students who need extra help and make a plan to provide that help after the minilesson.

In the personal essay unit, one of your teaching points addressed this very same thing. That's why we have used the phrase, "I want to remind you . . . ," not "I want to teach you."

The text that we've chosen to use as a model is available to you on the CD that accompanies this. If you teach this unit more than once, in subsequent years, you can share work that your own students have made. For now, we suggest you use the text we have provided because it undergirds this entire bend in the unit, and provides an overview for kids of the work you'll be asking them to do. You could, of course, invite your class to join you in thinking up ways to make their books even better than Naomi's and in that fashion, you can avoid letting the one mentor text control all that your students do over the next ten days.

Demonstrate the way that studying this book helps you develop an image of what you will be making in the end. Do this with one chapter in ways that set children up to replicate with other chapters and to begin writing their own chapter one.

Showing the class the cover of Naomi's book, I said, "Let's read Naomi's book, 'The Continental Army and the Battles of Lexington and Concord,' in that special way that writers have where they look at the finished product and think, 'How did the writer probably go about making that?' I wonder if chefs look at finished cakes and try to figure out the recipe for those cakes, because that's a bit what writers need to do. We need to look at Naomi's finished work and try to figure out how she made it, and how we could go about making something sort of similar.

"When you study an information book that has different chapters or parts, it is helpful to look at each part, asking specific questions of that part. We'll focus on the first part, the first chapter, so that you can be ready to write your own version of that tomorrow." I flipped a new page of chart paper over to reveal some questions that I knew would pay off, and said, "Let's start, then, by noticing some things about the first chapter."

The Continental Army and the Battles of Lexington and Concord by Naomi

Structure:
- All About the Bigger Topic
- All About the Focused Topic
- The Story of a Big Moment, a Big Decision
- Why this Focused Topic is Important

Chapter 1: All About the American Revolution

In order to understand about the Battles of Lexington and Concord, it is helpful to understand a little about the Revolutionary War because these were the first battles in that important war.

The Revolutionary War began in 1775 and lasted many years, until 1783. It was for the American colonies' freedom from Great Britain, their ruler at the time.

The king was making the colonists pay a lot of money in taxes. They had to pay every time they bought things like sugar or papers. The taxes were bad, but what made the colonists even angrier was that they had no say in the British Government. They couldn't even vote. James Otis made up the saying. He said, "Taxation without representation is **tyranny**." That means a ruler who would do such a thing is unfair.

In 1774, the Parliament of Great Britain passed really bad laws. This happened after the Boston Tea Party, when the colonists dumped tea worth more than $1000 (which was worth a lot more at the time!) into the Boston Harbor. The colonists had to pay for the tea. These were called the **intolerable acts**. Also, there was a law passed that colonists weren't allowed to have meetings or choose their own government. And British soldiers could come stay in anyone's home!

The colonists got very angry about these laws. Some men made a congress that stated what they thought their rights should be. They sent it to the king, but he ignored them. He was really angry about the Boston Tea Party.

Then, the British came and tried to capture the colonists' supplies, like gunpowder. That was what the Midnight Ride was all about. So the colonists found out about it, and the war got started at Lexington.

Chapter 2: All About the Battles of Lexington and Concord

The Battles of Lexington and Concord were the first battles of the American Revolution. These battles happened on April 19, 1775 in Middlesex County near Boston. They marked the beginning of military fighting between the British and patriots.

The Secret Plan

The British General Thomas Gage made a secret plan to sneak out in the early morning to go to Lexington and Concord. They wanted to capture Sam Adams and John Hancock who were colonial leaders and destroy all of the patriots military supplies.

But the patriots found out! Weeks before, the patriots heard that their supplies might be in danger, so they moved them from Concord. Sam Adams and John Hancock were warned about the planned attacked and escaped from Lexington before the British could capture them. The night before, they learned more details about the British plans and Paul Revere and other men rode off on horseback to warn the people that the British were coming.

Lexington

The first shots of the war fired minutes after sunrise in Lexington. When the 240 British soldiers arrived on the Lexington Green at 5:00 a.m., 70 Colonial militiamen, or soldiers, were waiting for them. They had been waiting for more than four hours. These Colonial militiamen were also called minutemen because they could be ready to fight at a minute's notice. The British soldiers warned the minutemen to move, but the minutemen refused. Suddenly, a bullet shot through the air and the fighting started.

The Battle of Lexington only lasted about ten minutes. The patriots retreated. 8 patriots died and 10 were wounded.

FIG. 1–1   Naomi's finished book provides a strong mentor text for the class.

> When studying each part of a mentor information text, it helps to ask:
>
> What do I notice about this part? What kind of writing is it?
>
> How is this part organized?
>
> What would I need to do to be ready to write something like this on my topic?

I opened to the first chapter, which I displayed. It was titled "The Revolutionary War." I looked puzzled. "Hmm, . . . think with me about this. So it is a book on the Battles of Lexington and Concord and it starts with a chapter titled, 'The Revolutionary War.'" I flipped between the cover, showing the title, 'The Continental Army and the Battles of Lexington and Concord' and Chapter 1 with its title, "The Revolutionary War." "What do I notice about this part? What kind of writing is it?" In an aside to the class, I pointed out, "I've got to think like that if I am going to make a similar book!" Then I said to the class, "While I think about that, will you turn and speculate about that too?"

The children talked for half a minute, and then I spoke over the hum. "Isn't it surprising that it starts with such a broad topic—the whole war? I'm wondering why. Let's read a bit and see if that will help us figure out what the author is doing here."

> To understand about the Battles of Lexington and Concord, it is helpful to understand a little about the Revolutionary War because these were the first battles in that important war.
>
> The Revolutionary War began in 1775 and lasted many years, until 1783. It was for the American colonies' freedom from Great Britain, their ruler at the time.

Summarize what you and the class have discovered so far by studying the mentor text.

"Oh! I'm beginning to get what Naomi is doing with this first broad overview. She's telling about the whole Revolutionary War, isn't she, so as to introduce us to the broader context of her topic. She is giving us an overview of the bigger picture, so that we can understand the one small part of it that she'll discuss in more detail."

ACTIVE ENGAGEMENT

Channel the class to continue studying the mentor text, this time with more independence.

"Writers, there are two other questions to think about," and I gestured back to the list of questions.

> When studying each part of a mentor information text, it helps to ask:
>
> What do I notice about this part? What kind of writing is it?
>
> How is this part organized?
>
> What would I need to do to be ready write something like this on my topic?

"Will you scan this section, and try to figure out how she has organized her information? While you do that, will you also figure out what you might need to do during today's workshop to get ready to write a section like this in *your* book, tomorrow? Work with each other."

You will need to decide if you want students to begin, in this unit, to take notes during your minilesson, or if you think their note-taking skills are still so rudimentary that this will distract them from listening. Certainly you don't want to let them call out to you, "Wait, I haven't finished writing that!" Here, in this instance, you haven't been especially clear over the sort of writing you imagine students doing. You may want to be clearer about it, or to not mention it at all. We need to guard against overloading minilessons.

Notice the way this unfolds. You first set kids up to surmise why there would be a broad overview before the writer zooms in on the focused topic. In a few seconds, you will practically spoon out the answer by reading aloud the start of Naomi's book, as it essentially tells children why the book starts with the broader topic. This, then, is a sequence of heavy scaffolding that is meant to be sure the whole class travels along this trail of thought.

The reason that I recorded the questions is that later in the workshop, I'm hoping students will continue to study Naomi's text, looking at other chapters of it, and I know that having these questions written down will scaffold them to approach those other chapters with these questions in mind. Notice the sequence of the questions—they are listed in order of how a person might typically ask them when studying a mentor text.

I listened in as partners talked.

Edward said to his partner, "She has headings in this section, like 'Causes of the War.'"

"Yeah," agreed Max. "And I think to get ready to write that, I would need to get some notes, like some dates, and important places, that kind of stuff. Maybe I would make lists of stuff that goes under each heading."

Recap what you hope the class has learned from studying the mentor text, and begin to talk up the importance of the homework that students will have a chance to do in preparation for tomorrow.

After a minute, I reconvened the class. "Writers," I said. "Many of you are noticing that Naomi's first section of her book is an all-about section, a bit like the information books you wrote last year, only instead of chapters she has subheadings within her section. And I am hearing that you are worried about writing an All About the Revolutionary War section for your books tomorrow—will you have enough facts? The good news is that you can spend some time later in our workshop, this evening, and even some time tomorrow, gathering notes and preparing. And your draft of Chapter 1 will be just that—a draft. It will be something you can come back to often to make it better."

LINK

Send writers off to continue developing a sense of this kind of information book as a whole, planning for the work they'll do over the next few weeks.

"So writers, I think you've realized that it won't be until tomorrow that you actually start to write your book. Today, you'll be getting ready for writing this kind of informational writing, in general, and getting ready for writing chapter one, in particular. I have a handful of copies of Naomi's book, and I'm thinking you could work in huddles of four to study her other chapters and get a big picture for what you'll be writing. You can study the other chapters in the same way that you studied chapter one. Instead of working as a class, work as a foursome, with each huddle of four of you poring over a copy of the book, putting Post-it notes on things you notice that Naomi has done and then after reading and thinking alone, doing some talking."

Coach writers in how to set up their notebooks so that they are ready to begin taking notes.

"As you study each chapter, will you set up your notebook so that you have a place to begin collecting notes for your version of that chapter?" What I recommend is dividing your notebook into sections, one for each chapter you plan to have. You might use paper clips, and put a paper clip on the first page of each new section, so the paper clips act like place markers. You can estimate how many pages you'll need for each section of notes, but my guess is around four to five pages should be just fine." I demonstrated what this might look like using my notebook.

I sent two partnerships to the science table, giving the four of them one copy of Naomi's book and some Post-it notes, and then I sent other groups of four to other spots around the room. "I'm going to admire your abilities to analyze *what* Naomi has done and *how* she has done it."

Obviously it would be better to duplicate so every partnership or every writer has a copy of Naomi's text. We recommend groups of four only to limit the amount of preparation you need to do for this session. But in general, this unit does require more materials and more preparation than usual, and you will absolutely want to access the materials we've developed on the CD. They will be invaluable to your students.

Plan to study your children's abilities to talk about the way another author has written. The Common Core spotlights this metacognitive ability, and we think for good reason. There are many people who can do something, but can't talk about why and how they've done that. Depth of understanding is important, and one way to support deep knowledge is to help children be reflective and articulate about what they do. The ability to talk about texts also has great carryover into being able to write about texts.

Organizing Notes and Angling the All-About

ON THE FIRST DAY OF ANY UNIT, the teacher's work is often once again reminiscent of the circus man, running between a score of plates, each spinning on top of a stick. One wobbles, and with a touch, the man keeps it spinning. Then another, another—and somehow the circus man reaches each plate just before it topples. You'll find that it's not easy to keep all your students engaged in their work, and the challenge will be especially great at the start of a unit when no one has any momentum yet. The good news is that by now, your students are experienced writers, and accustomed to working within the writing process. If you lead table conferences, you'll be able to reach many of your students today.

When you arrive at a cluster of desks or a table, take half a minute to just observe. Are students studying the mentor text? Have they found a way to position the text so everyone can see it? Are they both reading the mentor text and talking about what they see in it? Some tables will be essentially poking at the text, noting this or that part, but not really reading it, and others will be reading, with no discussion. Either way, you'll intervene. Your hope is that kids are collaborating on the project of developing some language and some thinking about the mentor text and about the implications that text has for the students' own writing.

Some writers will have begun studying the mentor text, and others could easily do so with some encouragement from you. If students are doing this, be sure to refrain from pointing out what you notice in the text long enough to learn what each individual is noticing. Some of your students will be interested only in the decorative touches—the text boxes, the zoom-in pictures, the call-out boxes—that sort of thing. Yet others will be noticing the ways the author has done the work they anticipate doing soon. This latter group, for example, might notice how the author of the mentor text introduces the chapter, perhaps noticing that in the introduction, the writer lets readers know what the upcoming text will especially teach.

You can decide whether you want to watch and coach as students progress through the mentor text, commenting on one chapter after another, of if you want to use

MID-WORKSHOP TEACHING
Making an Overall Plan and Organizing Note-Taking

"Writers, please gather in the meeting area because we have a lot to talk about now," I said. Once they were settled, I began. "Now that you have studied Naomi's book, I bet you are getting some ideas for how your book will go. I think a lot of you are planning to include the same sections that Naomi has included":

Possible Sections of an Informational Book

- All About the Bigger Topic
- All About the Focused Topic
- The Story of a Big Moment, a Big Decision
- Why This Focused Topic Is Important

"I'm thinking my book will be about the Boston Massacre, and it is going to start like Naomi's does, with an overview of the Revolutionary War, all about the bigger topic. Then, in the next chapter I will do what Naomi did and tell readers information that is all about the focused topic. Those first two sections will both be all-about writing with subsections. Then I will add a little bit of story—I liked the way Naomi did that and I want to try it too. And I'll end with sort of an essay about why my topic is important, maybe showing that it was a turning point in the war. I might add a chapter that Naomi didn't have, where I make a map of Boston."

"I'm hoping that today has reminded you of ways that people go about writing information books. I've listed the steps I think a writer needs to take—some of them we have already talked about, and some I will be teaching you soon. Let me read these, and you can give a thumbs up if you have already started work on it. If the step is something you have not yet done but can do soon, give some other cool signal—you make it up." (I suggested the kids make up the "about to do" signal, but meanwhile I raised a fist in a "Charge!" gesture.) I pointed to each step as I read it:

GETTING READY TO WRITE...
-- AN INFORMATION BOOK

1. Think about the topic ☐
and about parts of the topic ☐
you'll write about.   ⋮☰
→ Sometimes your resources and
sometimes a mentor text can help

2. Think about how your writing might go.
What kind of writing might each part be?

3. Plan a way to take notes and jot ideas
→ Make your plan match your image
☐ ⊢⊢⊢⊢ ☐→☐→☐ ⋅👁⋅

4. Take notes, fitting what you learn in your plan

5. Plan for teaching others, do the teaching

6. DRAFT!

"Right now, you will want to shift to work on steps three and four—taking notes. You have already thought about your topic and how your writing might go. If you haven't already, you'll want to divide your notebook into sections so that you have planning pages for each of the chapters that you will write—for the All-About the Revolutionary War chapter, the all-about your own specific topic, the small story chapter, and so forth. For now, you definitely need a planning page for the chapter you will write tomorrow.

"Sam has found some of the books we read earlier about the Revolution and he's rereading them really quickly, skimming them, to harvest specific dates and names that he's forgotten. My hunch is that all of you will want to do this work right now."

your time with the students to help them go from studying the mentor text to thinking about the writing they will soon be doing. Your mid-workshop teaching point will channel students to make the transition from reading Naomi's work to planning their own, but you may decide to help individuals make that transition even before you give the mid-workshop teaching point. After all, that decision will allow you to spend more time helping students become ready for the writing work they'll start doing tomorrow.

When I pulled a chair alongside Sam, I asked him what he was thinking he would need to do to get ready to write a book like Naomi's. He said that her first chapter had different subsections and he was thinking about the subsections he could put into his report.

"I think I could write all the subheadings I will have about the Revolutionary War on these pages of my notebook (and he showed an open spread of pages) and then I could write the facts for each subheading."

"Subheadings! You're really thinking like an information writer. You know that information writers don't just heave all their information into a great towering pile, but instead they have some ways to chunk it, to put different information into different buckets. So you are thinking to do the same with the quick note-taking you can do between today and tomorrow—you're dividing a few pages up with the subheadings that you expect to have in tomorrow's report, and then you are putting your notes into the right section, the right bucket? Good thinking," I said.

Then I spoke to all the students at Sam's table. "Writers, can I interrupt?" I asked and waited until they stopped working and looked at me. I asked Sam to show them his plan. "If any of you would like to try this out as well—setting up your pages with subheadings to make space for notes—go ahead!" In this way, a conference with one student allowed me to support a whole cluster of students.

Later in the workshop, you will need to focus on helping students take notes so they are ready to write an All-About the Revolutionary War section the next day. For example, I recently helped Abby, a proficient writer, think about how she might angle her All-About the Revolutionary War section so that it contextualized her specific topic. I knew that this would be too confusing for some of the children in the class, but wanted to see if I could teach it to Abby in a way that made sense for her. Because Abby seemed to grasp this idea quickly, I convened a group of other especially strong writers. "Let me share with you more about what I just heard from Abby. Like Naomi, Abby is going to write about the whole Revolutionary War in section one. But because Abby's book is about Betsy Ross and the flag, she has decided that she probably needs to tell a lot about important events that caused the colonies to not only go to war but to also want to have their own flag. So her all-about the war will be told in a different way than someone whose book is about George Washington and the Battle at Valley Forge. Right now, can you think about how *your* all-about section could be different because of your focused topic? Help each other with this."

Sharing Notes to Gather More Information

Explain that researchers often work in teams to compile knowledge, and channel children to share with others at their tables, thereby multiplying their notes and readiness to write.

While children were still at their work spots, I asked for their attention. "There's one last thing I want to tell you. Researchers often work in teams, helping each other compile knowledge. You're each going to be writing your own book, but it is really important that we help each other. Will you talk for a few minutes with the foursome at your table? One person, read off some of the categories you are thinking you will write about, and some of the precise, specific information you found that you might include. And the rest of you—take notes. If someone else has a name or a date that you want, take notes on each other's notes. You have seven minutes to do this swapping of information, and you'll have tonight to finish this research."

Orient students to the work they'll do tomorrow; in this case, fast-drafting the first section of the book they are writing.

"Tomorrow, it will be time to look over your notes, plan, and start drafting the first section (the one that is All About the Revolutionary War) of your book."

 ## REREADING AND NOTE-TAKING IN PREPARATION FOR WRITING AN ALL-ABOUT CHAPTER

There is a saying. To write with your hands, you must write with your head. Tomorrow, you'll just have a short time to plan out how your first section (All-About the Revolutionary War) will go, and then you'll begin writing it. To do that, you will need to come to school brimming with knowledge about the Revolutionary War. So tonight, reread whatever you can get your hands on about the American Revolution. Better yet, watch a videotape about the topic, or talk to a family member about the topic. You will definitely need to take notes, bringing them to tomorrow's writing workshop. (Be sure to keep a list of books or websites you use.)

Planning the Structure of Writing

IN THIS SESSION, you'll teach students that writers of information texts make a plan for the structure of their writing and then use this structure to organize research and note-taking.

GETTING READY

✔ "Structure of an Informational Book" chart from Session 1

✔ "Ways to Structure an All-About Section of an Informational Book" chart (see Teaching)

✔ "Getting Ready to Write an Informational Book" chart from Session 1

COMMON CORE STATE STANDARDS: W.4.2, W.4.4, W.4.7, W.4.8, W.4.9, W.4.10, W.5.2, RI.4.5, RI.4.9, SL.4.1, L.4.1, L.4.2, L.4.3, L.4.6

B EFORE PROCEEDING to discussing this particular session, we want to step back to discuss the whole notion that the students would be channeled to write all about a general topic. We expect this task might surprise you at first—why are they not working on their focused subject? There are a number of reasons. First, the information writing that students do on topics from their Social Studies curriculum is, in part, meant to help them learn content that is important to their studies. Writing about a broad topic such as the Revolutionary War is a way to help students organize and "own" their knowledge of that topic. Then, too, at the start of this work, we anticipate that students can write an all-about text on this broad topic more easily than on their focal subject, simply because the chances are good that their knowledge is a mile wide and an inch deep. This form will allow them to display their presumably somewhat limited knowledge. In a sense, then, the students are given repeated practice writing all-about texts on research subjects, and the first bit of writing is easier than the next. Finally, we do believe that their eventual book on the specific topic—the Boston Tea Party or George Washington and the Battle of Valley Forge—will benefit from the writer taking time to first present a summary of the context. Maxine Greene, Teachers College's most distinguished professor, has often told doctoral students that when writing a dissertation, first one presents the brick wall, pointing to a space where there is a missing brick. Then the student creates the brick—his or her research—and finally, the student slides it into its place in the wall.

You may ask whether the goal is for students to summarize. Summary is a specialized skill that requires a learner to both collect information and then to extract the most essential aspects of that information. There will be a time to teach that, but we don't feel that now, at the start of this unit, that's the work we want to focus on. Think of this instead as a variation on the mind-dump that third-grade teachers ask students to do at the start of their unit on information writing. "Put everything you know onto the page," we said to third-graders. Back in the third-grade unit, students were writing on subjects of personal expertise—on soccer or golden retrievers. So the fact that we essentially say the same thing in this lesson doesn't make this an easy challenge. You try it: take forty minutes and write everything you know about the American Revolution, doing so with subheadings that help you chunk and develop your information.

"The subheadings they choose for their all-about section should reflect some larger scheme, some logical structure for the entire book they are writing."

Another general note. If you try to write about the American Revolution, you will probably find that doing so reveals the extent of your content knowledge—and your students will find this as well. All of a sudden it will become clear that they aren't really sure exactly what those taxes were about, or what the name is for the people who sided with the British, or whether Sam Adams had a profession other than being one of the Sons of Liberty. You'll find that some students will feel paralyzed when they confront their shaky command of the facts. Be ready to urge these students on. For now, their writing can include phrases like "Sam someone-or-other (I forgot his last name)" and "this was called the Tea Tax (I'm not sure why). . . ." The fact that students are still learning about the topic in hand is not a mess-up—it is the reason why this writing is so vitally important.

In this session, then, students are invited to use their skills as information writers to fast-draft the first section of their information book. That first section will be their own version of "All About the Revolutionary War," and students will be asked to plan out this section, mapping out the subsections to match their plan for the whole book. In other words, the subheadings they choose for their all-about section should reflect some larger scheme, some logical structure for the entire book they are writing.

Structuring Notes and Writing All About

CONNECTION

Ask children to think over their writing work so far this year and so far this unit, in particular, and predict the work of today and the next few days.

"Writers, usually I talk for a moment at the beginning of writing workshop to help us think back on the work we have been doing and think forward to what comes next. Let me ask *you* to do that, instead of me right now. Think back over the writing and planning you've been doing, and think ahead to what you think you will be doing today. What do you figure you'll be tackling today and how will it connect to stuff you have already learned to do? Turn and talk."

Acknowledge their expectations and then go ahead and explain how the teaching you've planned fits into or challenges those expectations.

"Writers, I see you have definitely figured out how workshop goes, haven't you? Yes, you will, of course, use the plans you made yesterday to get started writing today. All of you plan to write a section that tells all about the Revolutionary War. Some of you talked about trying to do that in a way that sort of provides a context for your specific topic. Because you will be using this section to teach a lot of information, it will help to remember what you learned in other years about writing information books."

❖ **Name the teaching point.**

"Today, I want to remind you that writers, especially writers of information texts, take time to think over the structure for their writing. Writers choose structures that make sense for the entire piece of writing."

TEACHING

Offer students one template for structuring the subsections of their report and channel them to imagine the template you suggest might work for the all-about writing they're about to do.

"I'll show you what I mean. You know that I'm thinking of writing about the Boston Massacre, and that like you, I'm going to start by writing about the bigger picture of the Revolutionary War. And like you, I already came up with some things, parts, categories that I expect to include when I write all about the Revolutionary War, and have been sort of

The real goal at the start of a writing workshop is to get kids engaged mentally, so they are not tuned out. This is an unusual way to start—if it works, take note, because this way of starting a minilesson essentially gets kids doing the work that teachers tend to do in order to write the start of a minilesson. It makes sense to pass that baton to kids.

filing my notes into those categories. Information writers do this—they take notes in ways that matches their plan for the whole piece.

"Here's the thing—when writing about history, the most obvious way to get readers to see the big picture is by explaining what happened in order, from first to last. If you are organizing your All-About the Revolutionary War section that way, your subheadings are essentially ordered as in a timeline. If one of your subheadings around which you have been jotting some notes is titled 'the ending of the war,' and you have six subheadings, you might label that one number six. If you were going to organize your subsections as a sequence of events, which would you write about first? Next? Turn and tell your partner."

After a moment, I reconvened the children. "I heard you say that you might start before the war, perhaps writing about how people in Boston were forced to allow British soldiers to live in their homes, for example, and about the taxes, and the Tea Party. Then next you could write about the start of the war."

Suggest another template for structuring a big-picture section, each time explaining how students' notes should be organized to fill in that structure.

"Of course, you might not choose to organize your All-About the Revolutionary War section chronologically because the rest of your piece of writing wouldn't fit with a chronological retelling of the war in the first section. Instead, you might come up with several different categories within the topic of the Revolutionary War. Naomi did that in the example we've been studying. She wrote 'The Causes of the Revolutionary War,' 'Important Battles of the Revolutionary War,' and 'Important People of the Revolutionary War.' She chose that structure because it fit better, not only for that first section, but for everything she wanted to write about in her book.

"Right now, imagine you were dividing your All-About the Revolutionary War section into categories because that fits better with the rest of your plan. Tell your partner what two of your categories might be, and use your fingers as bullets to talk about what might go in each of those categories. Turn and talk.

"I know I've given you a lot to think about here, a few different ways to structure your all-about section of your book. In case you've forgotten, I jotted them all here on this chart paper. I'll leave it out for you to use in your planning. It's up to you to figure out how your plans will look, and then of course, how your notes will look."

Ways to Structure a Section of an Informational Book

- Chronologically—telling things in order from first to last
- Categorically—different categories within the topic
- Other?

The Common Core State Standards ask students to logically structure their categories when writing information writing. The expectations for this are low—it is enough for students to include just a hint that their subsections are chronological (by using a few time words, such as "not long after that" or "before too long . . . ," or that are they are organized by importance (by using some ranking words, such as "Most importantly, . . .").

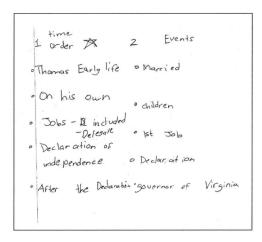

FIG. 2–1 Kim's notes, showing two different ways to organize her section, one chronologically (on the left) and the other by major events (on the right).

ACTIVE ENGAGEMENT

Ask students to choose (or invent) a structure for their first section and start planning how they will organize their knowledge.

"Right now, turn and tell your partner how you'll structure the All-About the Revolutionary War section of your book and how that will fit with the rest of your plan for your whole book. You already took notes in one way to structure this section—you already divided your notebook one way. Now see if that is the plan you want to keep. You'll have about five minutes to plan, and then you'll need to start writing that first section. Turn and talk."

LINK

Remind writers that information writers orient their readers by providing the context. They choose from a variety of structures, each one calling for a different kind of preparatory jotting and note-taking.

"Today and every day, remember that when you have a topic that feels like a great big armload of information, you can't just throw it right onto the paper. Instead, you need to ask, 'How will I structure my writing?' And once you figure out subtopics that you want to include, it helps to weigh different possible ways to sequence those subtopics. They may be organized chronologically, or categorically, or in another way. The important thing is that you take some time to think about how you will structure your writing so that not just the one section, but the entire piece, fits together. Every one of us needs to write, write, write, according to the plans we just talked through and jotted down, write, write write, without stopping. So get going—fast and furious!"

Ten minutes later I called, "Make sure you've stopped planning and have started drafting. So now, without a word, please get started on your book. You'll be writing like crazy, probably filling up four or five pages for your first section about the whole Revolutionary War in just the next half-hour. Go!"

Choosing and Writing within a Structure

THE CONFERRING AND SMALL-GROUP WORK YOU'LL BE LEADING during the start of this unit will continue to be a bit unusual because all of your students will be progressing in sync, which is not typical. By this time, your students will have settled on a plan for their first chapter, will have done some limited research, and will have started writing.

If you spot a few children listing subtopics in no particular order, you may want to collect these youngsters and tell them that once writers categorize, their next job is to think about the logic that undergirds those categories. You will probably want to look at the subheadings that students have collected and help them see what they are already gesturing toward. One student may seem to be writing about just a random collection of key events, with a chapter or two on other topics. Suggest this writer think of his subtopics as Key Events in the American Revolution, deleting the distracters. One item that will be essential to your conferring toolkit in this unit is the mentor text that demonstrates some of the writing moves you are supporting your students in trying. Chapter One of Josh Gregory's *Revolutionary War* has nice examples of clear, logically ordered subheadings.

It is likely that you'll find some youngsters have written what essentially amounts to a sentence or two about a score of little topics. The writer writes something about one subtopic, then jumps to the next, the next, and the next. You might say to a child, "When you get to a topic, push yourself to say more about it. Tell yourself you can't go to the next topic until you have written five or six sentences on the first one." You may want to suggest children pool their knowledge so that by working together, they can scrape up a bit more to say about subtopics.

If youngsters are reminded to paragraph whenever they turn to a new subtopic, the fact that their writing treats subtopics so lightly that it merits a new paragraph every two or three sentences can be a cue to young writers that something is wrong. Paragraphing can be about structuring and elaboration as much as editing!

MID-WORKSHOP TEACHING   **Keep Going: Writing with Volume, Even When Your Information Is Shaky**

Standing in the midst of the room, I said, "Eyes up here for a sec." I waited. "Some of you are wanting to get out your books and do some research. You are stuck on a name, a date, a place, and want to nail things down so they are correct. I know that feeling—but my suggestion to you right now is to push yourself to keep writing.

"So first of all, know that you can write things like this: 'And then Paul Somebody-or-Other went riding through the towns (what towns were they?) calling, 'The British are coming.' The person to the right and the left of you will be doing this as well, and later you can compare notes and help each other fill in the things you couldn't remember. You can also take what you write home and fill in some of the specifics.

"But what will not be okay is if you don't get a ton written today. I have two suggestions to help you write a lot. First, look back over what you have written. If you have put down a few facts about a topic and no thoughts about those facts—try saying to yourself, 'Slow down, say more.' If you recall that Paul Revere rode through towns calling, 'The British are coming,' then you have done the hard part. Now add onto that by saying what you think about it. Maybe you'll write—'I think it is odd that someone is famous for just riding around calling out a warning. Usually people who are famous have been important leaders. . . .' Or you might write, 'It must have taken a lot of courage to do as Paul Revere did. . . .'

Children talked, and I said, "I told you the important thing is that you write a lot, and one way is to write not just the facts, but your thoughts about the facts. The other suggestion is this: Put your pen to the page. Do that now." I waited. "Write, and keep writing. Don't stop."

Checking Writing for Breadth and Transition Words

Celebrate the sheer volume of writing that students did and suggest some ways to think about making the writing better.

After convening children in the meeting area with their drafts, I said, "Writers, shake out your hands! Nice work. Scan over what you did and think about what worked well, okay? What's good about what you did?" I gave writers a moment to think about that, and then asked them to tell each other their thoughts.

As children talked, I voiced over. "Writers, you are naming some good aspects of your work—but will you provide evidence to support what you are saying? Show your partner examples of where you did whatever it is that you think is good."

After letting children work for a bit, I spoke once more. "Now, writers, I want you to think about a few things that might nudge you to do even better work. First, when you try to write all about a topic, it is reasonable to ask yourself whether you actually did that. Did you cover the major parts? For example, did you tell the beginning, the middle, and the end—if not, jot yourself a note to address the parts you left out, when you have a chance."

"And secondly, when you use subheadings to help you stay within an organizational structure, sometimes you also need to use transition words that help the reader know how one part of your mosaic glues onto other parts.

"If your all-about is organized chronologically, you probably should have some words at the start of a subsection that clue in the reader to the fact that this occurred after the previous topic. You and your partner should look at whoever's piece has been organized by time and see if you already have—or if you could add—words like, *Before the Revolution . . .* or *Not long after that . . .* or *A while later. . . .*

"Meanwhile, if you or your partner organized your subsections categorically, you may end up sequencing them by importance, like 'most important,' 'more important,' and so forth; you should see words such as, *And even more important. . . .*

"Overall, you can use our chart about informational writing to help you remember the process most writers find essential. Take a moment right now to talk with your partner about transitions, about our process chart, and any other way you think would be helpful to check your writing."

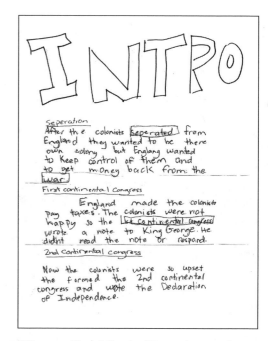

FIG. 2–2 Kim's introduction makes good use of subheadings.

WRITING YOUR INFORMATIONAL BOOK, BIRD BY BIRD

There is a famous book about writing called *Bird by Bird*. The author, Anne Lamott, got the title for that book from a time when her brother was about your age and was working on a research project about birds, which felt huge to him—a bit like this project probably feels to you. Anne described her brother as "immobilized by the hugeness of the task ahead." Then Anne's father sat down beside her brother, put an arm on his shoulder, and said, "Just take it bird by bird."

I can imagine that the notion of writing a chapter on the Revolutionary War probably makes you feel paralyzed. So I have some advice for you: "Just take it bird by bird."

Write one subhead. Then write that section, remembering as you do, all that you know about how to write well. Then write another subhead. Then write that section. Just write section by section, bird by bird, person by person, line by line. Tonight, write at least one subhead. Then do your best to write as much as you can in the section that follows.

Planning and Writing with Greater Independence

IN THIS SESSION, you'll remind students that writers take strategies they've learned in the past and apply them to new situations, working with more independence and skill each time.

GETTING READY

✔ A plan for the sections of your own informational book (see Minilesson)

✔ "Getting Ready to Write an Informational Book" chart (see Teaching)

✔ "Possible Sections of an Information Book" chart (see Teaching)

✔ A variety of sources for students to use when researching, including informational books and bookmarked websites

LEARNING A SKILL TAKES REPEATED PRACTICE. Someone could tell me how to do a backflip and even do one slowly, step by step, in front of me, but that doesn't mean that when I try to do one, I'll be a pro at it. Nor could I learn through demonstration to sing a concerto or to use Excel. Writing is no different. Becoming skilled at writing requires repeated practice.

This unit provides writers with opportunities to use and develop skills that they've been working on for years, using these skills to do work that would be challenging even for adult writers. In summer institutes at Teachers College, we often help adult participants write informational books, and even when they are invited to write on topics they know well, adults find this work enormously challenging. How much more difficult it would be for any of us to write about a topic that we are just beginning to understand!

The good news is that this unit is designed like a staircase, allowing writers to progress step by step. So far, you've helped your students review and practice the skill of writing all about a topic that they've learned about through research—the Revolutionary War. The fact that it was a broad subject meant that there was no scarcity of information on hand, and the fact that it was a shared subject meant that there was no scarcity of helpful partners. In this next session, neither of those scaffolds is a given.

Instead, in this session, students have the opportunity to apply what they've learned so far to a new situation, and doing so also gives them the repeated practice we all so sorely need whenever we learn something new. In essence, today you will put children in the same writing situation as you put them in during the previous session: they have a subject and they need to plan, research, and write about it. In the previous session, the subject was the Revolutionary War. In this session, the subject is each child's particular, self-chosen topic. You'll be expecting students to transfer and apply the skills you just taught about planning—then it was planning an all-about piece about the war, now it will be all-about writing about their focal topic.

COMMON CORE STATE STANDARDS: W.4.2, W.4.4, W.4.7, W.4.8, W.4.9, W.4.10, RI.4.1, RI.4.3, RI.4.7, RI.4.9, SL.4.1, L.4.1, L.4.2, L.4.3, L.4.6

Planning and Writing All-About with Greater Independence

CONNECTION

Let children know that writers often do the same kind of work they've done before, each time with more skill and more independence.

"Writers, for a second, think about learning to ride a bike. When you were little, maybe three or four, how did you ride a bike?" I paused to let them answer. "I think that you probably rode a tricycle, a bike that is easy for a little kid to ride, because it has three wheels, a lot of supports. Now think again—how did you ride a bike when you were a little bit older, when you were a kindergartner?" I listened to their suggestions and agreed. "Many of you are saying that you started riding a two-wheel bike, but you still needed training wheels. How do you ride a bike now?"

Of course, the children were clear that now they can ride a bike on their own, without training wheels. "You learned, little by little, step by step, the way to ride a bike on your own."

"That is the way learning goes a lot of the time, isn't it? You get a lot of help for a while, and then you get a little less help, and you do more on your own, and then, finally, with a lot of practice and feedback, you can do it yourself. That is the way it is going in this unit. You've had some practice looking at a text, planning your own sections, note-taking and drafting. Now it is time to do that again, more on your own, so that you know how—even when there are no training wheels to support you."

❖ **Name the teaching point.**

"Today, I want to remind you of something that you already know: writers take strategies they've learned in the past and apply them to new situations, working with more independence and skill each time."

Although almost every minilesson in all these zillions of units of study provides students with scaffolds and then removes those scaffolds, this is literally the first time I have talked to students about the way in which our teaching is designed. It makes sense, though, to let them in on the design for instruction, as this is probably the best way to make sure that everyone agrees the goal is for students to be able to do the challenging tasks with increasing independence.

We think it is important to not act as if we are teaching something new when we know full well this has been taught many times prior to now. Hence, the choice of the phrase "I want to remind you" instead of "I want to teach you."

TEACHING

Clarify the way that students will put today's teaching point to use. Let children know that in this case, they'll apply what they learned earlier as they write new sections of their informational book.

"For example, today you will not only work on finishing up your Revolutionary War section, if you need more time on that, but you will also get ready to write another section of your book, using the same skills and steps you have used to write the Revolutionary War section. Remember how we noticed that the second section of Naomi's book was all about the battles of Lexington and Concord? She had chosen a more focused topic of the Revolutionary War to home in on. Today, you will have a chance to move on to your second chapter. You chose a topic a few days ago, and today, you will collect notes and get your thoughts in order to write all about your focused topic. The subject is different but your planning process, the kind of work you do, can be the same."

Ask writers to study the anchor chart and think back over the teaching in this unit so far and see if it can help them figure out a wise way to tackle the work of today.

"Writers, you all know by now that every time we make an anchor chart together, the steps—or strategies or ideas or plans—on that anchor chart are meant to be helpful to you throughout that unit and even throughout your life. (In fact, if they aren't, that means we shouldn't have bothered putting them on the chart!) So, with that in mind, I'm going to bring your attention to the anchor chart that we started on the first day of this unit. Will you think about that chart and think about what you've learned in this unit so far and talk with your partner about a wise plan for your work today?"

As you may have noticed by now, most of the teaching sections throughout this series illustrate one of three methods: (1) Explain and give an example, (2) Demonstrate, or (3) Set up an inquiry. This teaching section is only Explain, and it is a bit on the inquiry side, since the children end up explaining the learning they need to themselves. We made this choice because children have already had both explanations and examples very recently—in the previous session. You too may decide at times to leave the example aside and shorten the teaching section to merely explaining. You will always need to make this kind of decision depending on the needs of your children.

Getting Ready to Write an Informational Book

1. Choose a topic.

2. Think about how your writing might go. What kind of writing might each chapter (or part) be?

3. Plan a way to take notes and to jot ideas for each part.

4. Take notes, fitting what you learn into your plan for the writing.

5. Plan for teaching others about your topic, and then do that teaching to rehearse for writing.

6. Draft!

"Today, I know, you might quickly revise or finish what you wrote yesterday, but most of your time will be tackling the *next* section of your informational book. We decided that for many of us the next section would be all about the focused topic. Chances are, you'll be doing the same kind of writing work you did yesterday (not the same work, the same *kind* of work). Look at the anchor chart and think, 'How will I work today; how will I get started on this next section of information writing? What kind of research and writing will I need to do today so that I can draft tomorrow?' Turn and talk."

I listened as children talked, and then reconvened them. "Writers, I heard some of you saying you'll look at the all-about section of Naomi's writing again to imagine how your next section will go. You know your next chapter will again be an all-about chapter, this time on your specific topic, but how will you chunk your information? What might your subheads be? Keep in mind that by tomorrow you'll be drafting the next all-about section—and proceeding just as you did when you planned and wrote your first all-about section. Very sensible!

"I heard others saying you'll jump in at number three on our chart. You'll think about how to take notes to match your plan. For example, if you choose to write about the people and places related to your event, you will probably structure your notes by those subtopics. If you choose to order your subtopics chronologically, then your notes might well include elaborated timelines—and so on. This plan seems very sensible to me also."

ACTIVE ENGAGEMENT

Ask writers to get started with this work here on the carpet as you go around and coach them for a moment, sending them off to work on their own, one by one.

"Writers, with your partners, go ahead and get started deciding how you'll do the work that is on the chart. You'll be starting with either number two or number three on our chart, or you'll be figuring out your own way to structure your notes and research for the next section of your information book. I'll come around and listen, and when I tap your shoulder, head off to your work spot."

I crouched alongside Max, who had written "George Washington Crossing the Delaware" at the top of his page. Max said, "I'm trying to do it by exactly what happened, in order. The first part could be about when they were planning to cross, then the next part would be how they got into position and went across, and then the last part would be they fought and defeated the Hessians." I asked him how he would take his notes, in that case, and he replied that he wasn't sure, so I pointed out that his plan was chronological so maybe he'd take notes in a timeline. He was excited about that, so I sent him off to work.

Knowing that others, like Max, would need to devote most of the day to note-taking to write on these more focused topics, I did a voiceover to the whole class. "Writers, Max decided that his writing will tell about an event in order, so he is going to organize his notes to time sequence. Max doesn't think he is ready to write his report yet, so he plans to spend a good part of today gathering notes, and I know that will be true for many of you."

You word this as if children are in the driver's seat, making big decisions, but actually during this first bend of the unit, you have spelled out your expectations with a lot of specificity. They are all writing a little book about a subtopic that the class has studied, and all the books have chapters that are structured differently. Two are all-about chapters—that is, information writing in the strictest sense of the word. Others are narratives and essays. Today you hope that when students return to all-about writing, this time on a more focused topic, they draw on what you taught them over the past few days. It's a fairly obvious message.

Time is of the essence. We mention two individuals here because that is the maximum number of individuals you'll be able to work with during the two-minute interval for students to work. Be sure you don't get yourself into the feeling that you need to reach many of your children individually during the minilesson, or you will surely go over the ten-minute ideal time frame for a minilesson.

I peeked over Lucie's shoulder. She had written "Boston Massacre" at the top of the page. "I'm going to write about all of the different parts of the massacre, but maybe not in time order," she explained, "like I might write a section that lists why it happened, then a section that tells who was there. That's all I have so far."

LINK

Remind students of the teaching point. In this case remind them to rely on all they already know in order to do the work in front of them better than ever before.

"So today, you will work just as information writers the world over do: you'll plan, research, and draft! And sometimes, you'll draft, research, and plan! As you work you'll see the need to do one or the other as most writers do. The key thing is to remember to build on what you know, calling on what you've learned about how to make your writing great. You can get started right here on the carpet."

Send students off to work once they seem ready, keeping those who need support with you for small-group work.

As I checked in with the students, I sent off those who had a viable plan to get going on their writing, and channeled others to get started while they were on the rug, where I could easily move among them. A group remained, and we talked through the fact that their first job would be to plan how their next section—and consequently their notes for it—would go, and then they could get started taking notes.

Predictable Problems for Researching and Note-Taking

As you confer on this day, you will need to be aware of the challenges that inexperienced researchers often encounter. Researching and note-taking require an understanding of how to determine importance, and this is especially true when people are reading texts that sometimes present a huge surplus of almost undigested facts. If you see some students recording every fact they read, often copying straight from the text, you'll want to convene a small group to address this topic.

You might start by telling students about your observation, then follow up with some questions to try to get to the heart of the issue. It could be that the source text is too difficult for some of the students to comprehend and they're copying directly because they really don't grasp the content at all. If you notice that this is true for some members of the group, the important thing will be to keep in mind that it probably will be true for everyone at some time. So teach the general strategy of monitoring for sense and discarding (or postponing) a text that is too hard. Usually if one reads a far easier text on the same subject first, that easier text provides enough knowledge about the subject that it is possible to then return to the challenging text. You might also learn that some of the students in the group are diligently copying the book they read onto their notes because they believe note-taking involves "recording the facts" and that is what they are doing—recording the facts, all of them.

In each of these cases, it will help if children talk freely about this, not worrying that they've committed a crime and could be hauled off to detention. Chances are good that they are trying to please and still learning what is expected of them.

Because it is predictable that in a research unit, some students will seem to be copying from the source, you will want to have a repertoire of strategies you can suggest as alternatives. We've mentioned one—suggesting children start by reading an easier text, then return to the challenging one. You will probably also want to coach students to read just a chunk of a text at a time, pausing after taking in that chunk to think, "What did that chunk just teach me?" Then, when reading on, encourage them to add

---

Researching for All Sections, Not Just the Next Section

"Writers, can I interrupt you for a second?" I said, speaking over the heads of still-working writers. Once the children had given me their attention, I continued. "I want to remind you that as you research, you'll save time if you are collecting notes for your *whole book*, not just this one section! Remember, on the first day of the unit, you made a rough plan for your whole book. Today, you are just starting the research for the section that is all about your topic. But we've also planned to write some other sections":

- a story, perhaps one involving a person coming to a big decision or turning point related to your topic

- a mini-essay that explains why your topic is important

"If you haven't set up places in your notebook for notes and thoughts about those sections, will you do so? And will you and your partner talk over what sorts of notes you might collect, knowing you'll be writing those other sections of your report? Let's take a moment now for you to turn and talk."

The children talked, and then I said, "Writers, I've been listening and I agree—for the story you will need details of what things looked like—the streets, the clothes, the schools. You are going to want to write bits like, 'John walked quickly down the cobbled street to the wharf where . . .' I also want to point out that good stories revolve around turning-point moments, or moments when people are torn in two ways, so be on the lookout to understand the tensions, the conflicts, what people were probably feeling related to your event, your subtopic.

"For the essay, you will need convincing reasons why your event was important. Think, 'What lessons were learned from that?' and 'How would things have been different had this not happened?' We'll talk more about these sections later, but at least keep them in your mind so you can be collecting for them as you skim and read."

the new information onto the existing information. You could also teach learners to teach someone else about whatever they are learning. This helps them gain voice over the subject. In all cases, it will be helpful to teach students to glean information from more than one source so that the content that they write is not a replica of any one text that they've read.

Just as you can predict that some children will seem like they are copying from the source and will need help with that, others will need other kinds of help with note-taking. If you see some children listing fact after fact, not appearing to digest anything, you'll want to help them at least organize their notes. For example, when I conferred with Yoshi, I saw that he'd recorded tons of undigested facts about the Declaration of Independence. "I am trying to get down all of this information and it's a lot to write," he said.

"Yoshi, you are right, it is a lot to write. It will also be a lot to mentally grasp. The thing is that because your notes are sort of like a swarm of little facts, it is going to be really hard for you to mentally get your arms around them. Can I teach you a huge step forward you could take toward having more useful notes?"

Yoshi was game, so I continued on. "You need to organize your notes. If I rattled off a bunch of things in a pile, you'd never recall all of them, but if I said, 'There are some office supplies' and then listed three, and some kitchen utensils, and listed a few, and some dog-grooming tools, and listed a couple—you could wrap your mind around the list of items much more easily.

I also explained to Yoshi that writers sometimes structure their notes (and their drafts) in a cause-and-effect way. "This happened, so that caused this to happen, and that caused. . . ." This is what he decided to do. (See Figure 3–1.)

Of course, you'll have other students who need very different help. For example, you are apt to find that there are some students who, when channeled toward a source that directly addresses the subject on which they are writing, still come away with very few tidbits of information, very few quotations. Citing the source text is an important skill and not one that most students have been taught. For example, some students will be apt to think that it makes sense only to cite sentences that they agree with exactly. So if they are writing about the Boston Tea Party and a loyalist describes that event as treason, because the young researcher doesn't see it that way, he is not apt to quote the loyalist. It's important, then, for you to demonstrate how you go about taking notes, showing students that it makes great sense, for example, to cite bits of language that reveal a participant's perspective on an event.

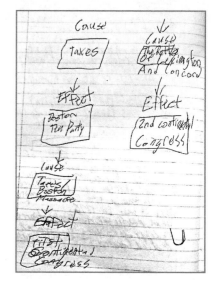

FIG. 3–1   Yoshi's notes

Organizing Your Notes and Creating a To-Do List

Congratulate writers and ask them to share their notes with someone who is not their partner.

"Writers, don't move out of your work spots. Listen, in a moment I'm going to suggest you share the work you did today with someone who is *not* your partner. So right now, get ready for sharing by taking a second to clean up your work. Make your notes tidy—if you have categories—label them. If you have written lots of ideas on Post-it notes, make sure each Post-it is stuck into the right section of your notebook. If you have written on a bit of lined paper, clip the paper into the right section of your notebook." After a few minutes, I said, "Okay, writers, will you share the work you did today with someone you don't usually share with?"

Ask children to learn from and add to the work they are sharing, giving themselves a To-Do list.

Once children were sharing, I called in a voiceover, "See if you can notice the other person's system—a way of taking or reviewing or combining notes. If there is something you admire, talk about it. Then, see if you can together do something cool with the notes. Maybe you can make arrows between things that connect, or number them in order of importance, or write marginal questions. Invent something admirable. Go." After a bit, I asked for the class's attention. "Finally, writers, will you give yourself a To-Do list? You might do this by rereading your own writing and starring the things where you need to learn more. Or you might jot some questions or subtopics you want to read about or write about."

SESSION 3 HOMEWORK

THE TO-DO LIST: A WRITING SCAVENGER HUNT

Writers, I wonder if you have ever been on a scavenger hunt? When you're on a scavenger hunt, you are given a list of things to find—your friends have a similar list. I'm mentioning the scavenger hunt because your To-Do list is probably a bit like a list for a scavenger hunt. See how many of the things you can find or do that are on your list—and bring notes or materials in tomorrow.

Teaching as a Way to Rehearse for Information Writing

IN THIS SESSION, you'll teach students that when writing to teach, it helps writers to do some actual teaching about their topic.

GETTING READY

✔ One student to share his or her work with the class (see Teaching)

✔ "Questions Teachers Ask When Planning to Teach" list (see Teaching)

✔ Chart paper and markers (see Active Engagement)

✔ "Getting Ready to Write an Informational Book" chart, updated to reflect today's teaching (see Active Engagement)

✔ An enlarged copy of the Information Writing Checklist, Grades 4 and 5, as well as individual copies for students (see Share)

COMMON CORE STATE STANDARDS: W.4.2, W.4.4, W.4.10, RI.4.1, RI.4.2, RI.4.3, SL.4.1, SL.4.2, SL.4.4, SL.4.5, SL.4.6, L.4.1, L.4.2, L.4.3, L.4.5, L.4.6

T HE GREAT PSYCHOLOGIST, Erik Erikson, has written, "We are the teaching species. Human beings are constituted so as to need to teach. Ideas are kept alive by being shared, truths by being professed." Those of us who have the great fortune of being teachers know that there is no way to learn more about a subject than to teach that subject. When we have the chance to teach others what we know, we come to know what we know—and what we do not know, as well. We learn the parts of our subject that will elicit a response from others, and we learn to rise to the occasion of those parts. We get that special glint in our eyes when we reach a good part of our teaching; we slow things down, become more detailed, building suspense, momentum.

Then, too, we come to anticipate the parts that will confuse our students. We approach those parts differently, aware that we need to carefully lay out the progression of thinking so that learners travel with us.

The wonderful thing is that children who want to write informational texts all have access to the power of teaching. The only thing that you need to do is to orchestrate time and people so that youngsters have an appointment to teach. Ideally, there is an interlude between learning about what one will teach and actually doing the teaching—because there are few more powerful ways to support rehearsal than to tell someone they have just a bit of time before they'll be teaching others. Perhaps you can find ways to elevate the teacher—prop that youngster up on a milk crate, suggesting he teach children sitting at his feet. Or give the child chart paper, a marker, a pointer, and ten minutes to prepare. The smallest props can do a world of good to create a drumroll around this event, and that will, in turn, invite children to rise to the occasion.

You've experienced this yourself: the first time you spoke at an open house to a room full of parents, the first time you talked about your teaching to your colleagues—and someone actually took notes! Give your youngsters the experiences that can allow them to write with an authoritative voice.

Teaching as a Way to Rehearse for Information Writing

CONNECTION

Note that the collegiality of shared inquiry keeps people wanting to engage in research, and support some of that by channeling students to teach others what they have learned.

I asked students to join me in the meeting area, sitting next to the partner that they worked with during the previous day's share session. "Today, writers, will you return to the person you talked to yesterday about your scavenger hunt, and show each other the notes you took, the things you learned or did? As you talk, tell each other what you learned that is especially interesting about the Revolutionary War."

The children talked for a bit, and then I voiced over. "I love that some of you are taking notes on what you are learning from each other! Researchers go through life like magnets, letting things stick to them. So yes, if your classmate tells you something interesting about the Revolutionary War, you need to think, 'Could I add that to *my* writing?' I circulated, listening to animated discussions about Molly Pitcher firing a cannon for her husband and William Dawes's bravery on the Midnight Ride. "You are all sounding like experts!"

There are a few reasons for this interlude. First, there is no better way to call for students' attention that to get them talking about the topic first. Then, too, the mark of good writing is that the voice of the writer comes through on the page. Many students write research that is utterly lacking in voice. So the simple act of making time for children to talk in pairs about the research topic will have far-reaching impacts.

❖ Name the teaching point.

"Today, I want to remind you that when you are writing to teach about your topic, as you are whenever you do any information writing, it helps to *actually do some teaching*. Knowing that you have an audience can help you figure out what you need to teach. And the questions people ask in real life are probably questions that *readers* will also ask, so it helps to try to answer those questions in your writing."

Of course, there is probably no single lesson that we could include in this series that has more power for us than this one. The fact that we (the coauthors of the series) teach is the single most important contributor to our writing. As we write, we see the faces, know the stories, of the teachers who fill our lives. When writing is a way to teach people we don't yet know but already care about, this transforms the writing.

TEACHING

Recruit the class to help one student prepare for teaching a familiar topic to another class, using this to demonstrate that preparing for teaching can lead a person to embellish notes and to anticipate interests and questions.

"Class, I need your help on something. Robert has been invited to go to Mr. Finnerty's room to teach his kids about Paul Revere's ride—and I know you *all* know a lot about that topic. So I'm hoping we can help Robert get ready for his teaching. If we can help Robert teach Mr. Finnerty's class well, I think that we can also figure out some things that will help everyone in this room teach better—and I'm talking about teaching in person, and also teaching on the page.

"I'm a teacher, so why don't I start by giving you some tips about what people do to get ready to teach. Before a teacher teaches, he or she needs to have a plan. The plan is usually a list of the main topics that I will teach, with notes about the important points. In a way, a lesson plan is the same as a plan for a piece of writing. It is important for you to read over the plan and to think, 'What do I want my audience to learn?' 'What will interest people?' I also think, 'What might confuse them, what I can clarify?'" I flipped to the next page of my chart paper pad, showing questions I ask.

Questions Teachers Ask When Planning to Teach
- What do I want my audience to learn?
- What will interest people?
- What might confuse them that I can clarify?

Debrief in a way that makes this a lesson not on teaching but on writing teaching texts, as the students are doing.

"Asking those questions helps me think of ways I can make my teaching as interesting and informative as possible. Writers do that as well, of course—and especially writers of information texts, because the goal is to write in such a way that the writing acts like good teaching."

ACTIVE ENGAGEMENT

Recruit the one student to share his teaching plan with the class, inviting the class to give feedback to help make the student's teaching plan as good as possible

"Robert, will you share your teaching plans with us? We'll all listen, trying to think about ways that your teaching can be as interesting and as informative as possible to the kids in Mr. Finnerty's class."

Robert clambered up on his knees. "See, I'm gonna teach about Paul Revere and so I thought I'd tell about the things that happened before that night, and then the lights from the church signaling to him, and then how he rode around to Lexington and all."

We trust that children will glean that the work with Robert is really not just about preparing Robert. It is, instead, all about students in general learning how to bring their knowledge of teaching into the writing they'll do.

When I want kids to return later to a list that I say aloud, I try to leave a written copy of that list. Making it during the minilesson can actually slow things down fairly dramatically, which is why I had my chart at the ready.

When you shift from the demonstration to debriefing, students should feel the different moves you are making just by the way your intonation and posture changes. After most demonstrations, there will be a time for you to debrief, and that's a time when you are no longer acting like a writer. You are the teacher who has been watching the demonstration and now turns to talk, eye to eye with kids, asking if they noticed this or that during the previous portion of the minilesson.

As Robert spoke, I jotted his plan:

Paul Revere's Midnight Ride

Before the ride
The signal
Riding to warn the patriots

I said to the class, "Let's remember that Robert needs to think first, 'What do I want my audience to learn?' To answer that, he had to think about all the main points of his topic and make sure his teaching addressed those main points. Do you think Robert's plan addresses the main points about Paul Revere and his midnight ride? Turn and talk to your partner."

I listened in while Grayson said to her partner, "I am writing about the Midnight Ride, too. And I think he has got to add more about what happened after. He got arrested by the British!"

After the children talked for a minute in partnerships, I voiced over, "Will you shift now to another thing that teachers think about—what will interest people? Have you got ideas for what Robert could do to be sure his teaching interests people as much as possible?"

"I have a good idea," said Mitchell to Lucie, "Robert should tell about how the guard at one of the houses told Paul Revere not to make so much noise. And he said something like, 'You'll get a lot more noise soon when the British come!'" Others suggested Robert add details like how Paul Revere wrapped his oars in cloth to muffle the noise.

I voiced over, saying, "So you are thinking that Robert's teaching—and eventually his writing—will be more interesting if he adds more details. Let's think about the third consideration teachers take into account—what might confuse the kids in Mr. Finnerty's class, and how Robert could clear up confusion."

"The kids might be confused about why he's such a big shot when all he did was ride around," Sam said, adding "and he wasn't the only rider. I'm confused about that, so I can't really fix it up. Why isn't William Dawes as famous?"

I reconvened the group. "I was able to hear a lot of what you were suggesting Robert could do, but Robert needs to hear your thoughts, as well. Tell them to Robert." A minute later Robert was being reminded that he hadn't told that much about what occurred after the ride (which was especially interesting in this case). I added that subtopic to the list of what Robert planned to cover in his teaching, and said, "It almost always happens that when you teach about a topic, new ideas come up. So the work Robert is going to do—adding that subtopic to his plans—is something every one of you will do whenever you are writing an informational text."

Soon others had suggested other "juicy bits" that Robert could add, and I pointed out that to add interest, they had all suggested details: quotes, anecdotes, quirky facts. Robert wasn't sure how to fit in a part of his teaching where he addressed people's confusions, so we suggested he include a part where he says, "You may be confused about . . . "

When you have set students up to follow a list, it is important that your teaching follow that list as well. Be aware that jumping about in the sequence of the list causes extraordinary confusion. So it might seem like no big deal to do that, but actually it is a big deal. Refer often to the list, too, just by touching a bullet point, so that you show children the way in which your teaching is built upon that infrastructure.

My coaching, of course, follows the list that I had introduced later and will add to the anchor chart when the minilesson is done.

and then address those confusions. I added on to the chart "Getting Ready to Write an Informational Book," a few of the specific strategies we discussed under step 5.

Debrief, pointing out that the steps writers took to plan for teaching are steps that will help with their writing.

"Writers, whenever you are writing an informational text of any kind, it helps to teach a real audience about the same topic on which you are writing. By thinking about the people you are going to teach and about building a lesson plan to help those people learn, you make your plans with the audience in mind right from the start. You'll find that when you need your thinking about a topic to help some people who are right there with you actually learn things—all of a sudden the presence of those people makes it really important that your teaching matters and that it works. So any time, when writing an informational book, your process will go like this . . . " As I read over the updated anchor chart, I highlighted the new information underneath step 5.

LINK

Set the class up to teach before they write, reminding them to use their teaching as a way to improve upon their writing.

"I want that magic for your writing. So right now, without a word, while you are still sitting on the rug, make a plan for how you will teach someone today. Just jot the topics you'll teach, in order, and then, after you make that plan, consider whether you've taught the important points, interested your student, and answered the questions that the student is apt to be asking. Once I see that you are ready, I'm going to give you a student—not your partner, but someone who hasn't talked to you about your topic.

"And remember, teaching about a topic can always help you rehearse for informational writing, now and always.

"As you teach or right after, jot some quick notes about how you'll change your information writing. Okay, teachers—plan!"

As children worked, I voiced over with some prompts. "After you run dry on one subtopic, say, 'Another part that I want to teach about is . . . ,' then add another paragraph!"

A minute later I voiced over, "I love seeing so many of you jotting specific facts and details (see Figure 4–1). You are right that information writing is built with the bricks of information, not just swirls of words."

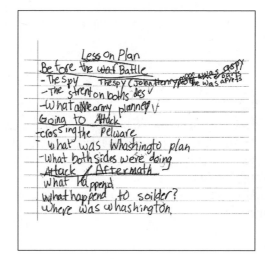

FIG. 4–1   Edward's teaching plan

Coaching Listeners

THE WRITING WORKSHOP WILL BE DIVIDED INTO TWO PARTS TODAY, and your conferring and small-group work will reflect that division. While children are teaching each other, you might make the decision to devote yourself entirely to working with the listeners. We all know what it is to talk to someone whose eyes are roaming as we talk, who seems to be waiting for us to cut to the chase and be done talking. On the other hand, we know what it is to talk to someone who listens raptly, who is so responsive to everything we say that it is as if that person is priming our pump, bringing more and more out of us so that we end up saying far more than we dreamt of saying. Your children will probably need help listening with that sort of attentiveness. You may decide that you can lift the quality of listening that is occurring in the classroom just by joining one partnership, then another, and in each instance, listening with rapt attention and responding as that sort of a listener does. Your model alone, however, may not be enough. You may need to ramp this up by whispering into the ear of some of your listeners. You might prompt, "Oh, that's interesting! Tell your partner to say more about that!" or "Wait! Are you confused? Ask your partner to say that again in a different way."

If you feel that almost every listening partner needs some direction, you might call out in a loud voice, "I need all listeners over here," and then give the listening partners a one-minute pep talk (quietly, away from the ears of the partners who are functioning as teachers).

Either way, after ten or fifteen minutes, you'll shift your class into writing, and then of course the kind of support you'll need to give will change. Be sure that writers are using their teaching to strengthen their drafting. For starts, it will be important that the structure that writers selected when planning their teaching is evident also in their

MID-WORKSHOP TEACHING
Teaching Others Should Prime the Pump of Your Writing

"Writers, in the old days, before the modern pipes we have now, people had to get their water from a well. Before they could pump water out of the well, they had to do what's called 'priming the pump,' that is—they had to give the handle a few pumps, like this," I mimed that I was pumping from a well. "Pump, pump, pump, and then the water would come spurting out. The teaching that you just did was sort of like priming the pump for your writing.

"You got yourself going a little bit—pump, pump, pump—by teaching others. Your teaching hopefully gave you lots of new ideas of what you could add to clear up confusion and to make things interesting. And now, your writing can come spurting out in a gush.

"Once you have primped the pump of your writing, pick up your pen and start writing. Be sure to think about ways to convey the important things about your topic, to interest your reader, and to answer questions he or she will be asking. We have about twenty minutes of writing left—plan to finish at least two more pages!"

drafting. One signal of this will be that they have clearly defined categories of information, and that they are grouping information into appropriate categories. Related to this, you can check in on their use of linking words and phrases.

Self-Assessment and Goal-Setting

Ask writers to reflect on all they already know about good informational writing, and use the Information Writing Checklists to set some goals for their writing.

"Writers, I want to remind you of one key principle of writing—and that's that writers bring forward everything they know about the kind of writing they are doing. I know you did some informational writing in third grade, and it's important that you carry that with you as you tackle these books. I also thought that it would be helpful to take a look at the goals for information writing that you'll be looking to master and exceed this year." I showed students the two-columned checklist.

"I know that you've seen a checklist like this before for the other writing units, but I just want to remind you how this works. In the first column are the goals for fourth-grade information writing. And in the next column are the goals for *next* year, for fifth-grade information writing. You might be thinking: What? Fifth grade? Next year, already? But you might be surprised to see that you are already starting to meet some of these fifth-grade goals. Right now, what I'd like you to do with the piece of writing that you've been working on today, is use this checklist to assess what you've done. Check 'yes' next to the things on the list that you are already doing and check 'starting to' if you're sort of doing it. Put a check in the 'not yet' column if you don't yet see evidence of that element in your writing." I gave students a few minutes to do this work.

"It looks like everyone is done. Now, with your partner, will you share one or two goals that you have for yourself? You can choose from any of the items on the checklist for which you checked 'starting to' or 'not yet.'"

Information Writing Checklist

	Grade 4	NOT YET	STARTING TO	YES!	Grade 5	NOT YET	STARTING TO	YES!
	Structure				**Structure**			
Overall	I taught readers different things about a subject. I put facts, details, quotes, and ideas into each part of my writing.	☐	☐	☐	I used different kinds of information to teach about the subject. Sometimes I included little essays, stories, or "how-to" sections in my writing.	☐	☐	☐
Lead	I hooked my readers by explaining why the subject mattered, telling a surprising fact, or giving a big picture. I let readers know that I would teach them different things about a subject.	☐	☐	☐	I wrote an introduction that helped readers get interested in and understand the subject. I let readers know the subtopics I would be developing later as well as the sequence.	☐	☐	☐
Transitions	I used words in each section that help readers understand how one piece of information connected with others. If I wrote the section in sequence, I used words and phrases such as *before, later, next, then,* and *after.* If I organized the section in kinds or parts, I used words such as *another, also,* and *for example.*	☐	☐	☐	When I wrote about results, I used words and phrases like *consequently, as a result,* and *because of this.* When I compared information, I used words and phrases such as *in contrast, by comparison,* and *especially.* In narrative parts, I used phrases that go with stories such as *a little later* and *three hours later.* In the sections that stated an opinion, I used words such as *but the most important reason, for example,* and *consequently.*	☐	☐	☐
Ending	I wrote an ending that reminded readers of my subject and may have suggested a follow-up action or left readers with a final insight. I added my thoughts, feelings, and questions about the subject at the end.	☐	☐	☐	I wrote a conclusion in which I restated the main points and may have offered a final thought or question for readers to consider.	☐	☐	☐
Organization	I grouped information into sections and used paragraphs and sometimes chapters to separate those sections. Each section had information that was mostly about the same thing. I may have used headings and subheadings.	☐	☐	☐	I organized my writing into a sequence of separate sections. I may have used headings and subheadings to highlight the separate sections. I wrote each section according to an organizational plan shaped partly by the genre of the section.	☐	☐	☐

The Information Writing Checklist, Grades 4 and 5 can be found on the CD-ROM.

30 MINUTES—JUST WRITE!!

Writers, you have done a lot of priming the writing pump. You've planned writing, taught writing, assessed writing, set goals for writing—the one part of all this that you haven't done enough is—*writing*! So tonight, set your clock to half an hour. Put your pen on the paper and start writing, and write, write, write for the full half an hour. If you aren't sure of a fact, just write "whatchamacallit" so that you don't pause to research anything.

In that half hour, you should be able to write at least a page and a half, and probably well over that amount. We'll admire what you get done tomorrow.

Elaboration

*The Details that Let People Picture What
Happened Long Ago and Far Away*

IN THIS SESSION, you'll teach students that writers improve their writing by adding details. History writers often try to include details that help readers picture what happened long ago.

GETTING READY

✔ Some of Jean Fritz's books to refer to when sharing information about the author (see Teaching) (This is optional.)

✔ Excerpts from Milton Meltzer's *The American Revolutionaries* (1993, 50, 51), or other nonfiction text related to the overarching historical topic your class is writing about (see Active Engagement)

✔ A variety of sources for students to use when researching, including informational books, articles, and primary sources

✔ A book related to the topic you are writing about (see Mid-Workshop Teaching)

✔ "Ways to Push Our Thinking" anchor chart, from *The Boxes and Bullets* unit (see Mid-Workshop Teaching)

✔ "Daily Life during the Revolutionary War" chart (see Share)

✔ Pictures related to students' topics (see Share)

✔ Chart paper and markers (see Share)

S EVERAL YEARS AGO, at one of the Teachers College Reading and Writing Project's summer institute on the teaching of writing, a teacher wrote a memoir about her divorce. I still remember one section of her writing. She described opening the door to her husband's closet, seeing it empty. Her toddler came and stood beside her, looking into the closet. "Who took Daddy's shoes?" he asked.

To me, that detail captures so much. The way that every bit of her home echoed with emptiness. The young child's perspective: "Who took Daddy's shoes?"

Memorable details bring writing to life. One of my all-time favorite lines is from Cynthia Rylant's *The Relatives Came* (1993): "It was hard getting used to all that new breathing in the house." I read that and felt the shock of seeing my exact experience there on the page.

Details like those bring to life the experience of divorce, of the relatives coming. As Richard Price has said, "The bigger the issue, the smaller you write." Ralph Fletcher tells about the day he noted that his fastidious father had threaded his belt so that it was outside one of the belt loops—that belt loop shocked Ralph into realizing something was amiss.

How crucial it is, then, for children to understand that if their goal is to bring to life a time and place that is utterly unlike our own, details become all the more important.

COMMON CORE STATE STANDARDS: W.4.2.b,d; W.4.5, W.4.6, W.4.7, W.4.9, W.4.10, RI.4.1, RI.4.3, RI.4.7, RI.4.9, SL.4.1, SL.4.2, L.4.1, L.4.2, L.4.3.a, L.4.6

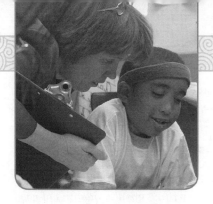

Elaboration

The Details that Let People Picture What Happened Long Ago and Far Away

CONNECTION

Celebrate the volume of writing that children have done, and meanwhile also acknowledge that just as writing fast and furious is helpful, so, too, it is helpful to pause in the midst of writing.

"Writers, yesterday we talked about the fact that teaching can be a way to prime the pump for writing, and my goodness, that is what happened for many of you! Thumbs up if you found that after you taught about your topic, it wasn't hard to do a lot of writing?" Many children signaled that. "How many of you wrote more than a page last night at home? More than two pages? More than three? Wow! Give yourselves a pat on the back." The children got their due recognition.

"Just as it is great to write fast and furious, it is also important to pause, to reread, and to even rethink what you have written. I know that first you are told to write quickly; now you are being told to pause and to reread—but actually those two bits of advice go together. An artist might sketch a portrait quickly in charcoal, and then, having sketched quickly, the artist pauses to say, 'How do I like it?' Sometimes the artist keeps going; sometimes the artist changes things."

"Shifting between writing and rereading is important no matter what kind of text you are writing. You'll always want to pause, to reread your writing, and to think, 'What's not so good that I can fix up?' Most of you have a goal from yesterday, and that is one thing you can fix up in your writing."

❖ **Name the teaching point.**

"Today, I want to teach you that often when you reread a draft of your writing, you will find that you've written in stick figures, without a lot of detail. One of the best ways to improve any piece of writing is to add details. Historians often try to give the details that help readers picture what happened in a long-ago and faraway time."

We've actually come to believe that one of the best ways to support revision is to encourage kids to draft more quickly. When a child invests a week in slowly writing what he or she hopes will be a perfect piece, that child is reluctant to revise. But if the piece was written in a day, the writer is often more game for revision.

Children did this same work when writing fiction. They learned to stop writing, to draw a line, and to think, "How else could this go?"

In the Common Core State Standards, elaboration is one of the key descriptors for each of the three kinds of writing that are valued—information, argument, and opinion. Of course, the ways that writers elaborate are not the same when a writer is writing a narrative or an information text, but in both instances, this is important.

TEACHING

Explain the importance of detail in history writing by telling about a well-known history writer who values details and by citing a few of the ones she's used in her writing.

"Jean Fritz, a famous writer of history books, once said, 'I dote on small details. In researching Ben Franklin, I read in one book after another that Franklin learned ten swimming tricks. What were they?' Fritz couldn't rest until she knew what those ten tricks were. She just *had* to know. After a long search, she uncovered all of the tricks—including one trick that involved Ben Franklin cutting his toenails underwater! Another of Ben Franklin's tricks was swimming with his legs tied together.

"Jean Fritz's obsession with details was not just *her* way. If you look at the most famous writers of history, many of them, like Jean Fritz, use details to make history come alive.

"When a writer of informational books wants to elaborate in this way, it helps to pause, and to say, 'What do I need to learn about?' like Jean Fritz did. Then the writer shifts from being a writer to being a researcher, looking for the details that bring people, places, and events to life."

Tell students to read, noting not just the main facts but also the intriguing details and particular stories that will enliven their writing.

"One way to get details is just to read like a magnet, letting intriguing details stick to you. Often the details don't seem like they are the important facts such as those that you'd be expected to produce on a test about this topic. They may seem quirky, even trivial. If you were reading to prepare for a test on the topic, you might not notice the details. But when you are a writer, you read as a writer, and that means you are a magnet for intriguing, quirky, odd details. A bricklayer builds with bricks. A writer builds with detail. Details are one of the most important materials you will use in any writing that you do—so make note of detail as you read."

ACTIVE ENGAGEMENT

Instruct the students to listen for details as you read an excerpt from an informational text and then discuss the ideas those details sparked.

"Let's practice reading for details, as a writer does. Let's read snippets of Robert Sessions's eyewitness account of the Boston Tea Party, recounted in Meltzer's *The American Revolutionaries*. As you listen to this, think about what you might want to record in your notes, to remember in your mind, to use later in your writing. Instead of focusing on the broad who, where, when, and what questions, pay attention to details that somehow seem to you to matter, to add up. Sessions describes the scene when he got to the Boston Tea Party this way":

Just as quirky details are important to strong history writing, they are also important to a strong minilesson. Kids want to learn, and thrive on hearing particular details. The qualities of good writing are also qualities of good teaching.

Everything was as light as day, by the means of lamps and torches—a pin might be seen lying on the wharf. I went on board where they were at work, and took hold with my own hands. I was not one of those . . . who disguised themselves as Indians, but was a volunteer, the disguised men being largely men of family and position in Boston. . . . Although there were many people on the wharf, entire silence prevailed—no clamor, no talking. Nothing was meddled with but the teas on board. . . . After having emptied the hold, the deck was swept clean, and everything put in its proper place. (1993, 50, 51)

"Will you tell each other some of the details you noticed, and what those details made you think? Turn and talk."

After children talked a bit, I reconvened the group. "I heard many of you talk about the way the ship was lit up with torches so that it was as light as day. A pin might be seen lying on the wharf. The powerful thing is that those details connect, don't they, to the next thing Sessions wrote about, which was the fact that the prosperous and well-connected rebels were disguised as Indians, but Sessions and others from less fancy positions weren't disguised."

Kids' eyes lit up, as if they were just now taking in the significance of that. "You see how the details—not just one detail, but several details—can click together like pieces of a puzzle to create the bigger picture. I'm getting a picture of how at the Boston Tea Party, the little guys took big risks. But then, the entire story of the American Revolution is about 'little guys' taking risks. That big idea is carried in the small details."

Channel writers to study their own writing with a critical eye, looking for parts that would benefit from more detail.

"Writers, right now will you take a second to reread the last bit of writing you did yesterday and notice how many details you have included? Notice, too, places where your writing seems a bit bare-bones. When you find a place that needs more details, star it so you know to go back and flesh it out later."

While partners talked, I crouched beside Natasha whose partner was absent. "Natasha, I noticed you made a star on this part. What are you thinking?"

"Well, it is about the patriots planning the Boston Tea Party, and I realized I didn't have a lot of details about it. I want to find out why the colonists were so mad about the tax on tea, and maybe how they planned the whole thing without people catching on to it. They must have had to be sneaky so the British wouldn't find out. I think that would be really cool to find out."

Debrief in a way that emphasizes the importance of detail.

After a minute, I voiced over to the class, saying, "I'm glad that you are being hard on yourself, writers. Jean Fritz didn't settle for just the general facts about Ben Franklin—she didn't just settle on knowing that he learned ten tricks. She wanted to know the specific tricks. Just like Fritz, you can try to find the details that will make your writing come to life."

The details of this scene are what pack the punch. Reading Sessions's account, one can't help but understand that the illumination at the wharf, where it was light as day, so light that a pin might be seen lying on the wharf—connects to the next detail. The prosperous and well-connected rebels were disguised, but not Sessions, and others like him. They took an extra risk. But then, the entire story of the American Revolution is about "little guys" taking risks. That big idea is carried in the small details.

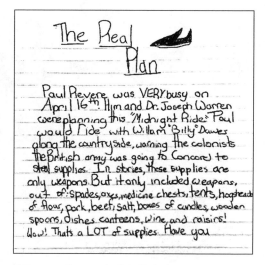

FIG. 5–1   Greyson's detailed passage

LINK

Send writers off to work by reminding them that details matter, while cautioning them that searching for details can consume a lot of time, and they also need to keep deadlines in mind.

"I hope that from this day forward, you always remember that details matter as much in informational writing as in personal narrative writing. But I also need to say that it is easy to get lost in the process of looking for one detail and before you know it, writing time has slid by. So balance looking for the details that will bring your writing to life, and pushing yourself to write, using all you know about informational writing."

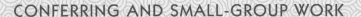

Conducting Research on the Internet

A S YOU CONFER ON THIS DAY, you may decide to spend some of your time chan-neling kids toward rich sources that will yield the kinds of details you taught them to value. If you are fortunate enough to have Internet-enabled computers in your classroom or access to a computer lab, you can concentrate some of your conferring time on helping students who are less Internet savvy to learn to conduct searches and home in on useful information quickly. The Internet is a resource like any other that takes some know-how to use properly. Even though many students are digital natives, more at home in the digital world than we are, they aren't always adept at using search engines effectively to find information on a specific topic.

You may want to prepare for this session by bookmarking search engines that will be helpful to them, such as kidrex.org, askkids.com, yahooligans.com, awesomelibrary .org, and onekey.com; as well as kid-friendly websites that provide historical content, such as kids.gov and americaslibrary.gov.

In conferences, small groups, or special "courses" you offer on using search engines to locate information, you may want to teach some of these tips to your students.

◆ If a web search doesn't yield fruitful results, an image search just might. For example, an image search of "George Washington and Valley Forge" yields images of the Continental troops trudging through snowy misery, Washington kneeling to pray for his men, and Washington walking through the makeshift camp, offering hope to the freezing, battle-weary soldiers. These powerful images have much to offer to students searching for the details of specific events. Additionally, these searches may yield other kinds of visual information, such as maps, that can help kids to add different kinds of detail to their writing.

◆ When conducting Internet searches, young people are apt to enter too many words (or words that are too tangential). Often, kids enter an entire question into the search box, such as: "What did Paul Revere's clothes look like when he

MID-WORKSHOP TEACHING
Coaching Writers to Grow Ideas about Their Notes

"Writers, I have a very important tip about note-taking. It is a tip I didn't learn until I was in college, but I wish I had learned earlier. Good note-takers don't just write fact after fact. Instead they pause, giving themselves space to grow ideas about those facts. Let me show you what I mean. I'm going to read you a little section from a book that tells about what happened after the Boston Massacre, and I want you to think about what you could write if you were recording not just the facts, but *your* thoughts. Get yourself ready to write 'This is important because . . . ' or 'The surprising/interesting thing about this is that . . . '" I opened the book and read:

> John Adams, a well-known patriot, was one of the lawyers who defended the (British) soldiers. He worked hard to convince the jury that the British soldiers were just defending themselves. In the end, the judge decided there wasn't enough evidence to find the soldiers guilty, so they were released.

"Start by writing, 'This is surprising because . . . ' and then keep going, fast and furious." After another pause, I continued, "Now try, 'To add on . . . ' and keep going, fast and furious."

I gave the class another moment, and then continued to call out prompts intermittently, such as "As I write this, I'm realizing. . . ." I ended by calling out, "All in all, what I want to say is that. . . ."

Then I asked children to talk as a class about what they thought after hearing the passage. Edward blurted out, "Why was Sam Adams defending the British soldiers? He was against the British. He's a Son of Liberty."

(continues)

Others chimed in. "And what did Adams say?" "Did he *have* to defend the British?"

"When you read as writers, the first step is to value the details, to let the stick figures in your writing become real. Then the next step is to wonder. To ask questions, as you are doing here.

"And I am hoping you saw that thought prompts helped you to think about your information. You won't always do that as you collect your notes, but when you find something interesting, you want to give yourself the space to grow some thinking. You may just want to reread your notes from time to time, boxing out intriguing parts, and then do this work to grow some ideas. I've left the 'Ways to Push Our Thinking' chart up from the essay unit for this very reason"—I gestured toward the chart, hanging on the wall. "Okay writers, back to work!"

went on the Midnight Ride?" The technicians behind search engines such as Google are constantly refining their search tools so that such a question might yield viable results, but the chances are good that if a child tries to search for answers to a sentence-long question, that will produce a dead end. It helps, therefore, to teach students to select a few key words, perhaps using only the main nouns from their original question. You can also point out to students that some search engines offer alternate searches at the bottom of a page of search results, and those suggested alternatives help kids refine their original search.

◆ It's important to caution students about the reliability of online sources. Anyone can publish a website these days—from professional historians to a first-grade class. Teach your writers to take note of the author(s) of the websites that they come across. If a website about the Revolutionary War says "Created by Mr. Hammond's Fourth-Grade Class," they can't be sure all of the information is wholly accurate. Another tip for assessing the validity of a site is to pay attention to how many advertisements are on the page. If the page is chock-full of ads, its purpose is to sell something, not necessarily to teach information. Sites that end in .org, .edu, and .gov tend to be reliable.

◆ Remind kids to keep track of the websites they use so they can credit these sources in their writing. It's important to clarify the difference between a search engine and an actual source. Many children list "Google" on their bibliography page. Google is a tool one uses to find information, but it is not a source itself. The websites one clicks on that give actual information are considered sources.

◆ Teaching a few keyword strategies can be helpful. For example, if a researcher types a phrase into a search engine, typically the results will contain any of those words, in any order. Typing the phrase *Most Famous Battle in the Revolutionary War* may return sites that are not about the Revolutionary War, but are about revolutionary tactics used in World War II. Putting quotes around the whole phrase tells the search engine to only return pages that have those words in the exact order. Additionally, using keywords such as "and" and "or" to search can be helpful. Searching for Washington *and* Jefferson will return sites with both of those terms. Searching for Washington *or* Jefferson will return sites with one or the other.

◆ As many of us who have found ourselves in the rabbit-hole of online searching can attest, the Internet can be a time-waster. Be on the lookout for writers who are spending more than ten minutes or so online, getting mired in the endless lists of results a search yields. At this point, kids should be collecting very specific details quickly, and then getting on with their writing. Periodically check the computer screens to make sure kids aren't returning to the search engine screen again and again, but are homing in quickly on a fruitful site.

Of course, not all of your conferring on this day will be spent teaching your fourth-graders to conduct research online. As in previous sessions where kids were gathering information from sources, you'll want to keep a watchful eye out for those who are simply copying right from a text. Many times this copying occurs because the text is too difficult for the particular writer. It may help to remind students who are copying directly from their texts that it is helpful to pause before jotting down notes, even going so far as to close the book or the website, and then take a moment or two to formulate what they might jot in their notes before putting pen to paper. If they have no idea what to write after closing the book or website, it could be a good indication that they need to track down a source that they can digest more easily.

Studying Pictures to Gather More Details about a Time Period

Channel students to study pictures related to their topics, noticing details about the time period.

"Writers, will you come to the meeting area so we can talk, and before you come, will you locate a picture you have, one that you can grab easily, related to your topic?" Once children had convened, I began. "We've thought a lot about the importance of details to your research. Details will become important in a new way starting tomorrow, because you'll be writing stories that teach readers about your topic, and you'll want to situate your stories in the world of those times. So you'll need to know details about the people's daily lives.

"I want to remind you that you can collect details not only from reading texts but also by observing. Remember that in order to write *Charlotte's Web* (1952), E. B. White spent days observing a spider in his barn? History writers can't observe the past, but you can study documents—paintings, photographs, letters, and the like.

"Writers, those of you who have a picture related to your topic, will you put it where a lot of kids can see it?" Soon the meeting area divided itself into clusters of kids, looking at one picture or another.

"Will your group study that picture closely now? Think of it as a secret map of the times, one that tells clues to those times, clues that have miraculously survived the generations and ended up in your hands. Tell each other the details about the time period that you can detect from the clues."

After some time, I said, "Daniel has noticed that men and women appear to be separate in his picture. Look at the objects in your pictures. Are they holding quill pens? A bayonet? Look again, and talk about what you see in the photograph that you could add to what you are learning."

After a bit, I said, "Let's collect some observations. You are all looking at glimpses of the same time period, so what can we as a class say about, say, the clothes worn by men and boys?"

"Wool stockings, up to their knees." "Leather shoes." "Hats with three corners."

"Girls and women?"

"Mop caps, aprons, gowns, tuckers."

This continued, until the class had collected details such as these, which I listed on chart paper.

Instruct students to envision the time period, thinking about how the details they collected can help shape the stories they will write in the next session.

"Writers, all of these details about daily life in this era bring to mind the stories of people who lived through the events we're learning about. These people had decisions to make, choices to wrestle with. One way information writers make history come alive is by telling the stories of people who lived in a particular era. Right now, think about one possible Small Moment story you might tell related to your topic. What might have been the decisions, the choices, that a person who lived through your event wrestled with? Could one of those become a story?" I left a bit of silence. "Thumbs up if you have one possible idea," I said. Then I continued. "Picture the story like it is a movie. Who is doing what at the start?" I gave the children a moment to think. "Now bring into your mental image as many details from the times as you can." Again I gave children a moment to envision. "Tell each other what is happening and how your knowledge of the times is shaping your story. Turn and talk."

SESSION 5 HOMEWORK

BRAINSTORMING NARRATIVE STORIES FOR YOUR INFORMATIONAL BOOK

Tomorrow you'll have a chance to move into another chapter of your informational book, this time writing a narrative about your topic. You just took some time in your small group to come up with one possible Small Moment story to tell. Tonight, I'd like you to take a look at your timeline, your notes, the writing you have done so far, and come up with at least three possible stories that you could include in your informational book. You don't have to write any of the stories yet, just come up with a list. Tomorrow you'll have a chance to write the actual narrative. But if you do some planning tonight, it will be easier for you to get right to work.

Daily Life during the Revolutionary War

- Clothing
  - men and boys: breeches, woolen stockings, leather shoes, and tricorn hats
  - women and girls: mop caps, aprons, gowns, and tuckers
  - Colonial soldiers: plain uniform of brown, red, or blue
  - British soldiers: fancy red uniform (called lobsterbacks)
- Food
  - Soldiers had a ration of salted meat, dry beans, and hard bread.
  - Most people ate simple foods, like corn, bread, salted meat, and few fruits.
- Money
  - Shillings
  - Pounds
  - Continentals—paper money worth about the same as a pound, released in 1775
- Kinds of shops
  - Silversmith
  - Gunsmith
  - Tailor
  - Apothecary
  - Blacksmith
- Language
  - 'tis—it is
  - 'twill—it will
  - ye—the
  - Sir—A way to address a man
  - Madame—A way to address a woman

Bringing Information Alive
Stories inside Nonfiction Texts

YOUR CHILDREN HAVE BEEN WORKING HARD, as have you! There is a lot of decision making and writing going on as these informational books come together. Let's take a moment to recap.

So far, your class has studied the kind of text they are going to write and planned how their own books will go, based on what they've learned. Then, they organized their thoughts and information to write a first chapter, one that gives the big picture of the Revolutionary War. Next, as they prepared to write a second all-about section (this time all about their own particular topic), they again jotted thoughts and took notes in a form that matched their writing plan. Then children used their notes to teach a partner about their topic, as a rehearsal for writing and as a way to see what further research they might still need. They spent most of the last workshop session drafting the chapter that is all about their topic. Some students finished with that work and began writing, researching, and setting up for the micro-story, the mini-narrative that will bring their topic to life. Other students won't be ready to do this work until tomorrow.

In an earlier session, we compared conglomerate rock (made up of different kinds of pebbles) to informational texts (made up of different kinds of writing). So far, you have coached children as they have made one kind of writing: category-based, all-about writing. Now, it's time to coach them as they make another kind of writing: mini-narratives. You can start this by bringing back to their minds all the things they already know to do to write effective narratives. Just because a story is in the middle of an informational text does not mean that story can be without dialogue, precise actions, internal thinking, and all of the other qualities of good narrative writing that children have been learning!

Today then, you will coach children to embed narratives within their information writing—by using all they know about narrative writing in the service of their cause: interesting their readers and teaching their topic.

IN THIS SESSION, you'll teach students that writers who are writing a story about a time in history think about the three most important elements in any story: character, setting, and conflict.

GETTING READY

✔ An excerpt from a familiar historical fiction book. We use *Number the Stars,* by Lois Lowry (1989). (see Connection)

✔ Chart paper and markers

✔ Chart paper with the title "Planning a Micro-Story that Will Be Embedded in History Research" to add to (see Teaching and Active Engagement)

✔ "Daily Life during the Revolutionary War" chart, created in Session 5 (see Mid-Workshop Teaching)

COMMON CORE STATE STANDARDS: W.4.2.b, W.4.3, W.4.5, W.4.8, W.4.9, W.4.20, RL.4.1, RL.4.3, RL.4.6, SL.4.1, L.4.1, L.4.2, L.4.3, L.4.6

Bringing Information Alive
Stories inside Nonfiction Texts

CONNECTION

Evoke a scene from a familiar historical fiction book to illustrate the work that writers will do today.

"Writers, today I'm going to help you get ready to write the story that will be one of the chapters in your report. This will be a bit like a small moment scene from one of your historical fiction books. I know you remember, for example, the scene in *Number the Stars*, when Jews are being rounded up and taken away. Because of this Ellen is staying over with Anne Marie's family so that she will be safe. She and Anne Marie are in bed, just starting to go to sleep, when they hear the Nazi soldiers come to search the apartment. You recall how they heard the soldiers ask, 'Who's in there?' and at just that moment Anne Marie catches a glimpse of the Star of David necklace—a sign of Judaism—around her friend's neck. "Take it off," she whispers, but there is no time. She has to make a decision—what to do. She grabs the necklace, pulls with all her might, and then clasps her hands around that star just as the soldiers come in to search the room. Anne Marie holds that star—later, when the soldiers are gone, she sees she has pressed it so hard that it is tattooed against her hand. That scene brings the whole of that history and heroism to life, doesn't it?

"You'll be writing your own scene, your own Small Moment story, only yours will involve the time in history that is the subject of your research."

Any historical fiction that your students know well will suffice here. The important thing is to conjure a small moment—just a scene or two—in which a character is faced with a decision or is otherwise embroiled in a point of tension.

❖ Name the teaching point.

"Today, I want to teach you that to write a story about a time in history, you need to think about the three most important elements in any story: central character, a setting, and a problem (or you could call it a tension, a turning point, a decision)."

TEACHING AND ACTIVE ENGAGEMENT

Remind writers of the questions people need to ask in order to write a story.

"Writers, this means that whenever you write even a micro-story, you need to decide whose story you are telling, what the tension or turning point or problem will be, and then you need to decide where exactly the scene takes place. That is, when the curtain opens, who is where, doing or saying what?

Coach students to consider the question, "From what perspective will I tell the story?" first in a class narrative, then in their own.

"Writers, I'd like to recruit you to help me with my narrative for my book on the Boston Massacre. Let's pretend we are all writing about it, although each of you should also be thinking of your own event. We need to decide whether we will write the story from British Soldier Private Hugh White's point of view—*I was being called all sorts of names by these colonial troublemakers*—or do we want to write as if we are someone different who also plays a part in the story? I'm thinking about what other character might play a part in a story about the Boston Massacre. Hmm."

At first, the children didn't think there was anyone else, but I pointed out that they could think about groups of people, and then tell the imagined story of one person from that group. They could, for example, tell the story of the crowd of boys who were shouting insults at Private Hugh White, or of one of the villagers in Boston who witnessed the event.

I asked, "If we told the story of one of the boys who decided to throw ice and yell insults at the British soldiers, can you think about how the story would go? How would it start?"

I listened in while Jude and Yoshi devised a plan. "It might start with them walking up to the soldiers and seeing them guarding the house," said Jude. "And then, they could start to make some snowballs and pack them real tight and get ready to throw them."

Yoshi nodded. "Yeah, and then one guy might say, 'Hey, let's all start throwing these at the soldiers, and then let's yell at them. Maybe we can get them to leave.'"

I reconvened the class and shared what I'd overheard Jude and Yoshi discussing, before continuing, "Will you think now about your own event? What are the different players whose story could possibly be told? Remember, just as we could give a name and a story to a nameless citizen in Boston who began to taunt the British soldiers, you could give a name and story line to a soldier in the Continental Army, or to a young boy who tags along with the Sons of Liberty, or to a well-known historical figure, like Paul Revere. Decide whose story you will tell. You can look back over your notes from last night's homework or come up with a new idea right now."

Recruit children to join you in thinking about the central tension that the main character in the class story might have been feeling, a tension that is related to the true facts of that event.

"So our first step was to decide on the perspective from which the story will be told. I think the second step is to figure out the central drama of that story:

"Next, we probably want to think about the major tensions that our character is feeling, the major decisions he or she needs to make. To do that, we need to think about what we know from history.

Perspective is a critical concept, and not one that many students learn a lot about in school. John Gardner, one of America's greatest writers, suggested that when teaching someone to write, it can help to ask them to describe a building as seen by a man whose son has just been killed in war. Gardner wrote, "Do not mention the son, war, or the old man doing the seeing. Then describe the same building, in the same weather, and at the same time of the day, as seen by a happy lover. Do not mention love or the loved one." This sort of exercise would be great training for reading and writing of historical research!

Planning a MICRO-STORY...
... That will be Embedded in
HISTORY RESEARCH

1. Decide whose story you will tell
   → What is that person's perspective?
   Patriot 👤 👤← Loyalist 👤← Redcoat

2. Decide on the major tension, conflict, problem

"Let's think together about the young boy who decides to join the group of protesting colonists and taunt the British soldiers. This boy likely wasn't a soldier or anything. He is just a boy, maybe about your age. He has decided to begin yelling insults and throwing snow and sticks at a group of soldiers, armed and in uniform. How do you think he felt? Turn and talk!"

A minute later I called on children, who buzzed with excitement. "Scared!" "Worried he would get in trouble." "Yeah, especially when the soldiers started to get angry." "I'd be afraid I'd get shot!"

"Now—the jobs are getting harder. Think not about the boy at the Boston Massacre but about *your* character, from your historical event. What were the main tensions your character was probably feeling, the main decisions he or she was trying to make? Turn and talk—help each other."

Recruit children into thinking of a small moment or two they can tell that will capture the main drama of their story.

"Before you actually write, remember what you have learned about small moment writing. You are going to want to write about one twenty-minute episode, or perhaps two, through which the story can be told. So for example, in our story about the boy at the Boston Massacre, the story probably won't start with him eating breakfast on the morning of the event. Instead, the story is apt to start closer to the action—what do you think we should have him doing at the start of our story?"

"Walking along the street and seeing the crowd?" Melissa said.

I nodded. "Try to see it with more detail. The boy, let's call him Peter, shuffling along on the side of the street, kicking a rock and watching the horses ride by. Then, hearing a rumble of voices in the distance, and seeing a crowd gathering near the customs house. Imagine him running closer, and seeing some men and boys he knows from the town gathered in a clump near the British soldiers. He begins to hear what some of the rumbling is about, they are saying to each other, what?"

"Let's get these soldiers?" ventured Edward.

"Yes, and what else?" I prodded.

"Let's throw some sticks at them and call them names, let's see if we can get them to leave the city!" said Lucie.

Channel the writers to do similar envisionment of a small moment that will become their story.

"Now writers, try the same work with your story. Think of the whole timeline, then zoom in on just two small moments that can carry the whole story. Turn and talk about that."

After a minute I said, "By now, you should have in mind the Small Moment story that you are thinking of writing at the start of your story. You'll be writing with detail—so writing this small moment will probably require a page or two, and then I assume you will jump ahead to a different small moment, which happens later."

In any story, readers expect something to happen—which really means that there will be a tension that builds, leading the reader to be on edge. The tension comes from conflict. Literary scholars will tell you the conflict can be a person with a place, a person with another person, a person with himself, herself.

LINK

Create an improvisation activity that helps writers begin imagining their story.

"Writers, imagine you are the character whose story you have decided to tell. Put yourself in the place where you are, at the start of the story. Don't say anything, but become that person by the way you sit." After a moment, I continued. "What you are wearing?" I gave them a moment to construct a mental image of their outfit. "Do something with your clothes—adjust your hat, wipe dust off your vest. . . . You are holding something—what is it? You are lost in thought, so you just turn that thing over in your hands, as you think." Again I left some silence. "What are you thinking about?"

"It is the start of your story. Where are you, exactly? What, exactly, are you doing? If you say you are carrying your lunch—what is in the lunch bag? If you are going to a meeting, what is the space like where you meet? Fill in the details." I left some silence. "What is going on around you? Changes are probably brewing; there may be tension, trouble in the air. What's going on?" I left more silence.

Use the guided imagery work to galvanize students to flash-draft the start of a small moment scene.

"Quickly, open your notebooks and sketch the place, and add yourself, and someone else, too. Show what you are you doing." I let some time go by. "Add the weather—is it sunny? gray? frozen cold, with deep snow?

"What are you worried about—and why?" I left some more silence. "Be more detailed in your worries—making stuff up, of course. What could go wrong? Be more exact and precise.

"Now, someone comes and says something to you. Give the person a name. Make the person talk. What does the person say? What do you do?

"Writers, flip to the page where you will be writing the Small Moment story and start writing. This is a twenty-minute moment. It will fill a few pages. Keep writing." As children worked, I tapped one, then another, another on the shoulder, signaling for them to return to their writing spots.

Planning and Launching into Drafting

ECAUSE THE KIND OF WRITING YOU WILL CHANNEL YOUR WRITERS TO DO on this day is a departure from what they have been doing, you may want to start your conferring by taking the pulse of your class. Move from table to table, studying your writers to get a sense of how they are getting started and what they seem to be struggling with. At first, you'll likely pay particular attention to how kids are planning for their writing. Are they making a story arc or a timeline to help plan how their scenes will go? Are they recalling the fiction work from earlier in the year and beginning with some character development, taking a minute or two to list some internal and external traits of their main character?

As you move from table to table, and you begin to notice patterns, you can deliver table conferences in which you compliment one writer who is doing something you'd like others at the table to replicate. You will especially want to encourage writers to plan for their story to involve just two to three fifteen- to twenty-minute scenes. In other words, instead of writing all about a soldier's entire experience at Valley Forge, you hope the writer decides to write about a moment in which he makes a decision to give an extra pair of socks to his friend, despite the bitter cold.

If you find some students are bringing lessons they learned during fiction into their planning, you'll want to celebrate that. You might say something like, "Can I interrupt all of you? Elizabeth has made a story booklet, and on each page she's jotted a few words to show what will happen in that part. She's now storytelling to herself. If you haven't done some planning to think through how each of your scenes might go, you might borrow Elizabeth's idea."

After not too long, you'll want to channel your writers toward drafting. Although it is very possible and sometimes prudent for narrative writers to spend days and days just on planning, in this case, the goal is for your writers to draft the entire narrative in about a day. It makes sense then, to aim to have your writers starting to draft after no more than about 20% of your writing time has gone by. As writers begin to draft, check to see if they are starting inside a moment, perhaps beginning with a small

MID-WORKSHOP TEACHING
Adding Historical Details to Stories

"Writers, can I stop you for a moment? Think back for a moment to yesterday, when we collected some of the details of daily life during this time period. We are writing stories not just to entertain our readers but also to teach them about the Revolutionary War time in history. Those kinds of daily life details will help readers to learn what life was like back then. You can look back at the 'Daily Life during the Revolutionary War' chart that we made if you need help.

"Right now, will you check your draft to see if there are places where you can add more of the details of daily life? Notice your descriptions of characters. Are there places where it would make sense to describe the way they dress? What about the setting? Where are your characters? What does the place look like? And what kinds of objects are in the scene? Take about two minutes to add these kinds of details to what you've already written, and think about where you might include them as you write on."

action or with a character saying something. Be on the lookout for writers who are launching into a summary of a moment, or those who are attempting to tackle a time span that is much too long. You'll want to gather these writers and redirect them early in the workshop.

As writers are drafting, look over their work and try to classify what is holding them back. You might find that many of them are summarizing, and not storytelling. This may surprise you, because if there was one thing that was stressed heavily in third-grade narrative writing, and certainly earlier this year in the fiction unit, it was the difference between storytelling and summary. While we cannot really tell you for sure why kids continue to struggle with this skill, we want to acknowledge you are in good company if you diagnose this issue in your classroom.

In one-to-one instruction or small groups, you can address this common problem. If a writer is struggling to write from inside a moment, you might suggest the writer grab a partner and do a quick bit of role-playing, so the writer and his or her partner act out what the characters say and do. You might also suggest writers self-assess to be sure their narratives are a balanced amalgam of action, dialogue, and internal thinking. If there is an overabundance or a dearth of one of these elements, writers can work to correct the imbalance. Then, too, mentor texts help. Encourage students to study Naomi's narrative, naming what she has done that they could try.

Edward

I was in a boat crossing the Ice frozen delaware rivier. Thinking should I jump off the boat, and die or strave to death hard to think about. The Boat is creacking, water is leaking and almost no food, very hungry and not knowing what to do. I stuck here in the delaware Riveir, little water is leaking, what should I do?... My latern is the olny sorce of heat. Helpppp! Sunddenlly my latern went out. dun dun dun...

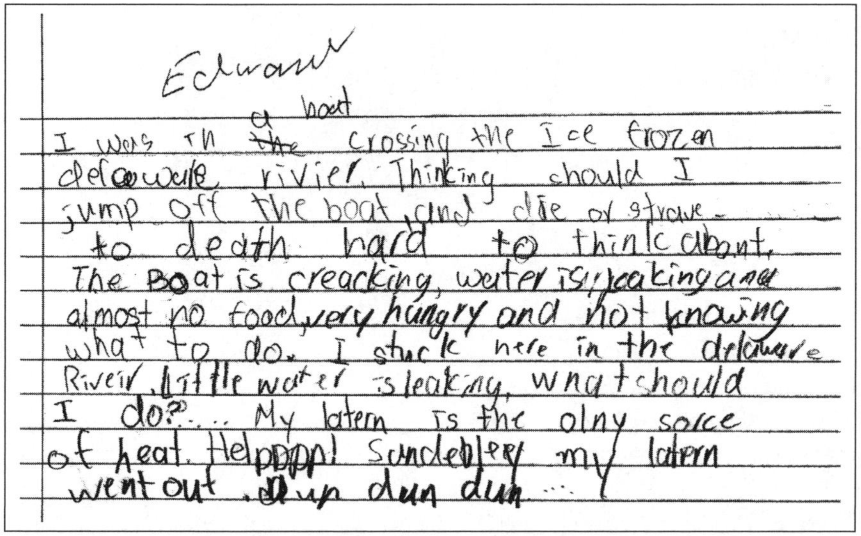

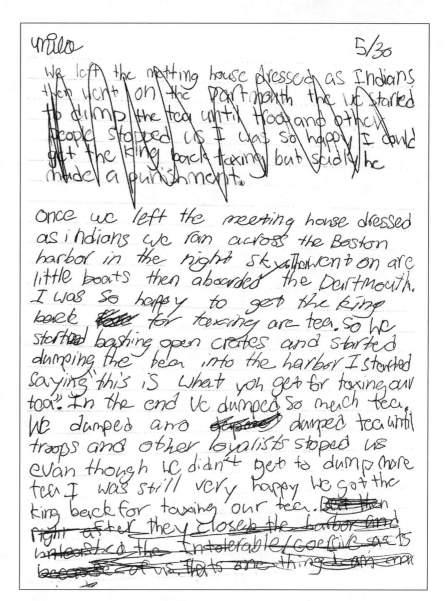

FIG. 6–1 Edward's draft of his narrative

Milo 5/30

We left the metting house dressed as Indians then went on the Dartmouth the we started to dump the tea until troops and other people stoped us I was so happy I could get the king back taxing but sadly he made a punishment.

Once we left the meeting house dressed as indians we ran across the Boston harbor in the night sky then went on are little boats then aboarded the Dartmouth. I was so happy to get the king back for taxing are tea. So we started bashing open crates and started dumping the tea into the harbor I started saying "this is what you get for taxing our tea." In the end we dumped so much tea. We dumped and dumped tea until troops and other loyalists stoped us evan though we didn't get to dump more tea I was still very happy we got the king back for taxing our tea. But then right after they closed the harbor and unleashed the Intolerable/Coercive acts because of us. That's one thing

FIG. 6–2 Milo's draft of his narrative

Learning from Classmates' Writing

Celebrate the work of one writer, pointing out qualities of his or her work that can inspire the class to make revisions that improve their own writing.

"Writers, let's gather in the meeting area. I want to share a part of Mirei's story with you. Mirei wrote the story of how Molly Pitcher in the Battle of Monmouth made the choice to take over her husband's cannon when he got shot in battle. Let's listen to Mirei read this part. Would you listen for the different ways she pulls the reader in, the ways she makes us feel as if we are there, on that day, alongside Molly Pitcher?"

Mirei stood and read (see Figure 6–3):

> One hot day I was looking out to see the beautiful sky, then I heard a drum beat. My husband and some other soldiers told me to move back. As they loaded the cannon, I picked up my pitcher and filled it with water. All of a sudden, we see a red sea of lobsterbacks marching in a perfect line coming towards us!

"Writers, doesn't that just pull you right into the moment? Let's take a closer look and see what Mirei does that others of us could possibly try. Would you turn and talk to your partner? What do you notice that Mirei has done that helps us to feel as if we are there, or that helps draw us in to this moment?"

I listened in while partners talked, then after a few moments I reconvened that class.

"Let's come back together. I heard quite a few of you talking about the sensory details that Mirei uses. That is, the details that pertain to one of the five senses. She talks about how hot it felt. And you know what, the weather at that battle was unbearably hot! She talks about hearing the drum beat. That's a very important detail, because that signaled battle was about to begin! And later, she talks about seeing the sea of lobsterbacks. Can't you just picture that in your mind's eye, all of the soldiers marching in unison? What Mirei did is something all of us could try. Right now, would you look at your story and think, 'Are there places I could add more sensory details? Could I add smells? Sounds? Sights? Feelings?' If you find a place, you might want to mark it with a star and a small note to yourself so you'll remember the kind of revisions you plan to make."

FIG. 6–3 Mirei's narrative

RESEARCHING TO FIND HISTORICAL DETAILS TO INCLUDE IN YOUR NARRATIVE CHAPTER

Now that you have begun writing your narrative chapter, you may be realizing that you have still more research to do. Part of writing stories is pulling your reader into the moment, and you do that through the details. When you are writing from your own life experiences, it is easy to recall those kinds of details. But when you are writing about a historical time period, those details may be a bit harder to come by, and it may involve some extra research on your part. Tonight, I'd like you to reread your draft. Look for places where you could add more details to make your reader feel like they are part of the moment, and make those revisions. You might find that you need to do more research to figure out what those exact details are.

Essays within Information Texts

IN THIS SESSION, you'll teach students that when writers are writing essays about historical topics, they think about all they know about essay writing: the structure, the thesis, and the supports. They also need to do research to find facts to develop and support their idea.

GETTING READY

✔ A copy of the mentor text introduced in Session 1, specifically the essay chapter, enlarged for students to see (see Teaching)

✔ "Parts of an Essay" chart (see Teaching)

✔ A copy of the plan and notes for the essay chapter of your informational book, enlarged for students to see (see Active Engagement and Conferring and Small-Group Work)

✔ Chart paper and marker (see Active Engagement)

✔ "Essay Frame Outline" chart, previously used in the *Boxes and Bullets* unit (see Link)

✔ "Transition Words" chart (see Mid-Workshop Teaching)

COMMON CORE STATE STANDARDS: W.4.1, W.4.2.b, W.4.5, W.4.8, W.4.9, W.4.10, RI.4.2, RI.4.5, RI.4.8, SL.4.1, L.4.1, L.4.2, L.4.3, L.4.5

COLLECT A STACK OF INFORMATION BOOKS, written for children, and leaf through them. You are apt to see that many of them contain a few chapters that resemble essays. For example, chances are great that a book on dolphins will have chapters on the dolphin's body, eating habits, life cycle, habitat—and then, as an extension of the habitat chapter, there is apt to be a chapter suggesting that if we do not take better care of Earth, the habitat of the dolphin will be compromised, and dolphins may be at risk. That "Be Good to the Dolphin" ending chapter has found its way into many information books on the dolphin!

Of course, our point has nothing to do with dolphins, or even books on endangered species. There are parallel ways in which information books on other topics will end. Perhaps instead of arguing that something is at risk and deserves protection, a final chapter will end by arguing that the subject of the book has not received the attention it deserves, or that it recently has begun to change, or that it increasingly resembles other things that are occurring. Whatever the exact spin on a topic might be, our point is that it is not unusual for information books to contain texts that are essays.

From the information books that they read, children learn ways in which the essays that are embedded into those texts are like and unlike the essays they wrote earlier. They will enter this unit, already sensing that the essays that are written in an information book are not written to expound on a personal opinion or preference (i.e., "I think it would be exciting to ride in the Pony Express") but instead, these texts argue that a conclusion is true, based on the evidence. The Battles of Concord and Lexington were important to the Revolutionary War. The Boston Massacre galvanized public opinion in favor of the war. The French played a far more important role in the Revolution than many people realize.

If your students struggle with this work, don't be surprised. Chances are very good that you didn't begin to write like this when you were their age. Your goal is not for them all to be proficient, but instead, for them to do the approximation work that helps them to develop their skills, beginning what will be a long learning journey.

Essays within Information Texts

CONNECTION

Tell about a "digital native" who tackled a totally new digital device with surprising proficiency, transferring what he knows to the new challenge. Suggest that similarly, children who are proficient writers can transfer what they know to new writing tasks.

"I went shopping with my nephew Taylor this weekend. I knew he wanted to go into the video game store because he's a video game maniac. When we got inside the store, there was a display with a brand-new game set up. Now, Taylor had never played this game before. He had never even seen it before. But when he got his turn to try it—you're probably already guessing this—he was amazing! He beat everyone to his right or left.

"When it was time for us to go I asked him how he did so well when this was a brand-new game that I knew he'd never played before. Taylor said, 'It was easy. It's similar to what I've done before, so I just apply that.'

"That got me thinking about you. Instead of being expert video game players, you are expert writers. You have written so many different kinds of writing over all the years of writing workshop. During this unit, you've reused a lot of what you have learned in other units, writing all about a topic, and stories. It's been challenging because you need to do that writing and those stories about this new content—the American Revolution—but still, the writing you have been doing you've done in the past. And today, you'll think about calling on another kind of writing, essay writing, and doing that within your information writing.

"But the essays you'll be writing require an extra twist because you'll be writing essays that are comprised not just of your own opinions and claims, but of information that comes from research.

"I'm going to show you that you can again call on what you know—about writing essays, but also about angling information to make a point. Just like my nephew Taylor can play video games he's never seen before, you'll be able to handle challenges you haven't handled before—and you'll do this in the same way. You'll draw on what you know to tackle what's new to you.

Oftentimes, the connection of a minilesson is a personal story that illustrates the kind of work students are about to take on. Using the example of my nephew playing a video game helps give children the impression that what I'm about to teach is totally doable, as familiar and approachable as a video game.

✤ **Name the teaching point.**

"Today I want to teach you that when you are writing mini-essays about your topic, you want to keep in mind all the things you already know about writing essays: the structure, the thesis, the supports, as well as hold in your mind what is different: using only facts to develop and support an idea. And you also want to be ready to do some work that might be new to you—finding information in books, and angling that information to make a point."

TEACHING

Channel students to notice the way the mentor text, written by another fourth-grader, shows that essays written to support a claim about history are similar in some ways, different in other ways, to the personal essays students wrote earlier.

"Writers, let's study the way that Naomi's essay is like the essays you wrote during the personal essay unit, and ways in which it is different. I'm going to read a bit of Naomi's essay aloud, and will you join me in thinking, 'How is this the same?' 'How is this different?'"

"I'm going to stop there. You get a sense for the essays you'll be writing. Will you turn and tell your partner what you are thinking about how this essay is like and unlike the essays you wrote earlier in the school year? Turn and talk."

Explain that while personal essays supported personal experiences, historical essays, written within information texts, support claims that are based on facts.

The room erupted into conversation. After a bit, I asked for the class's attention. "I heard most of you saying that this essay is based on facts—and some of you have discussed the fact that the personal essays were based on facts too. Let's take the 'I love ice cream' essay that you wrote during essay boot camp. If you write that you love ice cream because it has lots of flavors—you are right that it is a fact that ice cream comes in lots of flavors. But there *is* a difference. In the 'I love ice cream' essay (or the 'My father has been my best teacher' essay) the goal was to support a statement of personal preference and of feelings. Those essays were not arguing that the opinion expressed in the essay is *the* correct opinion. And that is the difference. The essay about the Battle of Lexington and Concord is contending that it is correct to claim that these battles were important. This claim is based on facts, not our opinions or our preferences."

Why the Battles of Concord and Lexington Were Important

The Battles of Concord and Lexington were so important to the war. They happened on April 19, 1775. They were important because they were all about the supplies for the war, and because they were the first battles of the war, so they pretty much started everything. Another reason they were important is because they proved the patriots weren't going to give up. Finally, a reason they were important is because they were a new style of fighting that the British didn't know about.

The British were marching to Lexington and Concord to find and destroy the Continental Army's supplies that they had secretly been hiding. If you know anything about wars, you know supplies are really important. The British had plans to destroy the supplies of the Continental Army before the war even began.

These were the first battles of the war and they started everything off. They happened on April 19, 1775, before any of the other battles . . .

Point out that historical essays are structured like the personal essays students wrote earlier, and ask students to label the component parts in a mentor essay, written by another fourth-grader.

"I also heard some of you say that this essay is structured like the essays you wrote in the personal essay unit. Why don't we see if the evidence supports that claim?" I unveiled a list of the components of an essay. "Right now, see how quickly you and your partner can locate and label the following parts of Naomi's essay.

As children got to work, I signaled for a few of them to work with me, in front of the class, labeling the component parts of the enlarged essay.

After two minutes, I called for the class's attention. "Writers, in two minutes you've found most of the parts of Naomi's essay! We've labeled parts based on what I heard you saying—see if you agree with these labels."

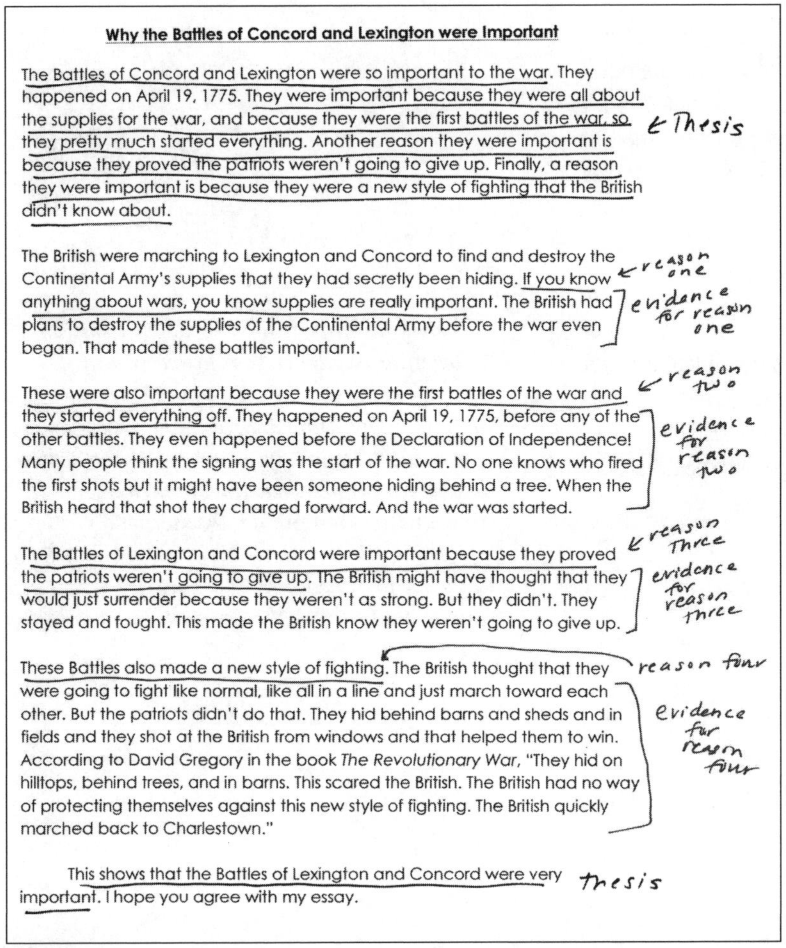

Parts of an Essay

- thesis
- reason 1
- reason 2
- reason 3
- evidence for reason 1
- evidence for reason 2
- evidence for reason 3

Why the Battles of Concord and Lexington were Important

The Battles of Concord and Lexington were so important to the war. They happened on April 19, 1775. They were important because they were all about the supplies for the war, and because they were the first battles of the war, so they pretty much started everything. Another reason they were important is because they proved the patriots weren't going to give up. Finally, a reason they were important is because they were a new style of fighting that the British didn't know about. ← *Thesis*

The British were marching to Lexington and Concord to find and destroy the Continental Army's supplies that they had secretly been hiding. If you know anything about wars, you know supplies are really important. The British had plans to destroy the supplies of the Continental Army before the war even began. That made these battles important. ← *reason one* / *evidence for reason one*

These were also important because they were the first battles of the war and they started everything off. They happened on April 19, 1775, before any of the other battles. They even happened before the Declaration of Independence! Many people think the signing was the start of the war. No one knows who fired the first shots but it might have been someone hiding behind a tree. When the British heard that shot they charged forward. And the war was started. ← *reason two* / *evidence for reason two*

The Battles of Lexington and Concord were important because they proved the patriots weren't going to give up. The British might have thought that they would just surrender because they weren't as strong. But they didn't. They stayed and fought. This made the British know they weren't going to give up. ← *reason Three* / *evidence for reason three*

These Battles also made a new style of fighting. The British thought that they were going to fight like normal, like all in a line and just march toward each other. But the patriots didn't do that. They hid behind barns and sheds and in fields and they shot at the British from windows and that helped them to win. According to David Gregory in the book *The Revolutionary War*, "They hid on hilltops, behind trees, and in barns. This scared the British. The British had no way of protecting themselves against this new style of fighting. The British quickly marched back to Charlestown." *reason four* / *evidence for reason four*

This shows that the Battles of Lexington and Concord were very important. I hope you agree with my essay. *thesis*

FIG. 7–1   Naomi's marked-up essay

Examine and explain the use of facts to support claims in the mentor essay, showing that students can find facts that are arguably evidence, and can discuss why the facts support the claim.

"Writers, I agree with you that Naomi starts her essay with a claim, supported by reasons. That first paragraph is sort of an outline for the rest of the essay—the rest of the paragraphs seem to follow that order. That is exactly how most of you organized your personal essays. But let's look at the way she uses facts to support her reasons."

> These were also important because they were the first battles of the war and they started everything off. They happened on April 19, 1775, before any of the other battles. They even happened before the Declaration of Independence! Many people think the signing was the start of the war. No one knows who fired the first shots but it might have been someone hiding behind a tree. When the British heard that shot they charged forward. And the war was started.

"This paragraph begins with a big reason why the battles were important—they were the first battles of the war. But look at the way Naomi brings in evidence. First, she names the date of them, and points out that date was before other battles. Then she added her own observation—these battles were before the Declaration of Independence. She doesn't just name this fact, she points out why it is relevant, saying that many people think the signing of the Declaration of Independence was the start of the war. Chances are good that fact wasn't something that Naomi read in a book. It was her own thinking, her own figuring out, that led her to say that."

Debrief by summarizing what you hope students have learned from studying the mentor essay.

"I hope you can see that Naomi proves that the Battles of Concord and Lexington are important by using facts that add up to that conclusion. The facts go with her idea—the Battles were important. This is Naomi's own idea. It is not something she found in the books she reads and just copied down. But it is both her idea and also what she argues is a *true idea*, learned from her research, that she sets out to prove. In this kind of essay, the evidence is mostly facts. But it's not enough to just plop in facts in any old way. The writer needs to carefully choose facts that go with each reason, and then say more about the facts to show how they support the reason."

When you shift from the demonstration to debriefing, students should feel the different moves you are making just by the way your intonation and posture changes. After most demonstrations, there will be a time for you to debrief, and that's a time when you are no longer acting like a writer. You are the teacher who has been watching the demonstration and now turns to talk, eye to eye with kids, asking if they noticed this or that during the previous portion of the minilesson.

ACTIVE ENGAGEMENT

Set writers up to try this work with the class book.

"Writers, I'd like to recruit your help with my book about the Boston Massacre. I've done a bit of work on it, and here is the structure I came up with."

The Boston Massacre was a key event in the Revolutionary War.

- It was a key event because it was a violent result of problems between the colonists and England.
- It was a key event because people could use it to make others mad enough to fight.
- It was a key event because it was the last straw before the start of the war.

I wrote the following on an empty piece of chart paper so I could write underneath it later:

> The Boston Massacre was a key event because people could use it to make others mad enough to fight.

"Writers, here is the first reason. I collected a few facts, but I'm not sure how they all really fit with this reason. Right now, would you and your partner look over these facts, and pick ones that you think would make really great evidence for this reason? Then, talk about what you might write to show the connection between the fact and the reason."

I listed the following facts underneath the reason, then signaled for writers to turn and talk to their partners:

> In 1768, 4,000 British troops were sent to Boston.
>
> Edward Garrick, a wig-maker's apprentice, started the trouble by arguing with a guard when he was sent to collect payment from a British officer.
>
> Paul Revere made an etching of the Massacre that showed the British soldiers killing the colonists on purpose, but this wasn't totally true.

I circulated among the writers as they discussed the facts and decided which would make for good evidence. I coached them while they attempted to articulate how to show the connection between the reason and the evidence.

After a few minutes, I reconvened the class. "Writers, I want to share something I overheard. A lot of you thought the third fact, about Paul Revere's etching, would make for a good piece of evidence for this reason. I heard Mitchell say that we could show the connection between this evidence and the reason by saying something like, 'The etching wasn't totally a true version of the Boston Massacre, but it made people angry enough to want to join the revolution!' I added what we just came up with to our draft."

If you feel that your minilesson is getting too long, you can always prepare your writing ahead of time, writing your reason across the top of your page and keeping the facts covered until you are ready for your students to work with them. It is not always essential that you write in front of the class.

The Boston Massacre was a key event because people could use it to make others mad enough to fight. Paul Revere made an etching of the Massacre that showed the British soldiers killing the colonists on purpose, but this wasn't totally true. The etching wasn't a completely true version of the Boston Massacre, but Paul Revere used it to make people angry enough to join the revolution.

LINK

Remind the students of all they have learned from their essay unit that they can apply to their mini-essay chapters. Unveil a chart from the essay unit, then invite writers to begin planning a frame for their essays.

I pointed to a chart I had hung on the wall and said, "Writers, I think you'll remember this trusty chart. You used it so much during the essay unit to help you remember how essays usually go. The mini-essay chapter that you're about to write is not very different from the essays you wrote before. It also needs to have a solid frame so it doesn't end up a pile of mush!

"Right now, before you leave the carpet, would you take a few minutes to start planning your essay? Think about what your thesis might be, and what your reasons might be. When I give you a tap, you can head off to get started."

I circulated among the writers, tapping those who had at least a clear thesis statement and were getting going on their reasons. I continued to send writers off until I had only a small group remaining who were struggling to come up with an idea for a thesis. I decided to keep these writers on the carpet for a small-group coaching session.

Essay Plan

(Thesis statement) because reason 1, reason 2, and most of all, because reason 3.

- One reason that (thesis statement) is that . . . (reason 1). For example, (evidence a), (evidence b), and (evidence c).
- Another reason that (thesis statement) is that . . . (reason 2). For example, (evidence a), (evidence b), and (evidence c).
- Although (thesis statement) because reason 1 and because reason 2, especially (opinion statement) because reason 3. For example, (evidence a), (evidence b), and (evidence c).

Essay-Planning Reminders

SCHOLARS FROM THE NATIONAL RESEARCH PANEL recently released a report listing the most crucial twenty-first-century skills to instill in our students. At the top of the list was transference. Today, you will nudge your writers toward this crucial skill as you teach them to bring all of their essay-writing knowledge from the previous unit to their work in this unit. To support transference, cite the personal essay unit as much as possible, even using the exact language that you used during that unit wherever possible.

It will be important in particular to be on the lookout for writers who are struggling to come up with an effective frame for their essays. Some produce a thesis that is so focused that they have a hard time supporting it across an entire essay. For example, Kim began with the idea that her thesis would be, "The Declaration of Independence was a turning point because it let the British King know that the colonies wanted to be their own country and it kind of started America being its own country." An essay supporting that claim needs to support both the first part of it and the second, and it would not be easy for Kim to provide evidence that the Declaration of Independence let the King know this or that. I advised Kim to try a more general claim: "The signing of the Declaration of Independence was a turning point in the history of the United States." With this broader thesis, Kim had no difficulty generating reasons that supported her argument.

Of course, once a student has figured out a claim and reasons—box and bullets: there are other ways to lift the level of the students' work. If their reasons feel as if they are a hodgepodge, you might remind them that essayists often write within parallel structure, and you might show your own structure for your essay:

The Boston Massacre was a key event in the Revolutionary War.

- It was a key event because it was a violent result of problems between the colonists and England.
- It was a key event because people could use it to make others mad enough to fight.
- It was a key event because it was the last straw before the start of the war.

MID-WORKSHOP TEACHING The Glue that Links Claims, Reasons, and Evidence: Transition Words

"Writers, can I interrupt you for a minute? I'm noticing that most of you have set up your essay so that early on you have a claim—and some reasons to support that claim. Listen for example to Milo's essay, and let's 'palm' the claim" (I pointed to my palm) "and 'list' the reasons" (I counted off one, two, three across my fingers). I nodded for Milo to read his essay (see Figure 7–2), and as he read, I followed the rest of the class in palming the claim, listing the reasons.

"The Boston Tea party is important. The Boston tea party is important because it made the king close Boston harbor. And it also got the king so mad that he let out the intolerable acts. And one more reason how the Boston tea party is important is the colonists paid for the tea."

> The Boston Tea party is important. The Boston Tea is important because It made the king close Boston harbor and it also got the king so mad that he let out the intolerable acts. And one more reason how the Boston tea party is important is that that the colonists paid for the tea.

FIG. 7–2   Milo's writing sample

"Partner 1, please read your opening paragraph to Partner 2, and will the two of you see if you can palm the claim and list the reasons in the same way, and if not, help each other. Then do the same for Partner 2's writing."

(continues)

The children did this. "You seem to be on top of that opening paragraph. Nice work. I want to shift to talk about how the next paragraphs of your essays will go, and especially, how they will be glued together. Listen to what Milo has done with his first body paragraph. You'll see that he's repeated his first reason—The Tea Party was important because it made the king close the harbor—and then he gave examples and other kinds of evidence. This time, listen to how Milo connects one example or one bit of evidence with another, and this time, let's signal whenever we see him doing this by going like this: I made a motion (and a sound effect) as if my two pointer fingers were being velcroed together. Milo, start at the beginning." We listened:

> The king closed Boston Harbor because of the Boston Tea Party. Because of this (Velcro), the colonists weren't able to get food delivered there. In addition to (Velcro) not getting food, they weren't able to get important supplies, for example (Velcro) soap or tools.

"Nice job. Will you reread your own second body paragraph, and make the signal whenever you see yourself using a transition word? If you don't have two or three in that paragraph, my hunch is that either you don't have a bunch of examples or pieces of evidence (making you need to use this glue) *or* you still need to insert more transition words. Here is a list of possibilities." I unveiled a chart with some common transition words.

Transition Words Chart

When you want to give an example:
An example that shows this is . . .
For instance . . .
One time . . .

When you want to add on:
Another example that shows this is . . .
In addition to . . .
Furthermore . . .

When you want to compare and contrast:
In comparison . . .
In contrast . . .
On the other hand . . .

When you want to show cause and effect:
For this reason . . .
Consequently . . .
Because of this . . .

While helping students develop the reasons to support their arguments, you might remind them of a specific strategy or two from the previous unit on essay writing. In that unit, you taught students to make a checklist for support in creating and checking their reasons, specifically to check if their reasons were parallel in structure and did not overlap.

If you notice a group of writers who could use extra support fine-tuning their reasons, you might gather them in a small group and offer them some tips. Remind them of some of the maxims of essay development they learned during the personal essay unit. Coach these writers to look for places where reasons are too similar and could be combined, or where they are phrased in such a way that they don't really match each other or the thesis.

Then, point out features of your writing and strategies you used to create it. For example, you might demonstrate how you checked for parallelism by adding *because* after the thesis to create a stem and naming each reason to be sure it fits. You could also point out that evidence that you could use to support one reason wouldn't really go with any of the other reasons, showing your reasons don't overlap. You might even point out that your reasons sort of go mad, madder, maddest . . . In other words, they go both in time order, and in order of how strong the colonists' feelings were.

More Head-Down Writing Time

Remind students of all the work they could be doing, and offer them the share time to continue their work.

"Writers, you've been doing a lot of work today—perhaps organizing your ideas, planning your essay sections, and even getting started drafting that section. Or, if you haven't gotten that far, you are probably revising and editing your all-about sections (on either All About the Revolutionary War or all about your topic). Or, you might be revising and editing your narrative about your topic that gives a real sense of those times. You might even be using the Information Writing Checklist to improve your work as you go! In any case, it is clear you have a lot of intense writing work going on. Instead of coming over to share together today, why don't you stay right where you are and just keep working—keep writing, writing, writing. You'll want to hold onto this writing momentum, this head-down drafting groove you are in, so that you can draft and write and revise even more tonight, too."

FINISHING UP AND BRAINSTORMING POSSIBLE TOPICS FOR NEW RESEARCH PROJECTS

Writers, I don't need to tell you what the homework for tonight is because you already have in your minds what you need to do to finish your information writing, don't you? Tell the person next to you what writing work you have before you, and what you still need to finish drafting, revising, or editing. Tell that person also what part of that work you think you can accomplish tonight. That will be your homework, of course! And there's one more thing too . . .

Writers, at the start of this unit, when I asked you to choose a topic to research, I had the feeling that some of you hadn't yet gotten yourself all that interested in a particular topic, and so you sort of went "eeny-meeny-miney-moe" to make your topic choice. You are probably thinking, "I wish that *now* was the time for topic choice, not earlier, because *now* I know a lot of interesting topics." Well, the good news is that you'll actually begin another, bigger research project in a few days, and you'll have another chance to choose a topic. Some of you may decide to continue studying the topic you've been pursuing all along—many famous history writers mine one subject for a lifetime, so that makes a lot of sense. Others will choose a topic that's new for you, but that might be a topic that a friend has been researching. Tonight, list three topics that you might be interested in.

As you do this, ask:

1. Is this a topic you are interested in, and expect you could get others to be interested in?

2. Is this a topic on which you can access information?

3. Is this topic focused?

Taking Stock and Setting Goals
A Letter to Teachers

ear Teachers,

At this point, as you are nearing the end of the unit, you will need to assess if most of your students are ready to move directly on to editing their entire piece, as we suggest in this session, or if they still need a day (or even two days) to continue drafting. We've found that sometimes students do need one more day at this point to finish their essay sections and fill in missing chunks or revise weak spots from earlier in their writing. By all means offer them that time! However, we don't want to belabor this first cycle of writing either. The goal of this bend is for the students to understand how the whole writing cycle of research and information writing can go, so that they can picture it in its entirety, tailoring the process to their own needs the next time around. So, yes, offer them one or two more days if the energy for writing is high and the books won't be finished without that time! On the other hand, we don't recommend you offer more than two days. Let these books be the baseline for what the students can do—the next books they write will reveal all the more growth! When you are ready, turn back to this letter in which we outline our suggestions for the last day in Bend I.

On this day, you will guide your students as they take stock of the writing they have done so far and as they set goals for the work to come. Of course, at this point in the year, you and your students will be familiar with the goal-setting process. You'll be able to turn the reins over to them more so than before, and will be able to hold them accountable for making grander revisions right away.

Part of what students will do today, in addition to setting goals for themselves, will be to study what they have written already with an editor's lens. In the connection, you will emphasize a key grammatical structure, the paragraph, and in doing so, you will hopefully not only hold your writers accountable for a form of punctuation they have been taught countless times before, you will also guide them to more deliberate organization and perhaps even greater elaboration. One reason among many that emphasizing the paragraph is important is that the Common Core State Standards for Informational Writing require

COMMON CORE STATE STANDARDS: W.4.2, RI.4.2, RI.4.5, SL.4.1, L.4.1, L.4.2, L.4.3, L.4.5

fourth-graders to "group related information in paragraphs and sections (WI.4.1a)," a marked departure from the corresponding third-grade expectation to "group related information together (WI.3.1a)." If your writers still aren't doing this, it's perfectly reasonable to be firm in holding them accountable until they do.

It is worth noting that directly after this session, students will begin a new project. You might feel it is important to spend another day or so on editing, based on your assessment of your students' writing. There is currently no session set aside for "publishing" or copying over students' writing to fancy it up in this bend, so if you decide this is warranted, add a session. Students will have an opportunity to do that kind of preparation for publishing later in Bend III.

MINILESSON

Not all connections need be congratulatory. Many times in your connection, you will name something writers are doing well to encourage them to do more of the same, or inspire the few writers who aren't yet doing it to give it a try. Sometimes, however, students need a gentle (or sometimes not so gentle) reminder to do something they've been taught to do countless times.

If you notice an error your students are still making, despite all of their previous instruction, make sure you show them you are perplexed at how they could still be making this error. For example, many of your students may not be separating their writing into paragraphs, something they most likely have been taught since the beginning of third grade, if not earlier.

You might start by saying something like, "Writers, I want to talk to you about a concern I have. I took your writing home last night, and I noticed one thing that totally perplexed me. I noticed that some of you aren't writing with paragraphs. You've got whole pages that are just one giant blob. I'm just so surprised by this. It's like you forgot to wear your shoes! And forgetting to wear shoes might have been something you would have done when you were really young, but now that you're so much older, you would never do something like that. I'm going to give you a minute to look back at your writing and check that you have written in paragraphs."

The Information Writing Checklist, Grades 4 and 5 can be found on the CD-ROM.

Information Writing Checklist

	Grade 4	NOT YET	STARTING TO	YES!	Grade 5	NOT YET	STARTING TO	YES!
	Structure				**Structure**			
Overall	I taught readers different things about a subject. I put facts, details, quotes, and ideas into each part of my writing.	☐	☐	☐	I used different kinds of information to teach about the subject. Sometimes I included little essays, stories, or "how-to" sections in my writing.	☐	☐	☐
Lead	I hooked my readers by explaining why the subject mattered, telling a surprising fact, or giving a big picture. I let readers know that I would teach them different things about a subject.	☐	☐	☐	I wrote an introduction that helped readers get interested in and understand the subject. I let readers know the subtopics I would be developing later as well as the sequence.	☐	☐	☐
Transitions	I used words in each section that help readers understand how one piece of information connected with others. If I wrote the section in sequence, I used words and phrases such as *before, later, next, then,* and *after.* If I organized the section in kinds or parts, I used words such as *another, also,* and *for example.*	☐	☐	☐	When I wrote about results, I used words and phrases like *consequently, as a result,* and *because of this.* When I compared information, I used words and phrases such as *in contrast, by comparison,* and *especially.* In narrative parts, I used phrases that go with stories such as *a little later* and *three hours later.* In the sections that stated an opinion, I used words such as *but the most important reason, for example,* and *consequently.*	☐	☐	☐
Ending	I wrote an ending that reminded readers of my subject and may have suggested a follow-up action or left readers with a final insight. I added my thoughts, feelings, and questions about the subject at the end.	☐	☐	☐	I wrote a conclusion in which I restated the main points and may have offered a final thought or question for readers to consider.	☐	☐	☐
Organization	I grouped information into sections and used paragraphs and sometimes chapters to separate those sections. Each section had information that was mostly about the same thing. I may have used headings and subheadings.	☐	☐	☐	I organized my writing into a sequence of separate sections. I may have used headings and subheadings to highlight the separate sections. I wrote each section according to an organizational plan shaped partly by the genre of the section.	☐	☐	☐

Once children have had a moment to check that they are paragraphing, you can continue toward the heart of your minilesson.

In your teaching point, you may want to emphasize the importance of self-reflection, then offer your writers a few questions to ask themselves. You might say something like, "Today I want to teach you that it always helps for writers to pause from time to time, to look back on what they have done over the past few weeks, and to ask themselves, 'Am I getting better at this? What do I need to work on next? How can I make sure that I keep growing as a writer in big and important ways?'"

You may find it fruitful to make an analogy, perhaps comparing getting better at writing to getting better at another activity, such as running or swimming. Describe a friend of yours (or yourself!), someone who is a competitive swimmer, or marathon runner. If describing a swimmer, you might explain that this friend competes in the 200-meter freestyle, and his goal is to beat the record at his swim club. He clocks his time regularly, and aims to get faster and faster. Explain that in the same way, getting better at writing takes this kind of goal-setting and focused practice.

As you unpack the anecdote, explain that your friend has a very clear goal, not just to get better at swimming, but to beat the best time at his club. He is doing specific things to achieve that clear goal, and he will know when he reaches it. Writers, like swimmers, show the most improvement when they are working toward very clear goals, when they know what to do to achieve those goals, and when they know how to tell that they have met those goals.

To encourage students to think about the expectations being set for them as informational writers, you might channel them to study the fourth- and fifth-grade checklists during the active engagement. Give them a minute or two to study each section at a time, underlining what they see as major differences between the two. Then, ask students to talk to a partner about the differences they notice between the two, and what they think these differences mean for them as writers.

After writers have had a few minutes to compare checklists, you can help them check their writing to decide whether they have indeed met the expectations of the fourth-grade checklist, or perhaps they are creeping into the fifth-grade side! Ask them to star places where they did whatever that checklist requires. You may want to ask your writers to give a show of thumbs if this is something they feel they could work on in the future, and commend the bravery of those who admit they have room for improvement.

If writers assessed one feature with your guidance, you'll want them to continue assessing other features without your input. If they have been through this process before, your writers may have learned to draw fireworks or many stars on goals that they especially need to work on. Once your writers have each identified a few areas that need attention using the checklist, encourage them to start a list of personal goals in their notebooks.

Your link should convey to writers the great responsibility and opportunity they have today. Today is their last chance to make these pieces the best they can be, as well as their chance to set the bar for the kind of work they want to do in their next book. As they determine areas that need improvement, they should make revisions right on the spot to make their current work even better.

CONFERRING AND SMALL-GROUP WORK

Today's session has the dual purposes of encouraging students to revise and edit their current books right away and supporting them in setting goals for their future work. You will need to balance your conferring between the two.

It will be important to remind yourself to not get bogged down by addressing every little error but instead to concentrate the bulk of your conferring on bigger teaching points that have a sweeping payoff. To get the biggest bang for your buck, you could plan to conduct mainly small-group coaching sessions today. Use the fourth-grade Common Core State Standards for language as a guide to help you to know what to target and how to group students. It is important to note that these standards are expectations for the end of the year, so don't panic if your students aren't yet meeting all of them.

Of course, today you'll also want to support the self-assessment and goal-setting that students are doing. Too often, students set goals without really understanding the steps they will need to take to reach those goals, which in turn, may defeat the purpose. It is also important to help writers set goals that are appropriate and attainable. You'll coach your students into setting goals not just to satisfy you, their teacher, but for themselves. They should come to know the satisfaction that comes from a job well done, a goal met. Encourage your writers to have clear but high standards for themselves, and steer them away from setting goals that are too lofty, too vague, or too paltry. A few strong goals with leverage beyond this one piece or even this one unit will do them much more good than a long list of weak or confusing goals. As you confer, aim to leave you writers not only with goals, but with a plan of how to meet these goals.

Because this is the last day your students will have to work on these pieces, you'll want to keep an eye out for those that need some extra nudging to reach the finish line. Gather a group of writers that are still drafting to support them in making a quick plan to finish, then in writing with high intensity and volume. "Writers, when you're working against a deadline, you have to plan to use your time wisely," you might say. "Because today marks the end of the time we have to work on these pieces, would you decide how much you can finish in this writing workshop? Then, make a plan to finish the rest for homework. For now, let's practice writing fast and furiously to try to meet our deadline." Then, have writers get to work while you're there to offer encouragement. "Keep going! Your hand should be flying!" After a few minutes of work, gather them back together and recommend they try to push themselves in this way on their own. Send them off with a reminder to save some time to study what they have done and set some goals for themselves after they have finished drafting.

MID-WORKSHOP TEACHING

You may decide to use your mid-workshop teaching point to address common grammatical errors you notice your particular group of students making. You'll also want to make sure energy is high and your students are working productively on this final day of the bend, so instead of stopping the students for a longer demonstration, you may instead take on the persona of a soccer coach, calling out one-liners from the sidelines in the form of tips and encouragements. "I notice some of you are forgetting the comma rules you already know. Right now, do a quick spot-check to be sure you used commas in all the right places." Or, "I just saw Kathryn checking the word wall to make sure she spelled *government* correctly. If you haven't already, be sure to double-check spellings of really important words like that." You can give these voiceovers throughout the session as you feel they are necessary.

SHARE

In today's share session, you will both celebrate the work that kids have done so far and rally them to launch themselves with purpose into the next round of writing. You may want to leave time for a slightly longer share session than usual. First, you'll want to think about how to celebrate your writers' enormous achievements. You may want to highlight the fact that the main purpose of the writing they are doing is to teach others about their topics. You could set partners up to read each other's pieces, leaving a few sticky notes on places where they learned something really interesting. Then, have each student say for the large group something they learned from their partner's writing.

Finally, to rally children toward their future work and support them with some public goal-setting, you might have each student share one important, lofty goal they have set for their next piece of writing that they think could make a big difference in their writing lives. Ask them to write their goal in their best handwriting on a note card, to sign their name, and post it in a public place, such as a bulletin board you've cleared for this purpose. In so doing, they are declaring to the whole community that they are committed to working on this goal. They might even make note of other writers who have similar goals and so they can plan to help each other during the next round of writing.

Good Luck!

Lucy and Anna

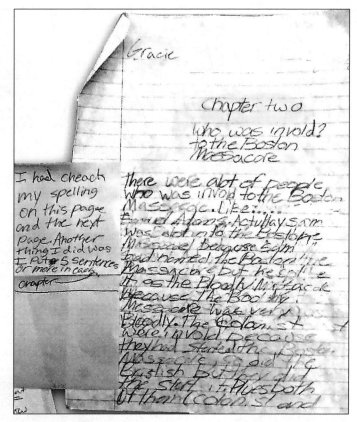

FIG. 8–1   Gracie's self-reflection

(1) All ABOUT THE BOSTON MASSACRE AND MORE!
BY GRACIE

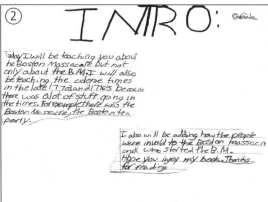

(2) INTRO:
BY Gracie

Today I will be teaching you about the Boston massacre but not only about the B.M. I will also be teaching the colonie times in the late 1770s and 1760s because there was alot of stuff going in the times. For example there was the Boston massacre, the Boston tea party.

I also will be adding how the people were invold to the Boston massacre and who started the B.M. Hope you injoy my book. Thanks for reading.

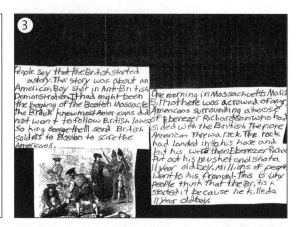

(3) People say that the British started a story. This story was about an American Boy shot in Anti-British Demonstration. It had might been the beging of the Boston Massacre. the British knew most americans did not want to follow British laws. So king george the III send British soldiers to Boston to scare the americans.

One morning in Massachuetts March 5, 1770 there was a crowed of angry americans surrounding a house of Ebenezer Richardson who had sided with the British. The more American threw a rock. The rock had landed into his house and hit his wife. then Ebenezer Richard put out his musket and shot a 11 year old boy. Millions of people went to his froneral. This is why people think that the British started it because he killed a 11 year old boy.

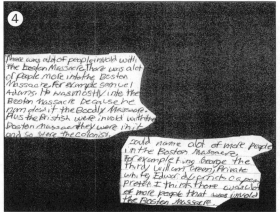

(4) There was alot of people invold with the boston Massacre. There was alot of people more in the Boston Massacre. For example samuel Adams. He was mostly in the Boston Massacre because he nom died it the Boodly Massacre. Plus the British were invold with the Boston massacre they were in it and so were the colonist.

I could name a lot of more people in the Boston Massacre. For example king george the third, William Green, Private white, Edward uprinck, a peper. prefer I think there was alot of more people that was invold the Boston Massacre.

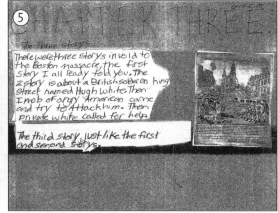

(5) CHAPTER THREE.
Gracie

The three storys

There were three storys invold to the Boston massacre. the first story I all ready told you. The 2 story is about a British soldier on king street named Hugh White. Then I mob of angry American came and try to Attack him. Then Private White called for help.

The third story just like the first and second storys.

(6) CHAPTER FOUR!

INTO of the Boston Massacre.

The location of the boston Massacre was in Boston, Province of Massachusetts bay.

The date of the boston massacre was March 5, 1770

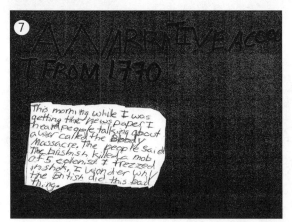

(7) A NARRATIVE ACCOUNT FROM 1770

This morning while I was getting the newspaper I heard People talking about a war called the Bloodly Massacre. The people said the British killed a mob of 5 colonist. I frezzed in shok, I wonder why the British did this bad thing.

(8) CONCLUSION
Gracie

who ever started the Boston Massacre was important because it was very valient. Another reason why it was important for someone to start the Boston Massacre was it was dangres to go outside for people cause you don't want to get killed.

My last reason, why it was important for someone to start the Boston Massacre was you don't want to started a fight cause sometimes when you start a fight it could get bigger.

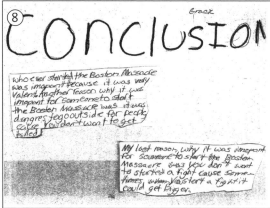

FIG. 8–2 Gracie's published book. Instead of an "All About the Revolution" opener, she chose to open with her "All About the Boston Massacre" section, which includes an embedded narrative. Her conclusion is her essay section.

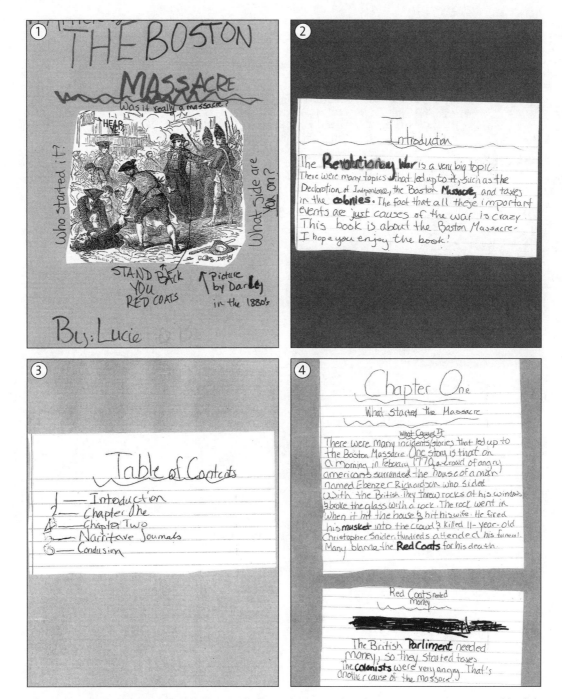

FIG. 8–3   Lucie's published book. She involved two letters rather than a narrative section and hadn't yet written an essay-like conclusion.

⑤

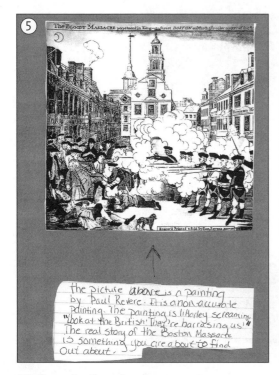

The Bloody Massacre perpetrated in King---Street BOSTON on March 5---etc. etc. etc.

↑

the picture above is a painting by Paul Revere. It is a non accurate painting. The painting is litterley screaming, "look at the British! They're harrasing us!" The real story of the Boston Massacre is something you are about to find out about.

FIG. 8–3   Continued

⑥

March 5th, 1770
Sara Prescott

Those colonists were at it again! Throwing ice & snow at our soilders was terribly rude of them. And, they've wounded my father, the private terribly. How I hope King George III will punish them deeply.

Love,
Sara Prescott
March 5th, 1770
Sara Longnington

I can not believe my own eyes! Those red coats killed 5 of our colonists! Can you believe that! How could they? And that is including my father, too! How can I ever forgive them?

Love,

Sara L.

⑦

Conclusion

The Boston Massacre was a turning point because it made the colonists even more angry. It really made them grow even more apart. Which side are you on? This might take a while, So choose wisley. I hope you enjoyed this book!

Writers Plan for Their Research

IN THIS SESSION, you'll remind students that when tackling a new piece of informational writing, nonfiction writers come up with a research plan.

GETTING READY

✔ "Getting Ready to Write an Informational Book" chart (see Teaching)

✔ Examples of two different research plans, one that is adequate and one that is problematic, enlarged for students to see (see Teaching)

✔ Post-it Notes (see Mid-Workshop Teaching)

✔ A variety of resources for students to use when researching, including lower-level books and videos

COMMON CORE STATE STANDARDS: W.4.2, W.4.5, W.4.7, W.4.8, W.4.9, RI.4.1, RI.4.3, RI.4.5, RI.4.7, RI.4.9, SL.4.1, SL.4.4, L.4.1, L.4.2, L.4.3

YOUR STUDENTS SHOULD BE ENTERING Bend II with momentum. They've each produced a rather respectable little nonfiction book. Granted, you led them along the pathway to that accomplishment, making many of the decisions that allowed them to now look back on such productivity. But remember, the fledgling bike rider forgets that she got started with your firm hand on her seat and is sure of only one thing: she did it! All on her own! Similarly, your students are apt to enter Bend II feeling brashly confident over their abilities to write informational books. Use that momentum. In the upcoming bend of the unit, your students will each write a second nonfiction book, and this time, they'll work with the increased independence that you and they have come to expect in later portions of a unit.

Your teaching isn't going to stop—far from it—but instead of carrying students along through a fail-proof, step-by-step sequence that you lay out for them, you'll mentor them in assuming the identities and living the life of being a history writer.

Before entering the bend, your students will have chosen topics for a second publication. We assume that many of them will have decided to continue with their original topic, and certainly hope you channel your less experienced students in that direction. Other students will presumably have chosen topics that you or their friends wrote about during the first portion of the unit. A few will be embarking on totally new topics.

Today, they'll make plans for how this upcoming text will go. This means that you'll coach them to engage in the messy, complicated work of creating a structure for their books and formulating a research plan. This, of course, is fundamental to the Common Core State Standards expectations for information writing, where fourth-graders are expected to "[i]ntroduce a topic clearly and group related information in paragraphs and sections" (20) and fifth-graders are expected to "introduce a topic clearly, provide a general observation and focus, and group related information logically" (20). You'll remind students to draw on all that they learned during Bend I. For example, perhaps students will again start their book with an All About the Revolutionary War chapter—perhaps, even, with the exact chapter that they already wrote.

It will be easy to remind students that as they think about possible chapters, they can think, also, about the genre in which those chapters might be written. Most of them will have written an essay in their first book, probably ending the book with "Why is this topic important?" and their new plans, too, may contain some chapters that are written as essays. If the child writing about the Boston Tea Party ends up wanting to write about how tea went from the fields of West Indies to the Boston Harbor, the child might write that as a how-to chapter. When channeling children to consider writing in a variety of genre, you needn't think that doing so compromises the unit's emphasis on information writing because in fact, informational texts generally combine genre, using all of them for the purpose of teaching information.

"Scientists generate a hypothesis before plunging into their research; researchers often write an initial flash-draft of findings that becomes the starting point in an inquiry."

While children develop a plan for their books, imagining some of the specific topics they are apt to write about, coach them to weigh the available resources. Children need not wait until they're developing research proposals as doctoral students to understand that before selecting a topic, one needs to assess available resources, including access to related videotapes and experts, and figure out a plan for developing expertise on the topic.

Teachers, you'll want to watch yourself a bit. Carry a radar-detector that beeps when you take control from the student, and let those beeps remind you to think, "What's the great harm with letting the student make this decision? What's the worst thing that could happen?" You'll find that many students want to relinquish control to you. They figure there is a "right way" and they want to do things "properly." You'll work to help them know that the right way is to be reflective, to make plans in pencil, expecting to outgrow those plans. For example, if you peek ahead to tomorrow's minilesson, you'll see that we waste no time before assuring students that the plans they developed were meant as temporary starting points. Scientists generate a hypothesis before plunging into their research; researchers often write an initial flash-draft of findings that becomes the starting point in an inquiry. If you see blatant problems with students' plans, you might let those problems remain, planning to help students, over time, come to some realizations about what works well and less well when conducting research.

By the end of this bend, your children will have another book, a bit like the one they produced in Bend I. Instead of publishing that book at the end of Bend II, they'll return to it in Bend III to lift the level in dramatic ways. The real achievement in Bend II will be the subtle but phenomenal difference between the first two pieces of writing. No matter how imperfect the final product that results from this upcoming bend, as long as it reflects a growing deliberation and independence on the part of your fourth-graders, it will be worth its weight in gold as a developmental milestone.

Writers Plan for Their Research

CONNECTION

Generate excitement for the upcoming bend by sharing with your students how proud and impressed you are with the informational books that they wrote in Bend I.

"Writers, last night, I got myself some coffee and started reading. I read and read and couldn't stop. I wasn't reading the novel I've been engrossed in. I was reading *your* writing! I couldn't stop!

"Was it just two weeks ago when you started this unit? What a journey you've traveled since then! Today begins the second lap around the track."

The message, of course, is important: I think about you on my time off. I enjoy reading your work. You are on a trajectory that is leading you toward important new places.

Discuss topic choice for students' new research book, reminding students that within any one topic, there are infinite possibilities for writing.

"I'm really excited that many of you have decided to write again about the topic that you addressed in your first book, because one thing I think we all learned is that those topics are so much more interesting than any of us realized—and there is so much to know about them. A subject—say, the Boston Massacre—is really a hundred topics. One could write about the causes of that battle, or about how that was just one of a few events that lit the fire of the war, or about the weapons that were used in that battle, or the consequence of that event—or a dozen other things. So now you'll have a chance to open up your topics and explore the subtopics within them.

"Of course, some of you have decided that you want to tackle a new topic, and that is okay too, as long as it is one you already know something about.

We'd initially suggested more idiosyncratic subtopics: a British soldier's experience of the Boston Massacre, how the geography of Boston played a part in that battle. You may still want to add those to your list. We deleted them because our hunch is that it won't be until Bend III that we can expect students to explore subtopics such as those. For now, we expect that the chapters in most students' books will reflect the subheadings in the nonfiction books they are reading. We'd be glad if they instead reflected students' own inquiries, but think that will be unusual.

"Give me a thumbs up if you have a topic in hand that you'll write about during this upcoming bend in the unit." Most students so signaled. "A few of you are iffy, so you'll want to resolve that straight away."

❖ **Name the teaching point.**

"Today I want to remind you that nonfiction writers don't just choose a topic and then pick up their pens and start writing. No way! They first make some writing plans—which often look like a table of contents. They think about different chapters they might write, and also think, 'What kind of writing might that chapter be?' 'That one?' Finally, they think, 'Do I already know enough to write that part? What can I do to get ready to write?'"

TEACHING

Remind writers of the steps for getting ready to write an informational book, then invite them to engage in a similar process as they begin to plan their second information book and their research.

"Let's review the steps writers take to get ready to write an informational book." I displayed the chart we had used in the previous bend.

> ### Getting Ready to Write an Informational Book
>
> 1. Choose a topic.
>
> 2. Think about how your writing might go. What kind of writing might each chapter (or part) be?
>
> 3. Plan a way to take notes and to jot ideas for each part.
>
> 4. Take notes, fitting what you learn into your plan for the writing.
>
> 5. Plan for teaching others about your topic, and then do that teaching to rehearse for writing.
>
>   - What do I want my audience to learn? (Add missing parts.)
>   - What will interest people? (Add quotes, anecdotes, quirky facts.)
>   - What might confuse them, that I can clarify? (Add, "If you are wondering . . ." or "You may be confused about . . .")
>
> 6. Draft!

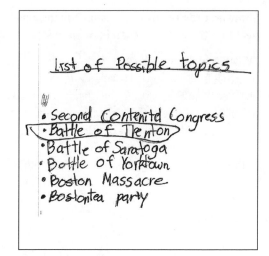

FIG. 9–1   Edward's list of possible topics

Of course it is not the case that all information writing is written in chapters. We have repeatedly tried to show students that they can use topic sentences and transitions instead of chapter titles and subheadings to create an infrastructure for information writing, and have repeatedly come from these efforts thinking that, at least when writing larger reports, students seem to rely on a table of contents and chapter titles. Of course, you can teach them to erase these in the final moments prior to publication if you think that is best. We tend to not vote for that.

Show an example of two research plans, one that is adequate and one that is problematic, asking writers to evaluate these and to plan improvements when they're called for.

"When you planned your last book, you used Naomi's mentor text as an example, and this time, you'll want to make a plan that is all your own, based on your own sense of what you want to teach about your topic. Many of you will probably decide to keep some of the things you did during the first bend in this unit—if your topic is the same, you could actually bring some of those chapters into this book, or you could write new and better versions of those chapters. Even if your topic is different, for example, you might start with your All About the Revolutionary War chapter. That's up to you.

"I thought it might help to study the plans other researchers have made, and to think about how to make plans that are as effective as possible. I've got two plans to show you. Will you and your partner think about which of these seem to you to be good plans, if either? And if one or both of the plans seem problematic, will you and your partner think about how to improve them?"

Plan I: Jason Topic: Valley Forge

	Name of Chapter	Genre	Kinds of Research I'll Need to Do
1	All about the Revolutionary War	all-about	Find a few more facts.
2	Setting up the Valley Forge camp: the layout and supplies and place	all-about and how-to	I have book on it. Map it?
3	The people: the soldiers who were there	all-about	not sure
4	What happened: George Washington helped his soldiers at Valley Forge.	an essay	I know a lot, but want specific details about what he said.
5	A turning point story (about the above)	a story	a story about how they were depressed, then GW helped
6	After Valley Forge	all-about	I need to find out more about this.

Plan II: Isabella Topic: People during the Revolutionary War

	Name of Chapter	Genre	Kinds of Research I'll Need to Do
1	The Lives of Men of the Revolutionary War	all-about	I know about lots of men but I don't know their lives, just why they were famous. I want to find out about men who were not famous.
2	The Lives of Women of the Revolutionary War	all-about	I know nothing about women, so need to study this.
3	Life in the Revolution	a story	I am going to read more about life.
4	How to Be a Good Patriot in the War	a how-to	I think I know all about this.

This may be confusing to students—the idea that they could bring chapters from the first book to this new book. It might be something you decide to bring up while you are conferring instead of now. You also will want to decide whether this is an option you want to offer to all your students. It could be a way to help some strugglers get a leg-up.

Notice that we've written this plan so that it is roughly chronological. We aren't, at this point, discussing the logical structure that undergirds this plan, but we'll bring that structure out before long in this bend. For now, you will probably want more of your examples to follow a time-related logical structure because that is far and away the most obvious way to organize writing about history. Of course, many people might not even see these chapters as being chronologically ordered. That's okay—for the point that we are bringing out is that instead of writing one chapter "All About Valley Forge," this book has opened that up to a collection of more focused topics, each written in a different genre. But underneath that, there is also a logical structure.

We rewrote this section of this minilesson several times, changing it after each time we taught it. We had to make the second plan more blatantly problematic each time. When contrasting what to do and what not to do in a minilesson, we generally find it helps to be over the top. In this instance, students are presumably learning the most by identifying what works about these plans. For this reason, we abbreviate the time for critiquing the problematic plan.

Channel students to reflect on which research plan feels more viable, and to use that question to develop a sense of standards for planning research. What does it mean to do that well?

After letting students talk a bit, I convened them and said, "Would you all, as a group, carry on a whole-class conversation about the two sets of research plans? Are there things both researchers have done that you think would be good for you to do as well? Does one set of plans seem better to you than another—and if so, why?"

The students agreed that they liked the way both research plans took big topics and divided them into smaller chapters, that both researchers thought about the kind of writing they would do in each chapter, and that the researchers thought about what they needed to learn to be able to write the chapters.

"Does one plan seem better to you than another?" I asked.

"I like that the first one, Jason's plan, has more chapters about the topic. Like, it's not just one chapter all about Valley Forge. It has a few chapters on Valley Forge—building the camp, who was there, what happened there," said Harris. Several students nodded in agreement.

"I think Isabella's plan, the one about people of the Revolution, seems hard," said Mirei. I signaled for her to say more. "I mean there are just so many people in the Revolution. I think it would take forever for her to get all of those facts."

I again pressed, and others joined into the conversation. Sam explained, " . . . 'cause, like, it seems she only knows about the famous men and she has a lot still to do. She'd need like a whole room of books for all of the people in the war. That chapter is too big. There is too much information that she'd need to find out."

Thomas added, "But I do like that she has a how-to part and "How To Be a Good Patriot" sounds really interesting, although it doesn't really go with the other parts."

Debrief, naming important points raised during the discussion that your students would do well to keep in mind.

I nodded. "You are raising important points. What I'm hearing is that Isabella would be better off narrowing her topic, perhaps to just one person, so she didn't have so much to cover. I'm also hearing that she should keep resources in mind, and choose a topic for which she has plenty of information quickly. You appreciate that both Jason and Isabella included a variety of genres in their writing and you like the idea of planning out possible chapters, and maybe even doing your planning in a grid like the one these researchers used." I gestured again to the anchor chart from earlier in the unit.

When you shift from the demonstration to debriefing, students should feel the different moves you are making just by the way your intonation and posture changes. After most demonstrations, there will be a time for you to debrief, and that's a time when you are no longer acting like a writer. You are the teacher who has been watching the demonstration and now turns to talk, eye to eye with kids, asking if they noticed this or that during the previous portion of the minilesson.

LINK

Send writers off with a vision of what they will do in the workshop today, and remind them to draw on all they already know about this kind of writing.

"Writers, a famous saying is 'a stitch in time saves nine.' What this saying means is that a little work done early on in a project can save lots and lots of work later on. Taking some time now to plan possible chapters of your book, to figure out the kinds of research you need to do, and to make sure you have adequate resources will save you time in the end. And of course, as soon as you have figured out your plans, you can get started researching! Off you go!"

Planning the Sequence of Your Instruction

Topic Choice, Tables of Contents, and Research Plans

OFTEN WHEN APPROACHING A DAY of conferring and small-group work, you'll have a sense of the teaching that you tackle, in sequence, almost as if your conferring time is broken up into subtopics. For example, when you begin working with students today, you can expect to start off helping some with their topic choice. Hopefully, by ten minutes into the day, you will be working with students on their research plans—which might result in some of them needing to go backwards and rethink their subject choice. Toward the end of today's session, you will probably help students organize themselves to take research notes.

For each of those, you'll want to have some possible teaching points in mind. For example, when your concern is focused on topic choice, you'll want to have in mind ways to steer your more and less proficient writers. If you want to help a student who struggles to have some success in this independent work, you might channel that student to think hard about applying the lessons learned during the first portion of the unit to this new work. Start by encouraging this student to stay with the initial topic—although if the student has lost interest in it, you won't want to insist. Then, too, think about helping this student to plan chapter headings that echo those that are commonly found in resource materials. If books on the American Revolution tend to have chapters such as "Boston Massacre," "Continental Congress," and "Native Americans"—then one of your less proficient writers would be supported writing about any of those topics. Similarly, if books give attention to a subtopic, that will make it easy for a student to do the same. During the first bend in the unit, we deliberately channeled students to write on fairly broad topics because we felt that would be easier for them than writing on more focused topics, given that students were not apt to have the detailed knowledge necessary to write a whole report on, for example, Paul Revere's horse. You may decide, then, to channel your more struggling students toward broader chapter topics.

Of course, you'll also want to channel your most proficient students toward topics that will pay off for them. For especially strong students, you might consider suggesting topics that don't reside in specific sections of the source books—for example, it would

MID-WORKSHOP TEACHING

Moving On after Planning: Note-Taking

"Writers, can I have your attention? By now you should have at least the start of a table of contents and some ideas for the kind of writing you'll do in each chapter. That table of contents will change as you read more about your topic. You'll want to get started doing some research and note-taking. Will you take out the notes that you collected earlier in this unit—even if your topic was entirely different? I'm going to give you three minutes to put some Post-it notes on your notes, marking places where you can point out things you did as a note-taker that worked well, that you want to remember to do as you continue taking notes." After a few minutes I said, "Show your partner what you did, what you learned."

I listened in as children pointed out to their partner the things they'd done.

Jackson showed Melissa a Post-it on one of his pages on which he'd written, "timeline."

Melissa, meanwhile, turned to one of her marked pages and said, "I think this was some of my best notes because I did it in boxes and bullets."

Jude, nearby, explained to his partner why he'd marked a large chunk of text. "I did some writing about my topic while I was taking notes. Some of it went in my book."

Children continued talking, and after a bit, I said, "You are saying really important things. And you are right, this time I shouldn't need to tell you to find a place in your notebook (or elsewhere) for your notes, to figure out a structure for your notes, like a timeline or sketch notes, or to take notes that are both boxes and bullets—summaries—and also contain bits of freewriting where you think about what you have gathered. If you are researching the same topic as you've already written about, of course you'll want to add right onto the notes you have already collected. Get cracking!"

be challenging to write about the finances of the American Revolution, or children's role in the American Revolution, or the relationship with France during the American Revolution. Then again, the truth is that a topic such as the Boston Tea Party is actually infinitely complex, for the student who sees the mysteries worth exploring.

You'll also want to be ready to help students plan their tables of contents and their research. One of the challenges will be to decide the extent to which students will be able to research the ins and outs of their topics. Assuming this writing is occurring during the writing workshop, not during Social Studies time, you probably will curtail the time for research somewhat, so that the writing workshop isn't totally usurped by reading and research. This means, for example, that when coaching a student who is preparing to write a full chapter about which children do and do not go to school during the Revolutionary War and yet another chapter on the subjects studied at the schools, you probably will need to nudge this student to write a chapter instead on schools during the Revolution, or on another more general topic.

As you prepare to help students think about their tables of contents, then, you'll need to point out to them that the writing process is a recursive one. The job of making a table of contents is never completed. New chapters emerge, old ones are set aside.

You'll want to have on hand ways to support students with their research. Remember that it helps, always, for a learner to read a simple, low-level book on a topic before diving into the most detailed texts. The simpler book gives the learner an overview of the topic, and the rule of thumb when learning about a topic is "the more you know, the more you can learn." Then, too, videotapes are a wonderful way for a student to get his or her mental arms around a topic. Learning from videotapes is not as easy as you might think, and surely students will need to watch the tapes several times before they are ready to record their learning. Another way to support a topical study is to set children up to work as research teams, helping each other and also talking about what they are learning.

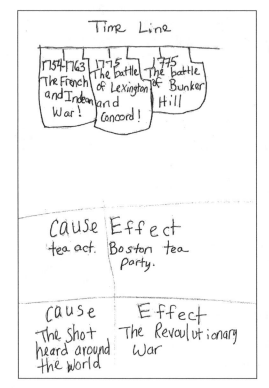

FIG. 9–2   Jackson's notes

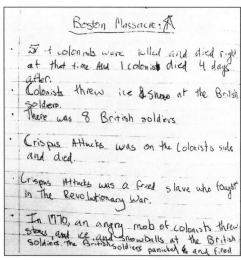

FIG. 9–3   Melissa's notes

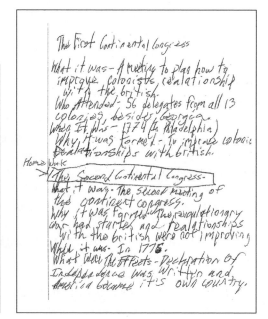

FIG. 9–4   Jude's notes

Creating Topic-Based Partnerships

Explain to the class that in research writing it is often helpful to be working with a partner who is sharing the same topic.

Standing in the middle of the room, I said, "Writers, if you read books by famous writers about their work, they say lots of different things. But pretty much every writer agrees that one of the most essential elements to successful writing is a true partner.

"You have always been in writing partnerships, but because you are launching new books and because you'll be doing a lot of research as well as writing, I've decided to launch new partnerships—these will be topic-based partnerships. When I call your names, join each other on the carpet, and you'll have the rest of writing time to talk to each other about your topic."

Channel students to discuss what they find interesting about their shared topic, using thought prompts such as "The thing I am realizing is. . . ."

After calling off the partnerships, and channeling most of the partnerships to the meeting area, some to other talk spots, I said, "Help each other learn more about your topic by pooling notes—and especially by talking about the bigger ideas you are growing from your research. Try saying phrases like, 'I'm realizing . . .' and 'The big thing I'm starting to think is . . .' Share with your partner the notes you marked earlier with Post-it notes, too."

RALLY WRITERS TO COLLECT, SHARE, AND COMPILE RESOURCES, INCLUDING VIDEOTAPES

Writers, tomorrow when you get to school, you will need to be ready to begin making a basket of resources on your topic—and the point will be that this is a place for your research partnership to combine resources. There are often two partnerships on a topic, so you'll combine efforts with that other partnership, in those instances. If you find any good resources at home, please bring them in. If you've read any books that seem helpful, please Post-it the good parts and put them in your basket (unless they are general resources that lots of groups will need, in which case we need to keep them in a shared place). I especially encourage you to search for videos you can watch at home on your topic—because it really helps a writer to have images to draw upon. Researching your topic will be *a lot* easier if you help each other find great information. As you do this, remember that writers are like magnets, looking for the specific stories, the intriguing details, the anecdotes that make a topic come to life. Be ready to share those with each other.

The Intense Mind-Work of Note-Taking

YOUR GOAL DURING THIS SESSION will be to channel students into doing the absolutely essential, bottom-line work of reading and writing for understanding. You will emphasize that when note-taking, the task is not to "record the facts," but instead, to understand what you are writing in such a way that you can explain it to yourself and to others.

One of the things we know about teaching students to *write* information texts is that this work has great reciprocity with teaching students to *read* information texts. The Common Core State Anchor Standards in Reading 1–3 emphasize the importance of students reading texts closely to determine what the text explicitly says, to ascertain the central ideas and related details, and to trace how the events and ideas develop over the course of the text. This focus on close, text-based reading is paramount in the Common Core.

Granted, the standards that I reference are reading and not writing standards, but there is never a better time to teach information reading then when students are engaged in research and writing about that reading. This session, then, is designed to help students read for what texts explicitly say, and to be able to ascertain key information and central ideas.

You will teach students to read a chunk of text, then to pause and think, "Let me explain to myself what I've just read." When the student goes to explain, he or she is apt to confront confusions. "Intolerable acts? What does that mean? Why are they called that?"

This session aims to teach students that when conducting research in order to write, comprehension will be an active, challenging process of detecting confusion, asking questions, rereading repeatedly, connecting the new to the known, hypothesizing, speculating—in short, of thinking.

Your emphasis will be more on reading and talking than on note-taking per se. The message is: when conducting research, a person reads and listens so that he or she can explain a subject to himself, to herself—and then to others.

IN THIS SESSION, you'll teach students that note-taking is not the easy part of research writing. When writers take notes, they need to understand what they are writing well enough that they are able to explain their notes to someone else.

GETTING READY

✔ "How to Take Notes" chart (see Teaching)

✔ Excerpt from *The Revolutionary War* by Josh Gregory, enlarged for students to see (see Teaching and Active Engagement)

✔ White boards and dry erase markers (see Active Engagement)

✔ Student copies of "Questions Teachers Ask When Planning to Teach" chart (see Homework)

COMMON CORE STATE STANDARDS: W.4.2, W.4.8, RI.4.1, RI.4.2, RI.4.3, RI.4.5, RI.4.7, RI.4.9, SL.4.1, SL.4.2, SL.4.4, L.4.1, L.4.2, L.4.3, L.4.6

The Intense Mind-Work of Note-Taking

CONNECTION

Tell students that when one of them had described note-taking as the easy part of doing research you couldn't shake the comment from your mind. Then explain the mind-work of note-taking.

"Writers, yesterday, when you were waiting for the bus to go home, I asked a few of you how the writing workshop has been for you lately, and your response was, 'Good, now that we're at the easy part.' I must have looked puzzled, because that was followed with an explanation: 'You know, 'cause now we're just copying down the facts and changing the big words into small ones.'

We find it helpful to name problems and tackle them as directly as possible. This connection cuts to the chase in part because the message is especially important.

"At home last night, that comment kept resurfacing in my mind. After supper, I started washing a dish, and as I soaped up the dish, I kept recalling that comment—'we're just copying down the facts and changing the big words into small ones.' I thought about it again and again. 'We're just copying down the facts and changing the big words into small ones. . . .' All of a sudden I realized I'd been washing the same plate for five minutes!

"I finally put the plate down, went to my desk, and started planning what I need to tell you."

❖ **Name the teaching point.**

"What I need to tell you is that note-taking is *not* the easy part of writing a research paper. When you take notes, you explain things to yourself so that you can explain them to someone else. Your brain should be exhausted from note-taking because you are thinking *so hard*, using every mind-muscle that you have. So if taking notes feels like the easy part of this work, something is wrong."

To highlight a point, it can help to dispute its opposite. That's what we are trying to do here.

TEACHING

Talk to children about the meaning-making work that you do when researching in preparation for writing.

"After I put that plate down and started working on this minilesson, I realized that one of the hardest things in the world is to teach someone *to think*. I want to teach you that when you read research to get ready to write, information comes in through your eyes (and maybe your ears) and then it goes into this thing called your brain—where something magical happens—but that sounds like hocus-pocus.

"Telling you your brain feels magical isn't going to teach you the intense kind of thinking that people do when taking notes—so I studied myself as I took notes and realized I do these things." I flipped to a new page of chart paper, where I had listed how to take notes.

If it feels like I am at my wits' end over how to teach this, you are right! If you can improve upon this, please do! But if not, it really is okay for the kids to see you struggle to find words and images that are big enough for the job.

How to Take Notes

- Organize information
- Think about the new information until it makes sense
- Connect new information with what I knew before

"I do all of that so I can explain the text to myself—and to others."

Demonstrate by reading a chunk of expository text and thinking aloud, explaining the text to yourself so that you can explain it to others. Struggle and show how you handle struggles.

"Let me show you what I mean by #1 and #2, for now. I'm going to read a bit from *The Revolutionary War* by Josh Gregory. Then I'm going to take notes. Please do this alongside me so you can see if your brain works like mine or not."

> *In 1774 Parliament began passing a series of laws that became known as the Intolerable Acts. These acts were designed to punish Massachusetts for destroying millions of dollars worth of property. Parliament then ordered Boston Harbor to be closed until the colonists paid for the tea they had destroyed.*

"Okay. What kind of notes would you take on that?" I gave them a moment to answer that question silently. "Watch what I do, and think to yourself, 'Do I take notes in that same way?'

"Hmm, . . . I could write some of this down but it doesn't yet make sense to me. What is this whole thing mainly about? I am lost. Let me read it again and try to get my bearings." I reread the start of the passage, pausing after reading "punishing Massachusetts for destroying millions of dollars worth of property." I said, "Huh? What are they referencing? I feel as if the author of this passage expects me to know something that I don't know. Let me look around this page and see if the rest of the page helps."

I scanned the page, and then said, "Oh—that's right. This comes a little after the Boston Tea Party. They are saying that these Intolerable Acts, these things are what England did to get back at the patriots for throwing the tea in the ocean. I get it. I could jot that down, but let me put more things together in my mind first."

Pause to name the intellectual work you are doing as you read an expository text in such a way that you can explain it to yourself and others.

I stepped back from reading, and said to the class, "Do you see that note-taking doesn't mean 'read, then write down some facts.' Instead, note-taking means 'read, and then try to explain the passage to myself.' I usually will find phrases where I don't know what they are talking about—like 'punishing Massachusetts for destroying millions of dollars worth of property.' Sometimes looking around the rest of the page will help figure out the hard parts. But always, I have to pause, think, and figure out what those parts actually mean."

ACTIVE ENGAGEMENT

Channel students to reread again, this time trying to put the whole passage together in such a way that they can explain it to themselves.

"Let's reread again, and see if we can 'get' what the passage is saying now so that we can explain it to ourselves and put it in our own words. There might be other parts that take some figuring out." I reread:

> In 1774 Parliament began passing a series of laws that became known as the Intolerable Acts. These acts were designed to punish Massachusetts for destroying millions of dollars worth of property. Parliament then ordered Boston Harbor to be closed until the colonists paid for the tea they had destroyed.
>
> British general Thomas Gage was named governor of Massachusetts. It became illegal for the colonists to hold town meetings or elect their own officials without permission from the British.

Coach students to pause to recap the text, doing so in a boxes-and-bullets fashion.

"Let me stop. Are you putting this together in your mind? You should be able to explain this to yourself, saying 'This is mainly saying that . . . (and I showed a hand, suggesting this represented a big idea) for example . . . , for example . . . , for example . . . ' (and I counted off on my fingers as I said "for example" . . .). Try it.

I gave the children a minute to turn and talk with their partners to recap the passage in this boxes-and-bullets format. Then I said, "You should be saying something like," and I used a fist and fingers as I continued: "The British wanted to get back at the Colonists, so they passed the Intolerable Acts (fist), which (1) closed the harbor, (2) made a British guy governor, and (3) made it illegal for the colonists to hold town meetings or to elect their own town leaders."

Notice that when reading aloud to demonstrate to kids, usually a very short snippet of text is sufficient.

There are few graphic organizers that I believe in more than the hand and fingers. This may sound silly, but I suspect if you try this, you'll see that it is more important than you imagined.

Again read on, trying to help students add what they learn next to what they have already learned.

"Let's read on and see if the British ordered yet more things as part of that punishment." I read, still holding fingers up as if expecting to add more items to the list. As I read on, I signaled these next items were, in fact, two more things the Intolerable Acts imposed on the Colonists:

> *The Administration of Justice Act required that any British official charged with murder be tried for their crimes in England rather than in the colonies. The colonists saw this as a way to legalize any murders committed by British soldiers in the colonies. The acts also saw the return of an unpopular law that allowed British officials to house their troops in colonists' homes.*

I paused. "Do you think you could explain this whole passage to yourself? Start with the Tea Party, and explain what transpired as a result of it." After a minute, I gave a thumbs up, as if to say, "Are you mostly grasping this?" The kids nodded.

"Partner 1, will you pretend Partner 2 doesn't know anything about this whole topic, and will you see if you can explain things to Partner 2? Start with the Tea Party, and then explain the consequences. As you do this explaining, try to be a teacher. Use an explaining voice, use your hands and fingers and face to make motions and gestures, and if you want to point to anything in the book, you can. Partner 1—turn and teach."

I listened in as the students taught each other. The fist-and-fingers organizer seemed to be working its magic for most. On occasion, there were students who were simply regurgitating facts straight from the passage. In those cases, I referred them back to the note-taking chart, reminding them that their job as a researcher is to think about the new information that they are learning and to connect it to what they already know. Pause, think, and figure out what this information really means.

Channel students to take written notes.

"Now, writers—and only now—I think you are ready to take notes on what you've read. But instead of each of you taking notes privately in your notebook, I'm going to distribute some white boards and marker pens. Those of you getting a white board, you will be the scribe. Talk with the kids around you to get ideas for what you might write in your notes, and how they'll go. Then take notes on the passage, making your notes be the quickest and best they can be. Get working!"

A minute later, I coached in a voiceover, "Taking notes has to be fast, so just another minute."

Before long, I reconvened the class. "Let's look at examples of your notes. As someone holds up one way in which notes could be taken, will you talk to your partner? What do you like about those notes? How could they be even better notes?" One child after another held up a white board, and children murmured their likes and critiques to each other.

The job, when teaching this, is to use gesture, intonation, and demonstration (where your thinking is so powerful and transparent that kids see you thinking) to convey the mind-work that is the focus of this minilesson. I've tried to detail the gestures that make sense to me, but you'll use whichever make sense to you. The important thing is to really truly be taking in this content, and for kids to see you doing that.

In our nonfiction reading workshops, students regularly read expository texts, then teach those texts to each other using an explaining voice, gestures, and references to pictures and charts. This has been extraordinarily powerful, in part because it makes reading into something more active.

Chances are good that you are going to need to nip at children's heels to move this along more quickly. Don't hesitate to do so.

If you have the children saying into the circle what they like or don't like about each other's notes, all of a sudden this becomes a very long-winded activity. Just show a few notes on white boards, and ask readers to share responses to what they see in a glance. Keep things moving along quickly.

LINK

Channel students to return to the initial question—"How is the work in the writing workshop going?"

"Now I have another question. Remember how I told you that yesterday, some of you told me note-taking is the easy part—you just copy down the facts and change big words to small words? I'm thinking that there must be some other way to talk about note-taking. So here is my question: How is note-taking going for you? Can you say your answers into the circle?"

"I'm curious," began Jude. "I mean, the Revolutionary War is like a story almost. There are so many things to learn about it, and I feel like I'm learning only little bits at a time. So each time I do more research, it's almost as if I'm finally getting it. And then sometimes, something that I've already learned starts to make even more sense."

Grayson chimed in. "I picked my topic, the Midnight Ride, because I was really interested in it. I thought it was pretty cool, Paul Revere and William Dawes, riding around, warning everyone of an attack that was coming. But I didn't know much about it, so I wasn't really sure how I was going to write about it. But researching and note-taking is helping me learn more, now I feel ready to write."

After a few more students shared, I sent the class off to begin working.

Supporting Intertextual and Cross-Text Synthesis

THE CONTENT OF TODAY'S MINILESSON IS IMPORTANT—and it is more challenging than might at first seem to be the case. You won't want kids to just nod and think, "I do that," without working hard to lift the level of their note-taking. Therefore, chances are good that your conferring and small-group work will channel students to apply the content of the minilesson.

You might gather a small group of children together and explain to them that you'd read that passage about the Intolerable Acts prior to the minilesson, and it had just sailed right over you. You could say, "I realize I needed today's minilesson because when I reread that passage about the Intolerable Acts for you, all of a sudden the whole thing fit together for me. I realized I'd missed half of what it said the first time I read it."

(continues)

MID-WORKSHOP TEACHING **Asking "Why?" and Saying "This Reminds Me of . . . " Can Help Nonfiction Researchers Grow—and Communicate—Meaning**

"Readers, can I bring your attention back to the shared passage from earlier?" I said, pointing to (but not rereading) the excerpt. "Readers, earlier, I pointed out to you that I do three kinds of thinking when I am note-taking." I referenced the "How to Take Notes" chart from the minilesson.

"We talked about the first two of these. Before today is over, I want to highlight the next way of thinking about texts." I pointed to the third item on my list, and read, "I connect new information with what I knew before." I added, "That work usually starts by me saying, 'Why?' and 'What's really going on?' Those questions lead me to connect to what I know—as I try to figure things out.

To get answers, I draw on what I know about life in general, not necessarily about those times. For example, it seems to me we might ask why the British responded to the Tea Party as they did. Those laws were pretty extreme—all those laws for some tea, thrown into the ocean?

"Try connecting to life now to understand this. Think, 'Are there any times in *my* life when I (or someone I know) acted a bit like the British acted in this situation?' Turn and talk about that."

Soon the class was awash in talk. Some suggested the British were acting like bullies, and that led to a long list of reasons and examples. Others thought that there are rules all the time in life—say, in baseball—and when people break the rules, they get in trouble. One child pointed out that the name, "The Intolerable Acts," couldn't be the *actual* name of the laws. "That'd be like naming your own laws, 'The Horrible Laws,'" she said.

After a bit of talk, I said, "Will you and your partner now talk in these ways about your topics? Ask 'Why?' and 'What's really going on?' and then, to find answers, see if you can make connections to *your* life that help you understand. Turn and talk."

The children talked, and then I intervened. "The talking and thinking you are doing in the air is what researchers do on the page as they take notes. So now, please stop talking about your topic, and instead—fast and furious for two minutes—write the same sorts of things as you have been saying."

Then you could suggest that the kids might all go back to a passage they'd read the day before and try to really turn their brains onto high and this time, reread the passage, trying to figure out what it meant, doing all the intellectual work we'd talked about.

As you watch children doing that work, you'll decide what aspects of reading you need to highlight. When we watched children do this recently, we were struck by the fact that they didn't seem to realize that thinking involves fitting what one already knows into whatever one is reading. If your youngsters don't seem to be doing this either, you might show them that as you read a page, you think about prior knowledge from the same book (or about the same topic) that might relate to that page. For example, if a child is reading about the Boston Tea Party and wants to pull in the information about the Intolerable Acts, the child might think both the British *and* the patriots seemed to be overreacting. One could argue that the British overreacted to the Boston Tea Party, and the patriots to the Intolerable Acts. Or the child might think about how the Intolerable Acts and the Boston Tea Party both seemed part of a slippery slope toward war. That might lead to the conclusion that both the British and the patriots made choices that led to war.

Partners can help each other see connections between texts. One partner might explain the text he or she has read, with the other partner listening to hear how what he read is similar or different. For example, one partner might explain that he read that the British didn't want the patriots to convene in gatherings but not have any sense of the reason for this, and another partner might have read that the British didn't want the patriots convening because they were apt to use those gatherings to rebel. That information could be combined.

You could also suggest that students can synthesize what they learn from one page with what they know from life. For example, a child might write that the way the patriots wrote about the Boston Massacre fanned the flames of people's anger in much the same way that reports of weapons of mass destruction did prior to our going into Iraq.

This synthesis work could be done through simply adding Post-it notes onto a page of reading—as long as the Post-it led to conversations.

Of course, to write about a subtopic, a student needs to draw together the pages from a scattering of resources on which that subtopic is tackled. You might suggest readers use especially odd colored Post-it notes—say, orange Post-it notes—on every page which detailed the punishments the British levied on the colonies. This will make these sections stand out from the sections marked with yellow Post-it notes. A reader might mark pages 34 and 56, and then a partner might add yet another page number from an entirely different book. Synthesizing information in that sort of fashion is essential to writing.

Assessing Note-Taking

Channel students to reread their notes from earlier in this unit, assessing whether those notes reflected the best of what they now know about note-taking.

"Would you go back and look at all the note-taking that you have done so far in this unit, and would you give your own note-taking a grade? Grade it a C, or an F, even, if when you look at your note-taking, it seems to you that you weren't really thinking at all—if you weren't organizing information, or connecting it, or explaining it—or most of all, really understanding it. Give yourself an A for places where your note-taking was an intense sort of mind-work."

I gave children a few minutes to do some, but not all, of this work. Then I intervened. "Will you show your partner one of your worst bits of note-taking, and talk about why it seems not great? Then show your partner one of your best bits of note-taking, and again, talk about it."

Recap what you hope students have learned.

After children talked, I said, "What I hope every one of you understands is that note-taking is *not* the easy part of writing a research paper. When you take notes, you explain things to yourself so that you can explain them to someone else. Your brain should be exhausted from note-taking because you are thinking *so hard*, using every mind-muscle that you have.

"So if taking notes feels like the easy part of this work, something is wrong."

TEACHING OTHERS TO PREPARE FOR WRITING

Tomorrow, you'll be starting to write a few of your chapters, so tonight you will need to get ready for doing that by teaching some people in your family about your topic. Before you do this, remember that teachers don't just teach anything that comes to mind, we take some time to plan our teaching first—and you should as well. Decide what chapters you are going to write first—and then plan to teach those chapters. As you plan, ask yourself the questions you learned about earlier.

Questions Teachers Ask When Planning to Teach

- What do I want my audience to learn?
- What will interest people?
- What might confuse them, that I can clarify?
- What will I teach that they can care about?

I have copies of this chart that you can bring home with you.

I want to add one more item to that list of things to think about. You should also remember that your goal is not just *to tell* the person all about this topic, it is also to make the person *care* about the topic. As you teach about the subject, watch your listener's face to get signs when he or she is going, "Huh?" For example, if you say, "When the British announced the Intolerable Acts . . ." you would probably see your listener's face go, "Huh?" So then say, "Let me give you some background . . ." Or "In case that's confusing, let me explain. . . ." You want to be a *better, clearer* teacher than the books you read.

Drafting Is Like Tobogganing

First the Preparation, the Positioning . . .
Then the Whooosh!

ear Teachers,

We're shifting the work of planning the details of this session onto your shoulders, and will use this letter to set you up for success. In Session 10, you helped students read for key information and for central ideas, tracing how the events and ideas develop across a text. That work, so critical to the CCSS, will continue whenever students are engaged in research—and will also influence students as they write, for they'll be trying to write in such a way that channels readers to focus on their key information and central ideas.

This means that some of the focus of your teaching will continue, even while your emphasis shifts from helping students read and research to helping them draft. This session is an important one, then, because you will be moving the emphasis of the class from researching to writing (although presumably they'll return to researching for later chapters).

Of course, some students began writing these new and improved books already. Your previous minilesson focused on note-taking, but that doesn't mean your students all worked on note-taking. Some probably already shifted from taking notes about a subtopic to writing a chapter about that subtopic.

The session we suggest for today adds heft to that transition from researching to writing. It is certainly understandable that you may have students who feel reluctant to make that shift from reading to writing, feeling unprepared still. In this session, you could blow the whistle; you could call, "Time to write!" You might suggest to them that writing is like tobogganing: You fuss around, positioning yourself, then whoosh, off you go!

MINILESSON

You might start the minilesson by saying something like, "Writers, have you ever tobogganed down a steep hill? Writing, to many professional writers, is a bit like tobogganing. You spend some time at the top of the hill, positioning yourself, getting ready for the ride.

COMMON CORE STATE STANDARDS: W.4.2, W.4.5, W.4.10, RI.4.1, RI.4.2, RI.4.5, SL.4.1, L.4.1, L.4.2, L.4.3,

You aim the toboggan. You calculate the projected path, and shift things a bit. You load on, check that nothing's hanging out, and then—whoosh, you are off! Faster and faster you fly, snow in your face, unable to do anything but hang on for dear life, on and on and on, and then, just like that it's over." You can then go on to explain to the students that they have been positioning themselves to write a chapter, getting ready for the writing ride, through all of their careful note-taking and thinking.

Today's teaching point could be another one of those "I want to remind you of something you already know" teaching points. Remember, not every minilesson is about teaching new information. Many times your students will need to be reminded to draw on all that they already know. Today is no different. Remind them that they already know a *ton* about how to write informational books. And that their job, when they are drafting, is to draw on all they know about writing informational books, and to write, fast and furious.

During the teaching section of your minilesson, you may want to direct attention to the "Getting Ready to Write an Informational Book" chart that you have been using throughout the unit. Point out that the chart has five steps on *getting ready* to write an informational book—and then there is just one step, step 6, that says "Draft!" That's not a lot of help for students as they embark on actual writing.

You might suggest that the class can collect what they already know about drafting to make a chart that can help with the work they'll be doing today. You might say that to help out, you started jotting such a chart, but you haven't come close to finishing it. Then you could show them a chart that you started prior to today's session that lists suggestions from drafting, setting them up for a turn and talk time to think, "What *else* goes on the chart?"

When thinking about the suggestions that you write and those you leave for them, you will want to remember to leave the low-hanging fruit for the kids. If there are three or four adages that you know are especially important to them, leave those, and add items the kids might not think about. We've noted some possibilities—though remember, you are charting tips that the class already knows, so select ones that will be familiar to your class.

As you look over the list, you should see that these are sequenced in a way that will help students. If you delete a number of these items, essentially leaving them to children to invent, you'll want to think about how to get their suggestions into the right order.

You may say to yourself that you don't want to mess up this list by deleting half of it, in which case you could decide to alter it a bit. Instead of recruiting students to coauthor the list, you could simply say that you went through past minilessons to collect this list, and ask them to use the active engagement time as a time to think about which of these items are easy for them to do, and which are challenging. Also, what parts of this list do they find especially helpful? What will be most important for them as they begin to draft? How do they plan to get started?

Today, you are expecting that all of your students write, write, write. To make this expectation clear, you could send them off, clarifying what you expect students to do, naming how much time they have, and saying, with urgency, "So get started."

Suggestions for Drafting

- Make sure your chapter isn't too broad. Break big topics into several subtopics.
- Start by drafting information you know especially well.
- Think, "What kind of a text will this be?"
- If it's an all-about chapter, make a table of contents for the chapter.
- Start the chapter with a hook, then let readers know how the chapter will go.
- Use words such as <u>first</u> and <u>later</u>.
- Say your plan: "I'll first talk about—then I'll . . ."
- When writing, remember to say more about a subtopic and to write in paragraphs.
- Am I teaching <u>information</u> (or is my writing full of a lot of hot air, and not that many facts, statistics, quotes, names, dates, stories . . .)?
- Will my writing make sense to a reader or will readers go, "Huh?"
- Is my writing written in my own voice (or did I end up copying from a book)?

CONFERRING AND SMALL-GROUP WORK

The checklist that students use to assess their progress needs to be something that you've internalized and apply to student work continually. It is helpful to assign yourself a particular lens to use, and to look with that one lens in mind. For example, you may look to see if students are approaching each of their chapters as if it is an autonomous text, and starting that chapter with an introduction. Does the introduction show some effort to draw in the reader, and if so, what are the methods for doing that that students are using, and are not yet but could be using? Then, too, you'll want to look to see whether somewhere in the introduction, the writer makes an effort to help readers anticipate how the text they're about to read will be structured. You will be teaching students about introductions in the following session, so presumably this will be something new and challenging for them. You'll want to notice which students are especially adept at this. What is it that they are doing to good effect? Then you'll want to think about whether you could have these writers share what they are doing with others, so that they might learn to do it as well.

Then again, you might notice whether students are incorporating a variety of information in their pieces. Are they writing with nuggets of specific information: numbers, names, places, quotes, or are they writing at a level of generality that essentially turns their information all into a homogeneous soup? If you notice a few students whose writing contains especially varied forms of elaboration, this will be an important resource for you. You can collect these snippets and use them to teach others.

You may decide to set up students who are doing something with high levels of proficiency to teach those who are in the "using but confusing" stage. You might hesitate to anoint some youngsters as teachers to others, worrying that those strong students also deserve to be challenged. If that is a concern, you should rest assured that one of the best ways to make sure a student owns his or her own knowledge and skills and can leverage that knowledge and skills to do yet more advanced work is to make sure that learner can explain what he is doing and why he is doing it to someone else. In fact, there is talk among Common

The Information Writing Checklist, Grades 4 and 5 can be found on the CD-ROM.

Information Writing Checklist

	Grade 4	NOT YET	STARTING TO	YES!	Grade 5	NOT YET	STARTING TO	YES!
	Structure				**Structure**			
Overall	I taught readers different things about a subject. I put facts, details, quotes, and ideas into each part of my writing.	☐	☐	☐	I used different kinds of information to teach about the subject. Sometimes I included little essays, stories, or "how-to" sections in my writing.	☐	☐	☐
Lead	I hooked my readers by explaining why the subject mattered, telling a surprising fact, or giving a big picture. I let readers know that I would teach them different things about a subject.	☐	☐	☐	I wrote an introduction that helped readers get interested in and understand the subject. I let readers know the subtopics I would be developing later as well as the sequence.	☐	☐	☐
Transitions	I used words in each section that help readers understand how one piece of information connected with others. If I wrote the section in sequence, I used words and phrases such as *before, later, next, then,* and *after.* If I organized the section in kinds or parts, I used words such as *another, also,* and *for example.*	☐	☐	☐	When I wrote about results, I used words and phrases like *consequently, as a result,* and *because of this.* When I compared information, I used words and phrases such as *in contrast, by comparison,* and *especially.* In narrative parts, I used phrases that go with stories such as *a little later* and *three hours later.* In the sections that stated an opinion, I used words such as *but the most important reason, for example,* and *consequently.*	☐	☐	☐
Ending	I wrote an ending that reminded readers of my subject and may have suggested a follow-up action or left readers with a final insight. I added my thoughts, feelings, and questions about the subject at the end.	☐	☐	☐	I wrote a conclusion in which I restated the main points and may have offered a final thought or question for readers to consider.	☐	☐	☐
Organization	I grouped information into sections and used paragraphs and sometimes chapters to separate those sections. Each section had information that was mostly about the same thing. I may have used headings and subheadings.	☐	☐	☐	I organized my writing into a sequence of separate sections. I may have used headings and subheadings to highlight the separate sections. I wrote each section according to an organizational plan shaped partly by the genre of the section.	☐	☐	☐

Core State Standards' leaders of making level 4 of any skill be not that the student can do work that is normally regarded as appropriate for the next grade, but instead, that the learner can not only do the work but can teach it to others.

MID-WORKSHOP TEACHING

If you use work time as a chance to look over students' work with an eye toward which items on the information checklist your students are able to do, almost able to do, and not yet able to do, you will certainly find a few items that merit extra attention, and the mid-workshop teaching point is a perfect time to give that extra attention. Simply tell children, "I've been looking over your work to see whether you are all meeting the expectations we have set, and I have two concerns I want to talk with you about." You will probably want to show the level of work that many students are doing, contrasting that with the expectations that you have for them. Then you'll want to give them some very practical tips for how they can go from what they are doing toward what you hope they will soon be able to do. It is helpful if you then channel partners to reread each other's work, looking for instances when the student hasn't yet met the expectations—and for instances when a student surpasses them. You can then ask partners to help each other make the appropriate revisions.

SHARE

You may want to use today's share to show students how, at the end of any writing time, you like to do a quick self-assessment. Model this by showing children how you reread the chart as if it is a list of things you want to watch for. Rather than using the entire list from earlier in the session, you might select a few key items, probably avoiding selecting items dealing with an introduction because that will be the focus on tomorrow's session:

Is my writing built with information, not just hot air?

Is my draft written in my own voice, not copied from a book?

Did I teach readers **information** (and not just give a lot of hot air)?

Will my writing make sense to a reader or will readers go, "Huh?"

The easiest way to demonstrate a teaching point that asks students to reread with the checklist in hand is to provide a piece of your writing, making sure that the piece contains lots of flaws, and then reread one paragraph with the suggested lens in hand, and ask students to join you in rereading the rest of the piece, planning revisions that you could make for that piece.

The piece that you provide should be short so that the share is quick—students can grasp quickly what it means to check that the writing is not just hot air, to check that it makes sense, and to check that it does not seem to have been copied from a book. For example, if your text was like this, the students could do all the requisite work:

> The aftermath of the Boston Massacre was a problem, it was not good at all. A lot happened that was stirring to emotions and this is important to the whole war because it affected a lot of things.
>
> Among the many forms of propaganda that were developed in the aftermath of the Boston Massacre, none precipitated more response than the etching done by the silversmith, Paul Revere.
>
> The Boston Massacre was a hard time and afterwards was lots of things like the etching and the stuff about Paul Revere. And then people didn't like what happened but it wasn't all true.

Once the students identified the problems with each paragraph, you might channel them to talk to partners about ways they could resolve those problems. In the first instance, students might suggest I return to sources to locate some more detailed information. Although it is true that we often suggest students close the source book so as to write "in their own words," it is necessary for a writer to have the bricks of information on hand before he or she writes.

Of course, in the second paragraph, the writing has gone to the opposite extreme. Students may notice their writing sounds as if it has been copied right out of a book. In this case it would help to teach someone before writing.

Finally, the third paragraph—the confusing one—probably suffers from organizational problems, and looking to see if the structure can be fixed will probably help.

Good luck with this day,
Lucy and Anna

HOMEWORK

For homework, you might say, "Tonight, write against the clock. Write at least another chapter. Start by positioning yourself for the toboggan ride. Figure out the plan for the chapter. Lay out some of the specific facts you will put into the chapter. Get ready to use thought prompts like, 'The important thing about this is . . .' Get ready to put some stories into your writing, like 'I can imagine what that was like. Perhaps so-and-so said such and such . . .'

"Plan to write three pages, so imagine that your subtopic won't be just half a page long! Then set your clock for twenty minutes of writing, and write fast and furious, without stopping. Stop after exactly twenty minutes, and tomorrow we'll talk about what you accomplished."

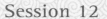

Developing a Logical Structure Using Introductions and Transitions

IN THIS SESSION, you'll remind students that when writing an informational text, writers need to organize information. In an introduction, writers let readers in on their organizational plan.

GETTING READY

✔ The research plan that you used in Session 9 to model an adequate method of organizing information, enlarged for students to see (see Teaching)

✔ Chart paper and marker (see Teaching)

✔ "Ways to Conclude a Chapter in an Informational Book" chart (see Share)

✔ An all-about chapter from your own informational book, written without a conclusion (see Share)

✔ Mini versions of the chart, "Ways to Begin a Chapter in an Informational Book" and "Ways to Conclude a Chapter of an Informational Book," photocopied for students to bring home (see Homework)

COMMON CORE STATE STANDARDS: W.4.2.a,c; W.4.5, W.4.10, RI.4.5, SL.4.1, SL.4.4, L.4.1, L.4.2, L.4.3

L EARNING TO STRUCTURE one's information writing is not an easy task. If this work is occurring before writing a chapter, it requires that the writer stand back and think over all that he or she plans to write in a section, then place all that upcoming information into a structure and writes to readers about that structure. Of course, that is exactly the work that essay writers do—but for your students, so far essays have been written about personal knowledge. Students had far greater control of and flexibility with that knowledge.

Today's minilesson, then, helps writers to foresee and foreshadow, for readers, the plan for how the upcoming text will unfold. Instead of writing paragraph one, sticking some good information into that paragraph, then thinking "What else do I have to say?" and proceeding toward the job of writing paragraph two, then again looking up to say, "Do I have more to add?," the writer who imposes an overarching infrastructure onto his or her writing is able to look over the whole tableful of information, to sort it into chunks, and to line those chunks up in some sensible fashion. Moreover, the writer is able to write about this plan.

This would be extremely demanding work, especially when writing with relatively thin amounts of information—as is apt to be the case for many of your students—save for the fact that students will probably be writing mostly about events that proceed chronologically. They can therefore fairly easily organize their information by time, writing about what happened before, then during, then after the event. That same structure could be renamed (and perhaps re-angled) into writing about the causes, the event, and the consequences. Of course, there will be other chapters—perhaps one that illuminates the weapons used, another that tells about the places involved, but it's not hard to find a place to hang them once one has the structure in place.

This is the first of three chapters that help students develop, foreshadow, and highlight their logical structure.

Developing a Logical Structure Using Introductions and Transitions

CONNECTION

Ask students to bring the writing they did when working under the clock last night, and to talk about what it was like to press themselves to write so much.

Once children had gathered in the meeting area with their homework from the previous night, I asked them to show their partner how much they wrote. "Writers, how many of you wrote at least a page and a half last night?" Most thumbs went up. "Two pages? Three?" There were still thumbs up.

"Lots of researchers say that students need to be able to write two pages in a sitting—in twenty or thirty minutes of actual writing during the workshop—and last night, a good many of you did that amount of writing. Can we talk a little about what you did that worked, that got you writing so much?"

I nodded for Jude to begin, signaling I didn't expect to be calling on people, and when Jude aimed his response toward me, I gestured for him to talk to his classmates. I actually left my seat at the front of the meeting area, sitting instead alongside the edge of the group.

Jude sputtered, "I just kept writing but my hand felt like it was gonna fall off."

Melissa added, "For me, it was good that you told me to figure out how many pages each part would be. I didn't have enough information so I added in some thought prompts, 'This is interesting because . . . ' and stuff like that."

"I made up a good trick. I put in a lot of lists like of the types of weapons because that took up lots of space," said Yoshi.

Ask writers to study the volume of writing they normally produce with the volume produced under pressure, using the contrast to highlight the need for increased amounts of productivity.

I nodded. "So here is my challenge for you. Will you look at how much you wrote last night—in twenty minutes—and will you compare that with how much you wrote yesterday, during our writing workshop? You had forty minutes—almost twice as long—for writing yesterday. Do a quick investigation and talk with your partner about what you notice."

It is vital to periodically emphasize volume as students move through the writing process. Research is clear that students' proficiency in writing is linked to the amount of writing they do. You'll want to continually stress the value of students setting goals and pushing themselves to write more and more.

FIG. 12–1 Melissa's draft, written for homework

Soon the class was engaged in spirited talk. "Writers, I heard an amazing number of you saying that you wrote more last night, in twenty minutes, than you wrote in twice that time in class! That's a problem, isn't it? Today you will have forty minutes to write, so you should mark out how much writing you can plan to get done in class today—it should be twice what you wrote last night. Make a goalpost for yourself on your page."

Clarify that more writing is not a goal unless the writing is also well done, suggesting nothing matters more than that the writing is organized.

"Of course, longer and faster writing *could* be worse writing, and it is really important that you combine more fluency in writing, with continued clear, organized writing. And the most important part of that is for you to work on making your writing organized. As the chapters in your book become longer and longer, it becomes more and more important that those chapters are well organized."

❖ **Name the teaching point.**

"Today, I want to remind you that when you are writing an informational text, that text—whether it is the whole book, or a chapter of the book—needs to be organized. There needs to be a plan for how the text will go. And usually the writer gives the reader some hints, early on and throughout, of how the text is organized. The writer often acts like a tour guide, taking readers along the trail of his or her information. And that tour begins with an overview, or an introduction."

TEACHING

Ask students to imagine giving others a tour of their school, bringing out the idea that they'd plan to tour "wings" of the school, and there would be logic behind their decisions. Draw parallels to the way writers plan a logical structure.

"Writers, I want to teach you something that isn't really about writing, just yet—then we'll come back to writing. Imagine that a couple of new kids moved into town and joined our class. And imagine that I asked you to take the group on a tour of the school. Right now, would you think about the main places you'd take them?" I waited for a few seconds. "Think about the order—how would the tour go?" Again I waited for a little bit.

"Someone, where would the tour head first?" I asked. A couple of children suggested the wing of the school with the gym, the music room. "And what might come next?" Other children suggested that next, the tour would go to their wing of the school—the grade 4 and 5 classrooms. "So, if you were the tour guide, you might say, at the start of the tour, 'First we'll visit some of the fun places—the wing of the school that has art, music, and gym, and after that we'll visit the grade 4 and 5 classrooms. Later I'll take you to the central office, where you take attendance information . . . ,'" I said, and the children concurred.

"Writers, when you write information texts, you are sort of taking learners on a tour of your subject. And the people on your tour expect you to give them an overview, early on, of how the whole tour will go. They expect a version of 'First

Practice writing, with feedback, is the single most important way your writers will improve. They must write a lot!

For most people, the structure that undergirds a nonfiction text is invisible, like the bearing beams of a house are invisible. The CCSS prioritize the need for information writing to be written with a logical structure, and this means that you will want to call students' attention to that structure. This session is one of many that does this work.

we'll visit the wing of the school with the fun stuff—art music, gym—and then we'll go to the fourth- and fifth-grade classrooms. A bit later we'll visit the central offices where you'll need to do some of your business. . . ."

Point out that just as learners expect the tour guide to overview the tour, the author needs to provide an overview of the structure of the upcoming chapter. Channel students to imagine how they'd describe the underlying structure that informs the Valley Forge book plan students studied earlier.

"And here is the thing: learners expect that overview at the start of your whole book, and again at the start of each chapter. Let's imagine how we might write such an 'Overview of the Tour' if we were writing the start to the Valley Forge book that we thought about a few days ago." I displayed the plan for that book.

Plan I: Jason

	Name of Chapter	Genre	Kinds of Research I'll Need to Do
1	All about the Revolutionary War	all-about	Find a few more facts.
2	Setting up the Valley Forge camp: the layout and supplies and place	all-about and how-to	I have book on it. Map it?
3	The people: the soldiers who were there	all-about	not sure
4	What happened: George Washington helped his soldiers at Valley Forge.	an essay	I know a lot, but want specific details about what he said.
5	A turning point story (about the above)	a story	a story about how they were depressed, then GW helped
6	After Valley Forge	all-about	I need to find out more about this.

"Will you think about what you might say at the start of the book to let people in on the plan for the book?" I gave the children a moment to think.

Coach to lift the level of students' efforts to name a structure that undergirds the book plan, supporting them to think in chunks and to name reasons for the sequence.

"If you are just listing all the chapters in order, that's not the best thing. Remember with the school tour, we talk about wings of the school, about chunks of rooms. The other thing is this: to give the overview of the tour, you want to try to think a bit about *why* the tour is going to go as is it. Like—for the school tour, we had in mind that first we'd take them to the fun stuff, and we knew those rooms were bunched together. Then we thought they should see all the classrooms for kids their age. . . . We let them in on the thinking behind the plan. To figure out what to say, we need to figure out what the underlying plan could be for the Valley Forge book. Let's think again about the chapters and see if we can figure out why they are ordered in this way." I listed off the chapters.

"If you were going to chunk these chapters, and say, 'First we'll learn about . . . , then we'll learn about . . . ,' how would you chunk them? Hmm. . . ."

The work you are doing supports not only the CCSS for information writing but also the standards for information reading. You are helping students to see the central ideas and supporting details, to think about the relationship between the structure and the meaning of a text. This is challenging work and will be the focus of a good deal of instruction over upcoming years, so you need not expect students to be skilled at this work yet.

Shift to demonstration, and demonstrate for students in ways that show them how you would go about doing the thinking you'd pressed them to try alongside you.

As hands shot up, I pressed on. "I'm thinking I might say, 'Before zooming in on Valley Forge, we'll get the big picture by thinking about the Revolutionary War in general.' Then we'll focus on a place that became important as a turning point of the war. We'll study that place from start to finish—first the setting up and populating it, then the events there, and finally the consequences that occurred as a result of Valley Forge.

"Turn and tell your partner your own overview of this book, and talk about how mine was similar to and different than yours." As children did this, I wrote some key phrases from my overview onto chart paper:

> Before (getting to X topic), we first got the big picture.
>
> Then we focused on (the topic).
>
> We studied—from start to finish—
>
> first the . . . , then the—and finally the . . .

ACTIVE ENGAGEMENT

Channel students to examine the chapter they wrote for homework to discern if there is an undergirding structure in it, and if so, to think how their introduction could forecast this.

"Right now, look at the chapter you wrote last night. Look first to see if there *is* a plan that undergirds the way the chapter is laid out. Have you written subheadings in the chapter that chunk it into parts, or could you? Do that first. If you have already done that, go ahead and think what you'd say as a tour guide, to let readers in on that plan."

Caution children that if they are struggling, their chapter probably lacks a structure, which simply signals a need for a chapter revision to chunk things more clearly.

After children worked for two minutes, I said, "If you are having a really hard time writing subheadings that actually label the chunks of your chapter, you probably need to rewrite it, this time making sure the chapter, like the book, follows a table of contents. This is very common for writers."

Add a final point. Being able to subhead a text is more important than actually doing so.

"One last thing I want to share with you. If you can chunk your chapter and make subheadings—you need to know you don't actually *need* those subheadings in your final draft. What you do need is the tour guide's overview of the chapter. You can borrow some of the phrases I said in mine." I referenced the phrases I had listed on chart paper.

LINK

Send students off with a reminder that informational writers need to provide their readers with an overview of the information they are presenting, in the form of an introduction.

"Writers, will you always remember that being a writer of an informational text is not all that different from leading a tour? You are taking your audience (in your case, your readers!) on a tour of all of the information you are trying to teach. Your audience is apt to learn more if you start in a way that explains what they will learn.

"Today, I know you have a lot to do. You need to write new chapters, and some of you will need to do research to write those chapters. Before you move to that work, take just a second to make sure the last chapter you wrote is chunked so that it could have subheadings inserted into it, and make sure you begin by giving readers a tour guide overview.

"As you move on to future chapters, you may find that your introduction is the last thing you write, because sometimes it's not until you have written a chapter that you know exactly how that chapter will unfold well enough to clue readers in."

Planning Small-Group Work to Help Writers Organize

THIS SESSION IS A BIG ONE. The work of organizing and categorizing information is a foundational skill of expository writing. Throughout this series, we teach organization in different ways and for many different purposes, purposefully cycling back to it while ratcheting up the level each time we revisit it. The work that your writers did in the previous essay unit lays the foundation for the work they will do in this session, and the work they do in this session lays the groundwork not only for future sessions in this book but for the upcoming unit on literary essay.

It's always helpful to have in mind some of the main things you plan to teach on any given day. Because it's so effective to support kids in front-end revision while they are planning and organizing ways their chapters could go, we recommend planning to get to as many students as possible. Small-group instruction will allow you to do just that.

It's likely that your writers will fit into one of a few predictable categories. You might have noticed some of these patterns emerging as you studied your students' writing over the last couple of days. One category of writers may be those who have yet to organize their chapters into sections according to content, and who need support with the basic skill of categorizing information. You might teach these writers to do some planning work in their notebooks, choosing a chapter and then making a list of all of the possible subheadings that chapter might contain. You may also teach them to go back to their drafts with these subheadings in mind, using colored pencils to underline information that fits into each subheading. Doing this will give them a quick visual reference to see how their information is organized. They might decide to reorganize their information, to delete certain subsections for which they don't have a lot of content, and to beef up others.

Another category of writers might be those who have organized their chapters into sections, but who may have placed some extraneous information in one section or another. It might be helpful to gather these writers with a section of your demonstration writing in hand, a section that you wrote with some extraneous information just

MID-WORKSHOP TEACHING
Reminding Students to Make a Plan

"Writers, eyes up here. You all are making decisions about what you need to do and are assigning yourselves the work you need to do. How many of you have started writing another chapter?" When more than half the class indicated that, I said, "Remember that it helps to lay out some of the information you'll be including in the chapter before you write so that you write with specifics. And keep in mind that you can write a page and a half in a day, *easily*. And finally, don't forget that it's okay to go back and write the introduction *after* you've written the chapter itself. But you do want to write with an organizational plan in mind. Keep writing!"

for this purpose. Be sure to create a piece of writing that contains information with some obvious errors, such as the one below:

The Beginning of the Boston Massacre

The huge event that is now known as the Boston Massacre began with what seemed like a small thing. A British soldier had refused to pay for a wig made by a local wig-maker. The wig-maker's apprentice, named Edward Garrick, made some nasty remarks to a group of British soldiers because of this. A British soldier named Hugh White overheard his comments, and the two got in a huge fight. After the Boston Massacre, Hugh White was put on trial. John Adams was his lawyer. The fight between Garrick and White led to other people getting involved, and the beginning of the Massacre.

Ask your writers to work in their partnerships to discuss whether all of the information in your paragraph fits. If you are using writing similar to the above, they will likely identify right away that the details about the trial don't fit in this section. Then, ask the group to work individually, and coach in while they search for information in their own writing that is misplaced.

A third category of writers might be those who have a sense of how to organize information but who need support in making this transparent for readers. Start by teaching this group that writers often begin a section of writing by letting readers know what the section is mostly about and what kinds of things they'll learn in that section. To do this, you might teach your writers to make a mini-table of contents for the chapter, and then to use this to write a few sentences that will help readers understand what they are going to be reading about.

Writing Conclusions
Wrapping Up the Tour

Point out that just as a tour guide wraps up a tour leaving the participants with something to think about, they too need to leave their readers thinking at the end of a chapter. Share possible strategies for writing a conclusion.

"Writers, today we talked about how important it is to organize your informational books. And one way to organize your writing is to write an introduction that gives your readers an overview of what is to come, highlighting some of the more important information. Just as a tour guide gives an overview of what stops will be along the way, highlighting key places, your introduction should do the same for your writing. But now, I want to think about conclusions. What is the best way to wrap up your chapter?

"I want to go back to thinking about the school tour you were giving to a new student. Would you just get to the last stop on your tour and say, 'That's it. Bye now'?" There were a few chuckles from the students, clearly entertained by my abruptness. "Nope, I didn't think so. Well, you don't want to end your chapter like that, either. Here are a few options for writing a conclusion that is just as powerful as the rest of your chapter." I flipped to the next page of the chart pad, where I had already listed out the possibilities.

Ask students to work with you to brainstorm possible conclusions for a chapter from your own informational book.

"Let's take a look at my chapter all about the aftermath of the Boston Massacre. It's pretty much done; it's just that I haven't thought much about my conclusion yet. I just sort of ended it. I definitely need more. I'll read it to you, and then we can work together to come up with some possible conclusions." I read my writing aloud.

Chapter 4: The Aftermath of the
Boston Massacre

The Aftermath of the Boston Massacre was serious. Many important things happened that helped lead to war. For example, many strong patriots tried to convince the colonists that the British soldiers had attacked on purpose. Also, the soldiers were put on trial and found guilty. And a final way the events after the Massacre helped lead to war is that the news of what happened in Boston spread through the colonies, making people very angry.

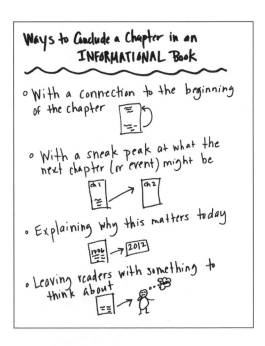

Ways to Conclude a Chapter in an INFORMATIONAL Book

o With a connection to the beginning of the chapter

o With a sneak peak at what the next chapter (or event) might be

o Explaining why this matters today

o Leaving readers with something to think about

One of the first things that happened after the Massacre was that patriots, like Paul Revere, wanted to convince people that the British soldiers were at fault. There was lots of propaganda being published that was trying to convince people that the soldiers killed people on purpose. For example, Paul Revere did an **etching** that showed the soldiers shooting right at innocent people. He did this to make people angry enough to want to fight the British.

Another thing that happened after the massacre was the trial of the British soldiers. Everyone knew that John Adams was a patriot, so they were very surprised when he decided to defend the British soldiers in their **trial**. He said that the **soldiers** deserved a fair trial, just like every-one else. In the end, two of the soldiers who fired on the crowd, Matthew Kilroy and Hugh Montgomery, were accused of manslaughter. Their punishment was to be **branded** on the thumb and kicked out of the army.

The anger in Boston started to spread through the colonies. People heard what had happened, and were starting to get ready to fight. Patriots began to get serious about making a plan to separate from Britain.

"Right now, please turn and talk with your partner about some possible conclusions that I could write. You can use any one of those strategies from the chart." I gave the class just a minute to brainstorm with their partners, and then chose a few to share their ideas with the whole group.

I gestured to Thomas, who said, "You could say something that's telling what is going to happen next. Like, I'm writing about the Boston Tea Party, so I know that it's another big thing that happened before the war."

"Ah, I see," I said. "So I could say something like, 'The Boston Massacre was just one event out of many that fueled anger and led up to the Revolutionary War. Another was the Boston Tea Party, which happened a few years later.'"

Next, I nodded to Lucie. "You could say why this matters. This chapter talks about propaganda, and I know that it got people convinced to have the war."

"Yes, that makes sense too," I added. "And I could talk about how people have to be aware of propaganda today, because people still use it to get others on their side."

Finally, I asked Jude to share. He said, "You could connect to the beginning of the chapter and talk about all of the ways the aftermath was really bad."

"Okay, so kind of a summary of the chapter, that makes a ton of sense," I said. "Wow, writers, you really came up with some powerful ideas. You left me with a lot to ponder. I can't wait to sit down and write! And I'm sure you can't wait to sit down and write your own conclusion as soon as you can!"

WRITING AN INTRODUCTION THAT HOOKS READERS

Today, we talked about how the job of the introduction is to give the readers an overview of what is to come. But really, that is only *part* of it. Besides giving an overview of the chapter, you also need to hook your reader. For tonight, what I'd like you to do is take a look at whatever source material you have been reading and see if that writer uses their introduction to hook the reader—not every writer does, of course, but *good* writers almost always do. After you look through your source material, go back to your own writing from today, and see if you wrote your introduction in a way that will hook your readers. If not, you will want to make some revisions. I'm handing each of you a copy of a chart with possible ways to write an introduction that will draw your readers in.

You will also need time to write (or revise) your conclusion in the ways we talked about. You'll see that our chart from earlier is on this handout, too.

Ways to Begin a Chapter in an Informational Book

- Asking and answering a question
- With a shocking fact
- With a small story (someone doing or saying something)
- With a connection to an earlier chapter

Ways to Conclude a Chapter in an Informational Book

- With a connection to the beginning of the chapter
- With a sneak peek at what the next chapter (or next event in history) might be
- Explaining why this matters today
- Leaving readers with something to think about (perhaps by asking a big question)

Text Features

Popping Out the Important Information

T HE TITLE OF THIS SESSION IS DECEPTIVE. At first glance, it will probably call to mind all the whirligigs that your students so enjoy adding: clip art, text boxes, a glossary, bold words. And yes, text features are one of the defining trademarks of informational writing—more so now than ever, as the Internet allows for more use of visual elements. But this session actually continues the emphasis of the previous session on the importance of developing and communicating a structure that undergirds information texts.

Your message today, then, is that writers use text features to highlight the central ideas and key information in their texts (and to subordinate the other information). You will begin

IN THIS SESSION, you'll teach students that writers think about the most important information and ideas that they're trying to convey in a chapter or a section, and they use text features to highlight that information.

GETTING READY

- ✔ An informational text that contains images as well as writing, enlarged for students to see. In this case we refer to Ben Franklin's letter to George Whatley (see Connection).

- ✔ Chart paper and marker (see Connection and Active Engagement)

- ✔ Section from your own informational book to use for modeling text features, enlarged for students to see (see Teaching and Active Engagement)

- ✔ "Ways to Highlight Central Ideas and Key Information in Your Informational Writing" chart (see Link)

"This session, like the others in this bend, is in many ways really a lesson in determining importance in disguise."

by asking writers to call to mind all of the kinds of text features that are found in informational writing. Just the very suggestion of text features may draw a palpable excitement from your crowd. "We get to draw!" they might think. "We get to search images on Google!" But your writers will soon learn that crafting text features that pack a big teaching punch takes a lot more than slapping on a few photos that were downloaded from the Internet.

This session, like the others in this bend, is in many ways really a lesson in determining importance in disguise. You will teach your writers to use text features as a way to show readers what each section is really about, to think of them almost like a highlighter, carefully crafting them as if to say to readers, "Hey! This matters!"

COMMON CORE STATE STANDARDS: W.4.2.a, W.4.10, W.5.2.a, RI.4.2, RI.4.5, SL.4.1, SL.4.2, SL.4.5, L.4.1, L.4.2, L.4.3

In Appendix A of the CCSS, the authors write "with practice, students become better able to develop a controlling idea and a coherent focus on a topic and more skilled at selecting and incorporating relevant examples, facts, and details into their writing" (23). This session seeks to maintain a spotlight on this important work. Students have several years before they are expected to be adept at determining and highlighting central ideas, but they will only develop these skills with repeated opportunities. This session, then, seeks to give them those opportunities—and to attach this difficult work to the fun of finding just the right images, constructing captions and headings, and making charts and diagrams.

This session also provides an opportunity for you to address the Common Core's recommendation that fourth-grade writers "include formatting (e.g., headings), illustrations, and multimedia when useful to aiding comprehension (CCSS W4.2a)." This standard, like the teaching you will do in this session, speaks to the high level of intellectual work that is called for when your writers research digitally and create visual texts. Modes of communication are becoming increasingly varied as more and more writers shift into a digital space, and it is important that we help our students develop the skills that are needed to communicate effectively in written form in our multimedia society. Not just any image will suffice, either. It is important to teach students how powerful the right image can be, how creating purposeful charts and visuals makes their writing much more robust and informative.

Text Features

Popping Out the Important Information

CONNECTION

Tell a story about a great researcher who used images as well as words to convey ideas, and point out that although many students "outgrew" drawing within the writing workshop, there may be reasons to return to it.

"Writers, Ben Franklin was not only a leading patriot, he was also a famous inventor. One of his most famous inventions was bifocal glasses. These are glasses that are split in half, right in the middle of the lenses, so that a person sees far away out of the top half and sees close up out of the bottom half. Ben wrote a letter to his friend George Whatley to explain how the bifocals worked—he wanted George to sell them. But here is the important part: Ben realized words wouldn't do the trick, so he drew a picture in the middle of his letter, adding labels to point out the important features. That letter and many of Ben Franklin's journals have survived through history—and repeatedly, he broke away from words to use precise little sketches to make a point. People study Ben Franklin's journals and letters as models of informational writing.

"I bet that when you were in first grade, your informational books always contained drawings. And I bet many of you began to use fewer drawings as you got older. Well—perhaps that should change. After all, walking in Ben Franklin's footsteps is not a bad way to go! And the truth is, more and more these days, informational texts rely on images and on text features of all sorts."

Channel students to brainstorm text features that are common in nonfiction texts. Chart these, and then caution students against throwing more and more text features into a text.

"Right now, will you think about some of the text features you've seen in nonfiction books and magazines? Just talk with your partner, listing possibilities across your fingers." The children found this easy, and exciting, too. As children talked, I kept one ear on what they were saying, and meanwhile jotted a list.

Although we refer to Ben Franklin, Leonardo da Vinci's journals are even more laden with images. You can easily access the journals of both these men online.

You will see that when possible, we tend to use anecdotes from the time period rather than from our own lives to warm up a minilesson and draw kids in. We could just as easily have shown a contemporary example, or a personal one. When you are immersed in the history part of this unit, you'll no doubt find tons of other choice morsels. Use them from time to time in your minilessons.

You'll want to decide whether you welcome your students using lots of images in their reports or not. We could imagine arguments either way. If you are interested in the connections between art and writing, you may want to read Looking to Write, *by our colleague, Mary Ehrenworth (2003).*

"Writers, I heard so many great text features," and I gestured to the list. "There are others, too, so add them to our list later."

Possible Text Features

- captions
- subtitles
- diagram
- timelines
- text boxes
- maps

"The idea of filling your pages with all those things feels pretty cool, right? Well, I want to give you a word of caution before you start piling all of that onto every page of your book!"

❖ **Name the teaching point.**

"Today I want to teach you that writers use text features purposefully. They think about the most important information and ideas that they're trying to convey in a chapter or a section, and they use text features to highlight what they're really trying to say."

TEACHING

Reiterate that slapping more text features onto a text isn't the way to go, stressing instead that writers use text features to highlight what is most important on a page or in a section.

"So that means that when informational writers get ready to add text features, they don't just slap on any old picture or timeline or text box or diagram that is somewhat connected to what is on the page. Instead, they study that part of their writing carefully and think, 'What I am I really trying to say here? What is the most important information that I'm trying to teach? Are there ideas I have about the information that I really want readers to know?' Only after answering that question can a writer think, 'What text features could I use to pop out that information, so I highlight the important stuff for my readers?'"

Marie Clay, the great reading researcher who founded Reading Recovery, used to visit us every two or three years. She'd walk through classrooms with us and give us feedback on our methods of teaching. Once, when we visited a room together, she said to me, "I don't think there should ever be a list that contains more than five items." Her point was that the lists we display in classrooms are not meant to be complete, they are meant to get students' minds going in a particular direction. Marie's focus was young children, and she may have been speaking only about classrooms for young children—I don't know. But I do know that her words come back to me when I make lists, and I try to remember that less is more. Of course I could have made a far longer list—and so could you. I wouldn't.

In third grade, students were encouraged to use technology to find images that they could add to their all-about writing. Their knowledge of text features, then, may harken back to that work a bit.

Although you will be saying that writers use text features to highlight important information and ideas, examples abound of writers using text boxes and the like in ways that distract from the information on a page. Nonfiction writing is often murky, and you'll want to teach students to read critically. On the other hand, there are instances when text boxes can be the way to present alternate views and voices. That can be something students learn to do in addition to the more central and important work of using text features to put some ideas into bold relief.

Read aloud a section of the informational book you are writing, asking students to join you in identifying the most important information and ideas and therefore, in weighing what might be better or worse bold headings to use.

I flipped the chart to reveal the section from my own book I'd copied previously. "Here is a section from the book I've been writing—many of you have helped with it—on the Boston Massacre. Would you help me look at this paragraph from the chapter on the aftermath of the massacre? Let's do the kind of thinking that will help us decide which text features we should add. We first need to think, 'What are the most important information and ideas in this section?' As I read this section aloud, let's think about what this part is really, really about." I read the following:

> One of the first things that happened after the Massacre was that patriots, like Paul Revere, wanted to convince people that the British soldiers were at fault. There was lots of propaganda being published that was trying to convince people that the soldiers killed people on purpose. For example, Paul Revere did an **etching** that showed the soldiers shooting right at innocent people. He did this to make people angry enough to want to fight the British.

"Writers, turn and talk to your partner. What is the most important information in that part? In other words, what is this part really about?"

After a few minutes, I reconvened the class. "I heard a lot of you saying that this part is really about propaganda, and that the patriots depicted the events of the Boston Massacre as even worse than they were so as to stir up anger toward the British. Paul Revere's etching that showed soldiers firing right at innocent people was one example. It wasn't accurate, but was instead propaganda.

"Now that we have a sense of what this page is really about, we can choose text features that pop out that idea. I'm wondering, for example, about what heading to use. Should it be, 'Paul Revere is an artist!' or, 'The British Massacred Innocent People!' or—what? Writers, would you help me choose a heading that communicates the idea I have about this part? Turn and talk."

Debrief, collecting examples of text features that would accentuate the most important information in the selected passage.

After the children talked for a minute, I asked for their attention. "You all were wisely returning to the most important idea—people used art and writing to make what happened that day feel like a massacre, when it wasn't, really. Patriots used propaganda—that's the word for it—to stir emotions up against the British. So—maybe we should call this, 'The Patriot's Propaganda Stirs Anger against British.' I hope you are thinking that now, and whenever you write, you can use text features such as headings to help readers understand the most important information and ideas you are teaching on that page."

Notice a few things about the teaching here. First, the section of teacher-writing that Anna and I use is extremely brief. The point can be made in short order, and we want to keep minilessons ten minutes or less. Then, too, notice ways in which we invite kids to participate in what is a bit of demonstration teaching. So here, the text is not the kids' text but the teacher's text, and this is the teaching, not the active engagement portion of the minilesson. We have every intention to essentially do the work in front of kids as a demonstration. But we know that if our teaching communicates "Sit back and put your feet up and watch me," then kids won't learn as much as if our teaching essentially says "Join me in trying this . . ." and then, once the kids are doing the work alongside us, we demonstrate how to do it really well. Of course, kids need time to do this too, so we follow this with the active engagement section of the minilesson where kids are each doing the work, in partnerships or alone.

Note that I am deliberately using over-the-top bad examples. Don't get tricked and think this is the best I could do. . . . Remember that you are trying to hit home some points. If you aren't fairly over-the-top, we find many kids don't grasp the point.

ACTIVE ENGAGEMENT

Ask kids to work in foursomes to think of other text features, making a mock-up of the page on chart paper.

"We might want to add some of the other text features we listed earlier—but I don't think we should just willy-nilly put in tons of stuff. Instead, it is important to decide what goes on the page, and why. How about I give the kids in this corner of the meeting area . . ." I gestured to show a group of about six students. ". . . this sheet of paper and one marker pen? Will you think together which of the text features you'd put around our paragraph? Then make a sketch of how you suggest our page go."

I then gave students in other quadrants of the meeting area their own pieces of chart paper and marker pens, telling each group they had only five minutes to capture their plan on chart paper.

While students worked, I coached, "Captions can help to pop out important information for readers" and "Words that are bolded on the page can also help to show readers what is important."

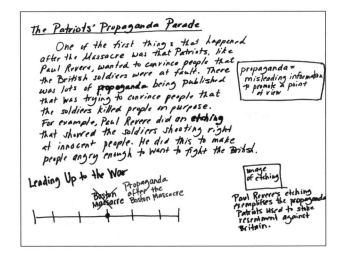

FIG. 13–1   Chart showing teacher writing after revisions suggested by students.

After the allotted time, I asked one person from each group to present their suggested layout, talking about one of the text features they especially cared about. Soon we'd collected these suggestions:

◆ a text box that defines propaganda, off on the side

◆ an image of Paul Revere's etching with a caption that says, "Paul Revere's etching shows the propaganda patriots used to make people turn against Britain."

◆ the words *progaganda* and *etching* in boldface

◆ a subheading, maybe titled, "The Patriots' Propaganda Parade"

◆ a timeline titled "Leading Up to the War" with the Boston Massacre on it, crossed out, replaced by the words, "Propaganda after the Boston Massacre"

I tried each of the suggestions on the writing I had done.

LINK

Put today's lesson into a bigger context by reminding students how it links back to the work they have been doing the last few days.

"So I know you all have a lot to do today. In addition to acting like a tour guide for your readers, setting them up for how each chapter will go, remember that you can add text features to your chapters. The chapters are rough drafts, so later you can worry about making the visual layout of the page work. For now, you'll want to think hard about the most important information that you are teaching. Make sure you write in such a way that when you ask, 'What's this part really about?' you'll have an answer. Thinking about the plans you made for how each chapter will go might help you, because you can think, 'What is this next part mostly about? And this one?' Determining what each part is mostly about will help you to develop your text features. The things that we've been thinking about the last few days—writing introductions and conclusions, thinking about text features—all those things are in the service of highlighting the central ideas and key information in your writing." I unveiled a chart that I had made to remind them of the important work they had been doing.

> ## Ways to Highlight Central Ideas and Key Information in Your Informational Writing
>
> * Write an introduction that gives an overview of what is to come and hooks readers.
> * Write a conclusion that summarizes the important parts and leaves readers something to think about.
> * Add text features that help to draw readers' attention to important information.

In fifth grade, readers are expected to read a text for central ideas—that is, for ideas that are furthered across a text, not just in one part. We think the phrase central idea *is far superior to* main idea, *especially when referencing texts that put forward a complex network of related ideas. Doing this work well is dependent upon readers being able to determine important information and ideas from more than one section, and then to synthesize across large swaths of a text. The work of determining importance that this session sets your writers up to do is an important precursor to what will be expected of them in fifth grade.*

Using Text Features Purposefully

TEXT FEATURES ARE APT TO BE INTOXICATING TO YOUR STUDENTS, and they're going to be ready to leap into the work of adding clip art onto every page of their writing. Your job during conferring and small-group time will probably be to do everything you can to make sure that their work with text features is part of a bigger effort to write in ways that bring home important points.

As you confer on this day, you'll want to keep in mind one of the main goals of this bend, which is teaching writers to be more deliberate about the way that they organize their writing. In all of the sessions in this bend, you'll want to keep an eye out that your writers are grouping information logically and making the logic of each chapter transparent to the reader, and that the details in each chunk of text fit together. Remember that the CCSS for fourth grade require students to group information in paragraphs and sections, and for fifth grade, to group logically. You'll want to aim toward that fifth-grade standard now for most of your students, so they have plenty of time to obtain and surpass the standard.

There is no question but that when you reread your students' writing, one of the most obvious weaknesses that you'll see (and you'll wish that they'd see) is that some sections will be a hodgepodge of facts, thus making determining importance difficult. Often students take the informal name that we use for information writing literally, and write chapters that are exactly what the title says—"all about" a topic. So the first job will not be to select text features that accentuate the most important information in a passage. Instead the first job will be to reread the passage and see whether there in fact is some central information.

You'll want to organize large groups of students and get them to check whether they have organized their chapters logically. You can do this in very concrete ways, starting with harking back to the teaching you did in the previous session. Say to them, "Try rereading your chapter the same way that you read nonfiction books when you are looking for a main idea. Read a chunk of the text—probably a paragraph but

MID-WORKSHOP TEACHING   Writers Work to Ensure They've Highlighted What Is Most Important—and Revise Accordingly

Standing in the middle of the room, I called for writers' attention. "Writers, I'm glad to see that some of you are adding text features to your writing. Can I see a thumbs up for those of you who have been trying to add text features to all-about chapters of your writing?" Those children so indicated. "For those of you who have been doing this, why don't you test out if your writing, and the text features, are working? Here's what you do. Think to yourself, 'What do I really want to get across in this part of my book?' and write the answer on a little sheet of paper, not letting anyone see what you are writing. Then fold that paper up many times so no one will see it. *Then* take your writing—complete with the text features—and give it to someone else to read, someone who is writing on a different topic and hasn't been talking with you about your writing. Ask that person to read your writing, and to tell you what he or she thinks the part is really about. Hopefully, that person's take-away will be what you were trying to get across!"

Realizing that many students' work wasn't yet ready to stand this test, I said, "Actually, I think we should wait and do this at the Share, and for now you should take the remaining fifteen minutes to see if you can have a section that could be put to the test in that way. So for now, give your writing your own test. Ask, 'What *are* the most important information and ideas here?' and then read your writing over as if you didn't know the answer. See if there are more ways to pop that answer out. I'm pretty sure that this might lead you to work on your introductory sentences to the passage, and maybe even your concluding sentences, as well as on your text features. Back to work."

sometimes it is two paragraphs—and when you get through it say, 'If I was to write a heading for that part, what would it be?' In the margin, write that heading. Then read on, through the next chunk, and do the same thing."

If students can't yet insert subheadings into their own information writing, despite the teaching you did in the previous session, then they have bigger problems than not accentuating important information and ideas. Those students will have neglected to write in a logical structure, grouping similar information together. This is a big deal on the Common Core, and needs to be a huge priority. Take those students aside, get them to rewrite their chapter entirely, starting with a table of contents for it. If you feel the need, you can instead channel them to scissor the existing chapter apart and reconstitute it under subheadings.

Of course, there are ways in which your conferring and small-group work can also support students to use text features more deliberately. You may want to carry with you the chart that students probably used in their third-grade informational writing unit.

You can suggest students look through their book, page by page, asking themselves, "Can any of these text features help my readers learn more in this part?" As they work you might coach, "Would a drawing help your reader here? Do you need a caption to explain that feature?"

Another way to help students use text features deliberately is by channeling them to study mentor texts. Just as students turn to their favorite authors and books to draw on the craft of writing, they can also use mentor texts to draw on the craft of text features. Guide students to note how authors use different features, and then as students do this, highlight their observations. "Sam noticed that this author used a map mark to locate all the battles." *The Revolutionary War* by Josh Gregory (2011) has some especially nice examples of text features.

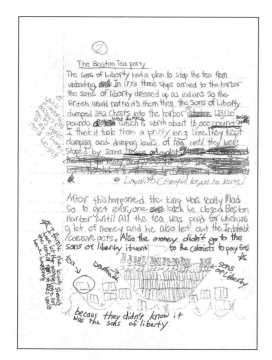

FIG. 13–2   Milo's sketch and labels

FIG. 13–3   Grayson's word section

FIG. 13–4   Edward's sketch

Testing that Text Features Highlight What Is Most Important

Set writers up to test their text features with someone who is unfamiliar with their writing.

"Writers, in a moment, we are all going to gather in the meeting area. Before you come, look over the work you did today and choose a section that is ready to share with someone. Now, think about the information you really want to get across in that section, write down the answer on a piece of paper, and fold it up. As soon as you're finished with that, bring your writing and the paper over to the meeting area."

After most of the children had gathered, I continued. "Usually you share your work with your partners, because they know your work the best. But today, I'm going to set you up to share your work with someone who doesn't know your work well. That way, you can test to see whether readers can figure out the ideas and information that you think is especially important. Right now, would the person in the partnership whose first name comes earlier in the alphabet stand up?"

Once those writers were standing, I continued, "I'm going to come around and pair you with the person you are going to work with today. As soon as I do, would you exchange the sections you chose to share? When you read someone else's writing, you should try to figure out what you believe that writer really wants you to walk away thinking."

As writers began to share their pages with each other, I voiced over, "When you think you have figured out what the section is mostly about, tell your partner-for-a-day your thoughts. Hopefully you are gleaning what the partner wants you to glean. If you have time, help each other accentuate that information, and those ideas, even more."

Point out what one writer has done that serves as an exemplar for others.

After it seemed students were beginning to be done with this, I spoke up. "Writers, can I have your attention for a moment? Gracie was studying the text features in a section of Edward's book about the Battle of Trenton, and she guessed that the part was mostly about how the

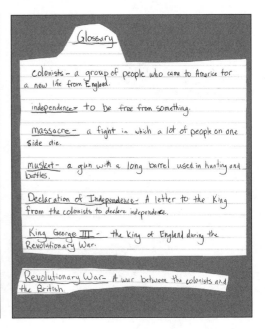

FIG. 13–5   Melissa's bold vocabulary words and glossary

Continental Army was able to surprise the British and Hessian troops. But you know what she realized? Edward's text features didn't just say that the Continental Army made a surprise attack. Edward also used a few pictures to quickly sum up *how* the attack happened. Take a look at what he did—he drew stick figures, one to represent the Continental Army, saying 'boo!' and two to represent the British and Hessians (see Figure 13–4). One Hessian's arms are up in surrender; another is saying, 'I'm too full!' to show this happened right after the British and Hessians' Christmas feast. What Edward did is something others might want to try—using text features not only to highlight the most important things that happened but also to hint at *how* those things happened."

DEADLINES CAN BE LIFELINES, MAKING WRITERS SPRING INTO ACTION

Many writers refer to deadlines as "lifelines" because they have a way of making a person spring to life. You need to be finished with the main chapters of your book within four days—so take that deadline as a lifeline. Tonight, I recommend you ask someone in your family to talk with you about a subtopic related to your report—perhaps a subtopic you'd planned to write, perhaps a new subtopic that you've been learning about. Plan to teach that person about your subject, and then to get into a conversation about your ideas (and your listener's ideas) related to that subject. As you talk, keep an eye on what interests that other person.

Then sit down and do what every writer does. Face the blank page. Write up a storm. You should be able to write two full pages in half an hour, writing fast and furious.

Quotations Accentuate Importance

Voices Chime In to Make a Point

IN THIS SESSION, you'll teach students that history writers add quotations to their writing to accentuate a central idea.

GETTING READY

✔ A draft of a student's all-about chapter from their informational book, or the chapter from your own informational book, enlarged for students to see (see Teaching and Active Engagement)

✔ An informational book on your class topic. We use *Liberty! How the Revolutionary War Began* by Lucille Penner (2002) (see Teaching)

✔ Sentence strips (see Teaching)

✔ "Ways to Highlight Central Ideas and Key Information in Your Informational Writing" chart (see Link)

✔ A chart with a list of elaboration moves (see Conferring and Small-Group Work)

COMMON CORE STATE STANDARDS: W.2.a,b,c,d,e; W.4.6, W.4.8, W.4.9, W.4.10, RI.4.1, RI.4.9, RI.5.1, SL.4.1, L.4.1, L.4.2.b, L.4.3

A YEAR OR TWO AGO, the Teachers College Reading and Writing Project was asked to develop a Common Core-aligned performance assessment that New York City could use to assess students' information writing. We were asked to assess a few standards, including Informational Reading Standard 1, which, for fifth-graders, states: "Quote accurately from a text when explaining what the text says explicitly and when drawing details from the text."

We developed the assessment focused on every standard *but* Standard 1. After all, it seemed clear to us that if students could find central ideas and supporting details and compare and contrast texts, they'd surely be able to quote from texts—and we figured we ought to focus our performance assessment on the more intellectually demanding work. We turned the draft of our performance assessment in for feedback from a review team—and the response we received was that they really wanted us to focus primarily on Standard 1.

That interaction was the first in a sequence of experiences that has led up to the understanding that there are some people—including the primary authors of the Common Core State Standards—who place a gigantic priority on students' abilities and tendencies to read closely and to incorporate actual citations of a text in any discussion of the text. The emphasis on text-based analysis made sense to us always (we've all been in classrooms where students read a text and then talk about the "text-to-life connections" in ways that leave the text itself behind in the dust). But we were a bit surprised that people were making such a *big deal* out of citing the text. How hard can that be? we thought. You open the book, you copy the words, you stick in the quotes.

Then my colleagues and I embarked on some serious work helping students engage in argument writing about information reading (leading to the final book in this series.) A lot of our instruction focuses on helping students realize the value of noticing and putting forth and coming to terms with differing views on a subject. As part of that, it has been essential for students to learn to cite the actual words that source A uses to forward his view, and that source B uses to forward hers. Once students are looking at the language choices the different sources use and at the different information they put forth, students can begin to analyze the different positions.

To make a long story short—we have been amazed to see that it actually is not easy to teach students to include quotations in their information writing. And the challenge is not so much teaching them to punctuate, or even to transition between summary and citation. Instead, there seems to be some resistance on the part of students to include quotes.

"To make a long story short—we have been amazed to see that it actually is not easy to teach students to include quotations in their information writing."

This minilesson, then, channels students toward using a skill that we have found is deceptively difficult. We try to link the work they do here to the way in which they learn to make characters talk within their stories, because students are very successful at doing that. And we try to continue the emphasis on writing well-structured texts that highlight important information and ideas.

Quotations Accentuate Importance
Voices Chime In to Make a Point

CONNECTION

Tell a story of a time when you had an idea that could have benefited from the support of others' opinions. Connect your personal situation to including citations that support the thinking writers put forth in their writing.

"I have to tell you about something that happened last night. I had a bunch of friends over, and I said to everyone, 'We should go bowling.'

"A few of us had already talked about it a few days earlier. We'd said that bowling would be fun, and cheap, and different. It'd be good for all ages. We'd even found a good place to do it. So I expected the others who'd made that plan with me would chime in."

"But last night, when I said, 'We should go bowling,' you know what happened? It made me so mad, *so* mad. This is what happened. I said, 'We should go bowling,' and—*nothing*! No one said *anything*.

"People gave each other awkward looks. It was totally silent. And I felt so silly for suggesting what was obviously considered to be a horrible, no good, very bad idea. But, hey—where were my supporters? Why didn't they speak up? Why didn't one of them say, 'Yeah, that'd be fun—cheap, too'? Why didn't one of them pipe in that it would be good for all ages? Or suggest the place we'd already selected?

"But no, I got no support. Nothing, nada. I was left, hanging out there by my lonesome.

"Has that ever happened to you? Have you ever *wished* there were more voices chiming in, more people adding their own two cents, building some momentum behind an idea?

"I'm telling you this because what's true in life is true in writing. If I want to build some momentum behind an idea in life, the best way is to have others speak up, saying, essentially, 'Me too,' and 'I support that idea,' and 'Count me in.' And that is true when you are writing, too. If you want to drive home the idea that it wasn't the Boston Massacre so much as the propaganda around that event that started the war, then you want to round up some people who say, essentially, 'I agree,' 'That's true,' 'Amen to that.'"

I got a real kick out of this connection, and actually sent it around to a few coauthors for their enjoyment. You won't be surprised that it's half true. When a group of coauthors and I spent a few weeks writing together, we did drive past a bowling alley and talked about how much fun it would be to take time out from writing to bowl. No one actually suggested such a preposterous idea—stop writing to bowl!—but had someone put forth the idea, that person would definitely have wanted voices to chime in.

The larger point here is that we need to humanize some of the strategies that researchers use. It has actually seemed to us that kids have a surprisingly hard time coming around to the notion that it is important to cite other texts. This is a Very Big Deal in the Common Core, so we've searched for ways to help youngsters feel more at home with this. This is one attempt to do so.

Name the teaching point.

"Writers, today I want to teach you that history writers add quotations to their writing for specific purposes. And one purpose—not the only one, but one important purpose—is to drive home a big point, to accentuate a central idea.

"Once a writer has decided on an important point he or she wants to make, the writer sometimes searches for quotes that get other voices chiming in, building the point up. In that way, quotations can work a bit like text features to highlight the most important information and ideas in a text."

TEACHING

Clarify to students that there are at least two kinds of quotes history writers use—those said at the time, and those written since, interpreting the time.

"Writers, I want to clarify one thing. When history writers talk of including 'quotations,' there are a couple of different kinds of quotations they mean. First, there are quotations that are actual words that someone said, usually a famous person. For example, if you are writing about the Declaration of Independence, and you want to show that it took courage for delegates to sign their names into that document, you could add a quote from John Hancock. While signing the Declaration, he said, 'There! His Majesty can now read my name without glasses. And he can double the reward on my head!' In an instance like that, you often do tell the context for the quote, as I just did when I said, 'While signing the Declaration of Independence, John Hancock said. . . .'

"You can probably think of quotes that are important to your topic. If you are writing about Paul Revere, for example, you might include those famous words, 'One if by land, two if by sea. . . .' And again, you'd want to tell a little about the context, so people know the quote is referring to the lights that would shine from the steeple of the Old North Church to tell Paul Revere how the British would be coming.

"Another kind of quotation is one where a writer quotes part of a book or website. For example, the book or the website might say, 'Of all Jefferson's many achievements, none was greater than his authorship of the Declaration of Independence.' One of you, wanting to show that Jefferson's work on this was important, might then write, 'In the book, *The Making of a Nation*, so-and-so claims that "of all Jefferson's many achievements, none was greater than . . . '"

Use a draft of an all-about chapter to practice adding quotes to support the central idea of the chapter.

"Let's practice adding both kinds of quotes. Julian has agreed to let us work with his first chapter, which is sort of an all about the Revolutionary War chapter. Let's look at one part of his chapter, and read this paragraph the way that we've been doing, trying to figure out what this part is really about. We'll double-check that the beginning sets up the reader, and add some text features while we're working on the quotes, if we can. Remember, our job is to think, 'What are the important information and ideas that we could bring home with text features and with quotes?'"

Julian read the section of his report, which I'd copied onto chart paper so we could return to it later in the minilesson.

> The colonists had to pay all kinds of taxes. They had to pay taxes for tea. They had to pay taxes for documents. They thought that if they paid taxes, they should have a vote. What made the colonists angry wasn't just the taxes but that they had no say in the British government. They thought it wasn't fair that they should have to pay taxes but they had no one like a senator that went to Britain and told their side. They had no one to represent them in the government.

"Will each of you name quietly, just to yourself, what you think the most important information and ideas were in Julian's paragraph?" I paused to let them name this in their minds. "Take this a step farther and think, 'If Julian is going to add a subheading—a text feature—to this, what might it say?'" Again I paused. Then I asked for contributions, and nodded when some children chimed in that it was mainly saying the colonists didn't want taxation without representation, and suggested that "taxation without representation" could be the subtitle. They had that phrase down pat, and it made sense. Julian added the subtitle.

Model going back to a source to locate quotations that will support the central idea of the chapter.

"So now it is as if I have a shopping list and I'm going to the store to get what I need. I need some quotes that accentuate the idea that the colonists didn't want taxes without getting a vote. Let's take this book"—and I reached for one of our standby sources, *Liberty! How the Revolutionary War Began*.

"Do I start on page 1 and start reading, looking for that quote?"

That was an absurd notion, so the children soon channeled me to scan the table of contents. "I'm looking for 'The colonists didn't want to pay taxes without a vote,' right?" I said, again voicing a preposterous idea. I corrected myself quickly, saying "Oh, no, I forgot that idea we talked about earlier about looking for key word. I'll look for taxes, representation, vote . . . "

I soon landed on a chapter called "Sneaky Taxes." "Let's skim this and look for quotations we could add," I said, and I read carefully.

> *The Sugar Act made [the colonists] even angrier. This act made it very expensive for the colonists to import one of their favorite products—molasses.*
>
> *The Quartering Act, the Navigation Acts, and the Sugar Act seemed to the colonists like sneaky ways of making Britain richer—at their expense!*

It is ideal, of course, to use a passage that you or one of your students have written, but you'd have to find the accompanying quotes and so forth, so you certainly could use Julian's writing. You could either pretend this was a passage from the first chapter of your report, or you could just talk about a student from another class.

If you have a document camera, you could also display the passage. Either way is fine; what is most important in this instance is that students are seeing you go back to a source in a purposeful way to seek out a citation that helps to drive home the central idea of your writing.

"There aren't any colorful quotes by people from that time, but we *could* probably use a snippet of this passage to get the author, Lucille Penner, chiming in on the idea that Julian wants to highlight. Think with your partner about what you'd suggest Julian write into his paragraph. Reread what Julian wrote, and think what, exactly, he might add."

As the children reread, I took a sentence strip and pasted it onto the end of Julian's text. The sentence strip said,

> 1) So and so, in such and such, says (writes) "_____"

I gave children a minute to do this, and then pointed to the sentence strip and dictated what I might write:

> Lucille Penner, in <u>Liberty! How the Revolutionary War Began</u>, says that the taxes "seemed to the colonists like sneaky ways of making Britain richer—at their expense!"

ACTIVE ENGAGEMENT

Channel writers to try their hands at adding a quotation to the same passage.

"How about if you try this without any help from me? Here is another passage from Penner's book that relates to this topic. See if you could cite something from this text—and figure out exactly what you'd say to add to Julian's writing."

> *People were Furious! Riots broke out in Boston. In other cities, there were many demonstrations and violent speeches against the British. To many, the Stamp Act seemed like the death of liberty. Americans didn't mind paying taxes to their local governments. That seemed fair because they elected their own representatives. But there was nobody to represent them in the British Parliament.*

I listened to Olivia as she told Griffin, "I think he can put in the death of liberty. Like the colonists were angry about losing freedom and then say 'the death of liberty.'"

I whispered to her, "Don't forget to write it in the air, to say exactly what you would write in the draft! And you could even show it with air quotes," I added, using fingers to make quotation marks in the air.

I moved on to Melissa, who was saying, "I would say, Lucille Penner says, 'Americans didn't mind paying taxes to their local governments. That seemed fair because they elected their own representatives.'" She finished by pantomiming an air quote. I gave her thumbs up and moved on.

There are lots of other source books that might provide you with even better material. We recommend Milton Meltzer's The American Revolutionaries: A History in Their Own Words *because this is full of primary sources, and of course nothing is better than going back to the source when quoting. For example, after the Intolerable Acts, fiery Patrick Henry cried out to the legislature, "We must fight! Is life so dear, or peace so sweet, as to be purchased at the price of chains and slavery? Forbid it, almighty God! I know not what course others may take, but as for me, give me liberty or give me death!" (1993, 53).*

Soon I reconvened the class, and we added a new quote to Julian's writing (as well as the one we'd decided upon earlier) and mentioned some others we could have added.

> The colonists had to pay all kinds of taxes. They had to pay taxes for tea. They had to pay taxes for documents. They thought that if they paid taxes, they should have a vote. What made the colonists angry wasn't just the taxes but that they had no say in the British government. They thought it wasn't fair that they should have to pay taxes but they had no one like a senator that went to Britain and told their side. They had no one to represent them in the government. Some colonists called the taxes "the death of liberty." Lucille Penner, in Liberty! How the Revolutionary War Began, says that the taxes "seemed to the colonists like sneaky ways of making Britain richer—at their expense!"

Debrief by reminding students of the multiple strategies they have at hand to organize their informational writing and highlight central ideas.

"Writers, I hope you have learned that one reason to add quotations to your writing is to highlight the information and ideas you want to get across. So you now have four strategies for highlighting this—giving an overview in your introduction, writing a conclusion that leaves readers thinking, using text features, and using quotations. I'm hoping you've learned that first you decide upon what is most important to accentuate, then you skim and search to find a section of a resource that might help, then you harvest a carefully selected quote. It is a little tricky to figure out wording that connects the quote into your writing, and I'll be helping you do that, when you need help."

LINK

Remind writers of all the ways they know to highlight important information in their texts.

"Writers, over the past few writing workshops, we've talked about several ways you can help readers to understand the most important information you are trying to teach. Let's look back at the chart we started the other day." I went ahead and added on what we learned today about adding quotations.

"In addition to adding quotations today, you can also be working on other ways to help readers understand what is most important. Don't forget to add all of these things to the new chapters you are drafting, and to go back and check for all of these things in the chapters you've drafted already."

Ways to Highlight CENTRAL IDEAS and KEY INFORMATION in INFO writing

- Write an introduction that gives an overview of what is to come and hooks readers
- Write a conclusion that summarizes the important parts and leaves readers something to think about
- Add text features that help draw readers' attention to important information
- Add quotations that support information and your central idea

Growing Ideas
The Three-Column Approach

I N THIS SESSION, YOU TAUGHT YOUR WRITERS TO USE QUOTES not only as a way to restate important information, but also as a way to underscore some of the ideas they are starting to grow about what they are learning. This is a subtle but important shift. The big work your writers will be doing, then, will not be finding and adding quotations. The big work will be finding quotations that further a particular *idea*, and showing readers how this quotation fits with what the writer really wants to say about the information.

Some writers might be struggling with this work because they have yet to move beyond listing facts in each section. To do the work of highlighting ideas, they must first grow ideas about their topic. If you notice that some of your writers are struggling to do this work, you might want to gather them in a small group and teach them a strategy that might help them to think more deeply about the information they are writing about.

"Writers," you might begin, "I gathered you together because you have a *ton* of information in many of your sections, and it seems like you could use some help thinking about what you really want to say about all of that information. I have a tool that writers often use to help with that very thing. A way to start is by dividing a paper into three parts, like this." I showed them how to fold a piece of lined paper into thirds, lengthwise. "Then, in the first column, write 'information.' In the second column, write 'I wonder,' and in the third column, write 'ideas.'

"To start, pick a section that feels like it has a ton of facts, but you're not sure what you really want to say about those facts. In the first column, record as many of the facts as you can. You don't have to write them out completely, just bullets will do. Then, in the second column, write some of what you are wondering about those facts. Let me show you a quick example of this. In my version, I have a few facts about Private Hugh White, the British soldier who was on duty when the whole thing started. Here are a few of my facts:

MID-WORKSHOP TEACHING   **Drawing on Everything You Know about Information Writing—Especially What You Know about Structure**

"Researchers, eyes up here." I waited. "As you continue to add quotations, I want you to remember two guidelines that always help informational writers: 'say more' and 'write with information.' Right now, reread your writing and think whether you are 'saying more.'" I gave children some time to do this. "If you find yourself writing something in a sentence, then jumping to something different, go back and add a caret, right now. I'll show you what to do next." I gave children a moment to do that.

"Now, if you have written one sentence about—say, who some of the delegates were to the Constitutional Convention, or anything—instead of jumping to another topic, think to yourself, 'I need to say more about this.' To say more, add whatever details you know. Zoom in to something more specific. Think about what quotes you could add that pertain to that." I gave children a minute to think of something more specific and add that to their writing. I knew some couldn't, so I soon voiced over, saying, "You can also say *your thought* about the information you just shared. Start with one of those prompts, 'This was important because . . . ' or 'It is important to note that . . . ' or 'Such and such didn't happen, instead . . . ' or 'This makes me realize that. . . .' That is, after a bit of information, you can make a comment or share a thought. But don't just write a sentence or two about one topic, then jump, jump, jump.

"Second guideline. You are a bricklayer, building with the bricks of information. No one wants a house made of hot air, or just breezy chatty comments. You need to piece together information. With a partner, list ten kinds of information, then do a quick search for which of those kinds you have in your writing. I'll be making my own list up here, but don't look at it until you've made you own. Go!"

(continues)

> I recruited a nearby partnership to help me and together we jotted this on the white board:
>
> | | |
> |---|---|
> | quotations | anecdotes |
> | names | descriptions |
> | dates | definitions |
> | specific places | reasons |
> | exact numbers | a timeline of actions |
>
> "If you only found a few kinds in your writing, make a plan to 'say more' and to 'write with information.' Make a quick list on the top of your page of the other kinds of information you plan to add. Okay writers, back to it!"

- Private Hugh White was stationed outside the Customs House.
- He was taunted by a group of young men.
- He swung his gun and hit one man on the head.

"So now, I can write some things I'm wondering about in the second column. I'm wondering, for example, what the young men were saying to Private White. I'm also wondering if he hit the man on purpose. I'm going to write those things in my second column.

"Now, we also have this third column. I'm going to start answering my own questions and by doing this, I'm going to grow some ideas about the information on my page. I am thinking the young men might have been saying very insulting things to Private White. I know from other research this kind of thing had been going on for quite some time. I imagine Private White might have gotten fed up. I'm thinking that Private White might have been so fed up with being taunted that he got very angry. If the young patriot men weren't taunting the British soldiers all the time, Private White might not have gotten so angry. Aha! I think I might have my big idea! I know what I'll write in the third column—'Private White was pushed to the brink by the patriots.' Writers, did you see how looking at my writing this way, through this three-column approach,

led me to have a new idea about the information? Now, I can go back to my text and think, is there a way I can use quotations, and maybe even text features, to help readers understand what my central idea is?"

After this demonstration, channel your writers to give this work a try using their own texts. Before sending them off, quickly get them going on finding quotations or planning text features that help highlight the new understandings they reached.

Keep in mind that the past sessions have been about highlighting important information and ideas, but they are also designed to support elaboration. One question we get so often is how to teach writers to "say more." In informational writing, when a good portion of the detail comes from outside sources, it is often a challenge for some writers to say much at all. Today is a great day to do a quick, informal check-in, looking specifically for how writers are progressing in their elaboration moves.

You might create a chart with the elaboration moves from the fourth-grade checklist that you have already taught your class. These things likely include:

- ◆ Using a variety of detail (facts, definitions, concrete details, and quotations)

- ◆ Using a combination of known information and information from outside sources

You might even want to add a few items to your chart from the third-grade informational writing checklist, if you think some of your writers have not yet mastered them:

- ◆ Writing at least a few sentences in each of the sections

- ◆ Using headings and subheadings to distinguish between parts

With your chart in hand, you can do a quick sweep of your class, jotting down students' names who fit each category, making sure to leave a couple of spaces for other issues related to elaboration that you notice.

When you see two or more students, that would make for an excellent small-group coaching session. Where there is just a single name, you will know right away what to target in your research and conferring. Where there are no names, you breathe a sigh of relief—for now anyway!

Keep on Writing!

Explain that you will be skipping the share so as to squeeze in more time for writing.

"Writers, you only have three more days to draft this book. Then we're going to devote some time to editing before we shift to another bend in the road of informational writing. When we make that shift you'll still be working on these reports, but you'll be taking it to a whole new level, adding on another chapter or two. So, from what I see today, I'm thinking that most of you could use a bit more time on the drafting part of your work. I'm going to suggest that right now, you shake out your hand so it gets a quick break. Then I'm going to ask you to reread what you have written so far, and to use that rereading to prime your pump so that you can get another page written in the next seven minutes. That is, instead of a share, I'm giving you extra time to write. Make a mark where you are. Then start by rereading, then write fast and furious. After seven minutes, we're going to look at how much you get written. Go!"

As students worked, I looked over their shoulders. I saw, for example, that Kim was working furiously on a section about Thomas Jefferson writing the Declaration of Independence. She wrote:

> It took Thomas 17 days to write 1,337 words. It also took him many drafts to find the one that worked. There were three main sections. Section one was about people being born with rights. The second section was about people being able to choose your own government. The 3rd section was about being born with rights. It was completed on July 2nd and accepted on July 4th.

After five minutes, I stopped the children, and asked them to count how many lines they'd written. After determining what they were able to write in seven minutes, I suggested that this data could help them make a reasonable goal for the amount of writing they could accomplish at home that night.

> Thomas Jefferson was asked by John Adams to write the Declaration of Independence with help from the 2 continental congress.
> It had 56 [signatures] from delegates from the 13 colonies. It took Thomas 17 days to write 1,337 words it also took him many [drafts] to find the one that worked. There were 3 main [sections] Section 1 was about people being born with rights. The 2nd section was about people being able to choose your own government. The 3rd section was about being born with rights. It was completed on July 2nd and accepted on July 4th.

FIG. 14–1   Kim's writing during the share

GIVING CREDIT TO THE QUOTE SOURCE BY USING CONNECTING PHRASES

Writers, it is important that you always give credit to the source of your quotes. One way to do this is to use a connecting phrase, such as:

"According to the book such and such by so-and-so,"

"The author of the book, . . . , says . . ."

"According to the website, . . . , by . . ."

In this way, readers know whose idea it was, and they also know that you, the author, did your research. Tonight as you continue to draft, be sure that you are giving credit to the quote sources. You should also go back and reread what you have already written, and make sure that any quotes you have included are attributed to the proper sources.

Using All We Know to Craft Essay and Narrative Sections

ear Teachers,

Today, we suggest that you might remind your writers that the plans they originally created for their books often contained chapters that would not be structured as all-about chapters, but would, instead, be small essays or stories. Although it is not necessary that students drop everything and work on those chapters today, the deadline for completing these books is not far away, and certainly many of them will be turning to those chapters soon.

MINILESSON

It is traditional that in a connection, you often connect today's teaching with what has gone before—and sometimes, the work that builds on a particular minilesson is not the work of the proceeding day, but work from earlier in the unit or even the year. Today's session builds on students' work during the first bend of the unit. So you'll want to recall that work in your connection.

Today also harkens back to the first session in Bend II, and to the plans that students made. You might suggest students look back on those plans, noting whether they'd initially intended to devote a chapter to narrative or to essay writing. If so, today's minilesson will help with exactly the work they'll be doing—otherwise, the lesson can be stored away and used whenever they *are* writing narratives and essays within an information text.

Your teaching point might be something along the lines of, "Today I want to remind you that writers always approach new work equipped with a toolkit of strategies that they have learned from previous work. When a writer of an information book decides that some chapters or sections should be written as stories or essays or how-to's, for example, the writer then draws on his or her knowledge of those kinds of writing to write those sections."

To demonstrate this teaching point, you might quickly demonstrate how you mine the tools of the classroom, looking for possible strategies you could give yourself that might help you as you approach these different kinds of chapters.

COMMON CORE STATE STANDARDS: W.4.1, W.4.2, W.4.3, W.4.5, W.4.6, W.4.8, W.4.9, W.4.10, RI.4.1, RI.4.7, RI.4.9, SL.4.1, L.4.1, L.4.2, L.4.3

"Watch me," you might say, "as I get ready to write a chapter that has a story format. First, I'm going to take a look around the classroom, looking for tools that might help me. Let's see—what could I use?" Pause for a moment, giving writers some space to do this kind of thinking alongside you. Then, make a big show about realizing there are charts on the wall that lay out tips for this kind of writing, such as the chart you used in Session 6, "Planning a Micro-Story that Will Be Embedded in History Research."

You might continue by pointing out that studying the charts on the wall isn't the only way writers can mentor themselves. They can also draw on writing they have done in the past, studying what worked well that they could try as they do this same kind of writing again. Show writers how you might study the story you wrote in Bend I, pointing out parts that work well that you could replicate.

To demonstrate, you might use part of your own writing; just a snippet of a story related to your topic should suffice. If using the Boston Massacre as your topic, as we are in this book, your demonstration writing might sound like:

> I stood on my tiptoes and peered out of the window to see what was going on. I heard loud voices and shouting coming from the street below. The window of my bedroom looked out to the court-yard in front of the Boston Customs House. For weeks, I'd been watching the Redcoats stationed outside marching back and forth. I'd also noticed that a gang of men had been giving them a very hard time, shouting insults and even throwing sticks at them. It seems the situation here in Boston is getting worse by the day, especially since the government just passed a new law saying we have to pay taxes on practically everything, even things like paper and glass.

Then, you might make a big show of studying your writing carefully, mining it for ideas. "I like how I begin with a small action," you might say. "That really puts readers right in the midst of the story. Also, I think it works well that I added some of the historical details, like in this part where I say that people were angry because they had to pay taxes. I'll have to be sure to include little historical details in the story I begin writing today, to help my reader get a good sense of what this time period was like. And starting with a small action, that might work for my new story, too!"

You might set your students up to give this a go as they ready themselves to draw on what they know to write chapters that are written as essays. Prompt them to look around the room, noticing what tools are available to help them with essay writing. It is likely that they will notice the "Essay Plan" chart from your earlier unit on personal essay writing, and that you referred to in Bend I.

Similar to the way you looked back at a story you wrote in Bend I to study it for narrative writing ideas, you could also give students an opportunity to work in partnerships or small groups, mining a mentor historical essay. You can create your own, based on the focused topic you are using in your classroom, or of course, feel free to use the one that we have created about the Boston Massacre.

As you deliver your link today, it will be important to support repertoire and independence. Encourage your writers to work through trouble by drawing on the resources you named earlier, as well as on each other. Point out that they can always ask a partner for help if they run into trouble.

Planning a MICRO-STORY...
... That will be Embedded in HISTORY RESEARCH

1. Decide whose story you will tell
   → What is that person's perspective?
   Patriot   ← Loyalist   ← Redcoat

2. Decide on the major tension, conflict, problem

CONFERRING AND SMALL-GROUP WORK

On this day, you'll want to draw on your own toolkit, your own repertoire of strategies from your previous work. You will be supporting writers who are working on a number of different genres. To prepare yourself for these conferences and small groups, you may want to think about some of the conferences and small groups you have conducted in the past to support your writers with narrative and essay writing. These are short lists of tips that you might want to have in your back pocket while conferring with writers who are working within narrative and essay structures.

Teaching to Support Narrative Writing

- Writers draw on story structure as they draft. They often think about the way that stories typically go. Is there a character who encounters trouble or struggle? Does this happen early on? Does the trouble escalate before it gets better?

- Narrative pieces aren't just about the events that happen. They are also about the character's response to those events. Writers can revise to bring out the main character's response to events, to bring out the internal as well as the external story. What was the character thinking, wondering, noticing, wanting to say, pretending? How does the character respond to some of the personal events, and how does he or she respond to historical events?

- Writers *craft* details that will support the meaning or heart of the story. We can reread our piece, paying attention to each of the details we've included and asking ourselves, "Does this support the meaning? Can I change it, take it out, or add in another detail that reveals the meaning of my story even more?" Also, when writing about history, writers make sure some of the important details are about the time period.

- Often any one moment is important in relation to other moments and to a time in history. A young boy waking up to the shouts of "The British are coming!" is important because of the times that the boy heard his parents talking about the trouble brewing among the colonists. In these instances, flashbacks or flash-forward can bring the secondary moments into the story.

Teaching to Support Essay: Filling Essays with a Variety of Evidence

- Evidence that works particularly well in essays about history includes quotes, small anecdotes, lists, events, and dates.

- Writers often include lists made of sentences. (The patriots planned where to meet before the Boston Massacre, they planned how they would disguise themselves, and they planned what to do in case they got caught.)

Essay Plan

(Thesis statement) because (reason 1), (reason 2), and most of all, because (reason 3).

- One reason that (thesis statement) is that . . . (reason 1). For example, (evidence a), (evidence b), and (evidence c).

- Another reason that (thesis statement) is that . . . (reason 2). For example, (evidence a), (evidence b), and (evidence c).

- Although (thesis statement) because reason 1 and because reason 2, especially (opinion statement) because reason 3. For example, (evidence a), (evidence b), and (evidence c).

- Writers often include quotes from other experts or from famous people of the time period. (After the Boston Tea Party, Patrick Henry said, in a speech to encourage Virginia to join the Revolution, "Give me liberty, or give me death.")

- Writers often include idea blurbs arguing their point of view. ("I think dumping the tea in the harbor was a bold move. The colonists did what they felt they had to do to get the attention of the British, even though there might have been more peaceful ways to solve the problem.")

- Acknowledge counterarguments. ("Many people think the patriots chose to dress like Mohawk Native Americans just to trick the British. But I think they chose this disguise because it was a symbol of freedom.")

MID-WORKSHOP TEACHING

Today, your students will be working on a variety of things—researching, writing all about chapters, determining importance, crafting narratives, essay writing. You may want to be brief with your mid-workshop teaching, and be thoughtful in selecting a topic that could work for students across the board, no matter which genre they are working within. It might be a good idea to go back to the "Language" section of the Information Writing Checklist, looking to see if there is a particular bullet on the list that your students could use a reminder about, or more focused teaching on.

SHARE

A possibility for the end of this session could be for you to give your students an opportunity to work with their partners for a bit. You may want to remind them that partners can rely on each other when times get hard. Suggest that they box out parts in their writing where they really struggled. Have them show each other these parts and talk through their struggles, and then channel partners

The Information Writing Checklist, Grades 4 and 5 can be found on the CD-ROM.

Information Writing Checklist

	Grade 4	NOT YET	STARTING TO	YES!	Grade 5	NOT YET	STARTING TO	YES!
	Structure				**Structure**			
Overall	I taught readers different things about a subject. I put facts, details, quotes, and ideas into each part of my writing.	☐	☐	☐	I used different kinds of information to teach about the subject. Sometimes I included little essays, stories, or "how-to" sections in my writing.	☐	☐	☐
Lead	I hooked my readers by explaining why the subject mattered, telling a surprising fact, or giving a big picture. I let readers know that I would teach them different things about a subject.	☐	☐	☐	I wrote an introduction that helped readers get interested in and understand the subject. I let readers know the subtopics I would be developing later as well as the sequence.	☐	☐	☐
Transitions	I used words in each section that help readers understand how one piece of information connected with others. If I wrote the section in sequence, I used words and phrases such as *before, later, next, then,* and *after.* If I organized the section in kinds or parts, I used words such as *another, also,* and *for example.*	☐	☐	☐	When I wrote about results, I used words and phrases like *consequently, as a result,* and *because of this.* When I compared information, I used words and phrases such as *in contrast, by comparison,* and *especially.* In narrative parts, I used phrases that go with stories such as *a little later* and *three hours later.* In the sections that stated an opinion, I used words such as *but the most important reason, for example,* and *consequently.*	☐	☐	☐
Ending	I wrote an ending that reminded readers of my subject and may have suggested a follow-up action or left readers with a final insight. I added my thoughts, feelings, and questions about the subject at the end.	☐	☐	☐	I wrote a conclusion in which I restated the main points and may have offered a final thought or question for readers to consider.	☐	☐	☐
Organization	I grouped information into sections and used paragraphs and sometimes chapters to separate those sections. Each section had information that was mostly about the same thing. I may have used headings and subheadings.	☐	☐	☐	I organized my writing into a sequence of separate sections. I may have used headings and subheadings to highlight the separate sections. I wrote each section according to an organizational plan shaped partly by the genre of the section.	☐	☐	☐

to offer each other some tips. At the end of these partner conferences, give your class a moment or two to reflect on the advice they garnered and to create a "self-assignment box" with a list of all they plan to do as a result of their partner's advice.

HOMEWORK

You might say, "Writers, we are nearing the end of this bend in the road. You have spent lots of time writing all-about chapters for your informational book, and today you may have started to draft either a narrative or an essay chapter for your book. Tonight, you will need to draft another chapter. Choose whichever genre you did not work on today in class. Set the timer for thirty minutes and write, write, write!"

Good luck!

Lucy and Anna

The Other Side of the Story

IN THIS SESSION, you'll teach students that history writers need to remember and address more than one side of a story.

GETTING READY

✔ Published informational books for students to look through in small groups (see Connection)

✔ A sample of a student narrative written about a historical event (see Connection and Teaching)

✔ Chart paper and marker (see Connection)

✔ A copy of an illusory image, projected for students to see (see Teaching)

✔ "Daily Life during the Revolutionary War" chart from Session 5 (see Mid-Workshop Teaching)

✔ One student's writing to share with the class (see Share)

COMMON CORE STATE STANDARDS: W.4.3, W.4.5, W.4.8, W.4.9, RI.4.1, RI.4.3, RI.4.4, RI.4.6, RI.4.8, SL.4.1, SL.4.4, L.4.1, L.4.2, L.4.3

YOUR YOUNG WRITERS already know the power of stories. These writers have already embedded narratives into their history books. In this session, you up the ante. You teach them that writers can use the power of a story to depict two sides—and multiple perspectives—in history.

The work that you are teaching students to do is not for the faint of heart! Those that take up your instruction will be asked to use all that they know about the qualities of good narrative writing: writing bit by bit, zooming in on small moments, showing rather than telling the reader in the service of bringing out multiple perspectives. They will be required, also, to draw on all they know about developing a story arc—setting a scene, establishing a main character, developing a problem or a rising tension, and carrying this through to its resolution. But the real new work that this will accomplish is to add a layer of depth to children's ability to understand and write about history.

On the way to becoming true historians, children learn that one story can never be the only story. Children mature into readers and writers of history when they realize that any telling of history involves multiple perspectives: the Native American as well as the white settler, the loyalist as well as the patriot, the women and the children as well as the men. Historians uncover the silent voices in history.

This session should ignite conversation—and questions. In the final bend of this unit, students will hear that it is critical to value the questions that can drive research. They will be coached to frame musings as researchable questions. Were the patriots really justified in dumping exorbitant amounts of precious tea into the Boston Harbor? Was the propaganda created after the Boston Massacre a necessary step in helping the colonies gain independence? And were all of the Redcoats taking advantage of the colonists and trying to make life miserable?

The Common Core State Standards for Reading Literature ask that fourth-graders "Compare and contrast the point of view from which different stories are narrated." This lesson takes a big step in that direction.

The Other Side of the Story

CONNECTION

◆ COACHING

Overview the important role that stories have within information books by asking students to note all the narrative they can find in information texts.

As the children convened in the meeting area, I distributed some published information books to a scattering of them. "Writers, you'll see that I have given you information books. Would you share with kids sitting near you? The challenge is to scan through the book and see whether the author included a story, and if so, how that story was put into the book. Study what you see, and be prepared to think about what this means for the books you are writing."

There was a buzz as children looked through the pages. Some started reading word for word, so I voiced over. "You are going to need to just glance at the pages, maybe read a starting line, turning through the pages to pick up clues that tell you, 'This is a story.' When you get to a story, study it more closely."

After a few minutes, I said, "So what are you noticing?"

The children commented that many of the information books contained stories, and that all of the stories seem to be filled with facts, and taught about the topic, even though they probably were actually "made up." I nodded, and pointed out that we could have looked for other genres as well, and would probably have found a lot of different kinds of writing, all embedded in information texts. "I know many of you have been writing stories within your own books, so I know you will want to remind yourself of what you already know about writing stories within history information books."

Obviously we recommend you select the texts that you will distribute so that when students look to see if they contain embedded stories, the answer is yes.

Read the story a student wrote, making sure the story you read offers a different perspective on a familiar tale, and sets children up so they can, at the end of this minilesson, tell the same story from yet one more perspective.

"Let me read you a bit of the story that Grayson is working on. Will you let it jog your mind so that you remember tips you've already been taught?"

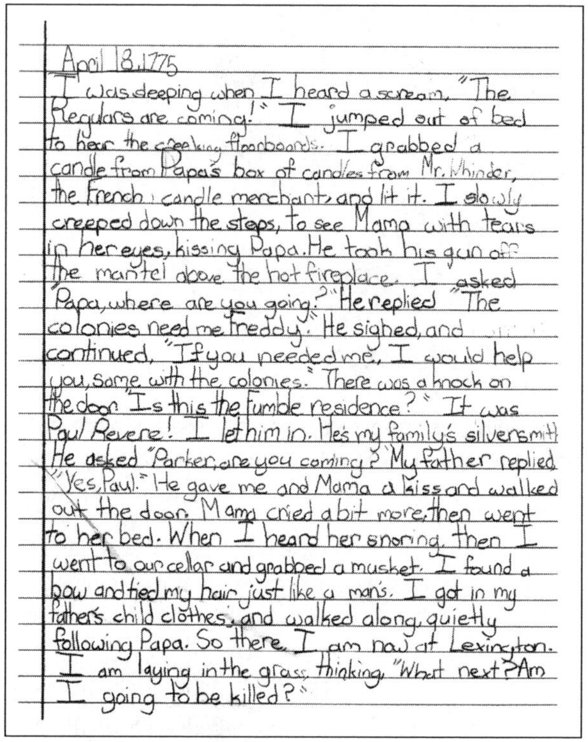

April 18, 1775

I was sleeping when I heard a scream, "The Regulars are Coming!" I jumped out of bed to hear the creaking floorboards. I grabbed a candle from Papa's box of candles from Mr. Whinder, the French candle merchant, and lit it. I slowly creeped down the steps, to see Mama with tears in her eyes, kissing Papa. He took his gun off the mantel above the hot fireplace. I asked "Papa where are you going?" He replied, "The colonies need me Freddy." He sighed and continued, "If you needed me, I would help you, same with the colonies."

There was a knock on the door. "Is this the Fumble residence?" It was Paul Revere! I let him in. He's my family's silversmith. He asked, "Parker are you coming?" My father replied "Yes Paul." He gave me and mama a kiss and walked out the door. Mama cried a bit more, then went to her bed. When I heard her snoring, then I went to our cellar and grabbed a musket. I found a bow and tied my hair just like a man's. I got in my father's child clothes, and walked along, quietly following Papa. So there I am now at Lexington. I am laying in the grass thinking, "What next? Am I going to be killed?"

I paused at that point. "What has even just that little bit of Grayson's story made you remember about methods for writing powerful history stories? Stop and jot." The room was quiet as children scrawled.

After a minute, I said, "You are listing important things. You are right that you need to remember to have a central character, a setting, and a problem, a turning point or tension. And you are right, too, to remember that to start the story, you need to think, 'Who is doing what, where' and then let the story spin out. And yes, you'll be writing about a small moment or two.

FIG. 16–1 Grayson's narrative, trying on a new perspective

Obviously, you always have a choice to call "Turn and talk" instead of "Stop and jot" or vice versa. There are advantages to each. In general, we tend to do more stop-and-jot as students grow older.

"I jotted on this chart some of what I saw in your writing."

Methods for Writing Powerful History Stories

1. Imagine you are a character, then let the story spin out.

2. Think about a character w/ traits, wants, who encounters trouble that gets worse and worse.

3. Think of a story as 2–3 scenes or small moments, glued together with narration.

4. Sketch the plot in a story booklet, then touch each page and story-tell the whole story of that page. Make other story booklets to try other sequences.

"Today, I want to teach you one more thing about writing stories related to history, and this is a very important point that relates to story writing—but is bigger than that. In fact, it is one of the biggest things I could ever teach you."

❖ **Name the teaching point.**

"Writers, today I want to teach you that to write (and think) about history well, you need to remember that there is always more than one side to a story. When trying to understand an event in history, it is important to ask, 'What are some other sides to this story?'"

TEACHING

Use the student's story shared earlier to point out that others could have written about that same event from different perspectives, and would have therefore included different information.

"Writers, during the first bend in this unit, we pretended we were all writing about Paul Revere's ride, and we talked about how you could tell the story of Paul, nervously carrying out his important mission, or of someone, sleeping, who heard the cry. We talked about how important it is to decide, 'Whose story will you tell?'

"And my point, today, is that you can look at the same set of facts and see them differently based on whose story you are telling. Just now, instead of hearing Paul's story—about the muffled oars, about the responsibility on his shoulders—we hear a young girl's story, the daughter of a minuteman. This story, from her point of view, shows that she thinks about the relationship between her parents, about her mother's cries, about their good-bye kiss, and about her own role in the war. She doesn't think a lot about what her father brings or doesn't bring with him to war, what the look on his face suggests.

"Paul's story about knocking on the door of this particular house may have included that Paul saw the young girl, leaning over the banister, listening in. He may have tried to get the parents to talk in the kitchen, out of earshot to the young girl, knowing that if she listened in, if she ended up joining the army, she'd be risking her life."

Use the iconic picture that can be looked at in a way that reveals one thing (a chalice) or an altogether different thing (two faces) to point out that perspective determines what one sees.

"Writers, I want to show you a picture." I projected the well-known image that can be seen as a vase, or, if one looks differently, as the profile view of two faces, looking at each other (see Figure 16–2). "Tell your partner what you see." The room erupted into chatter, as different students registered their different understandings of what they were seeing.

"It's a cup, I mean, like—a wine glass," said Milo, as if the only challenge in the activity was to name the container depicted in the picture.

"Huh? A glass? That's two people looking at each other," Robert said, just as certain. The two boys looked at each other, flummoxed that they were seeing something so absolutely different. Then each looked back, trying to see what the other saw.

Debrief in a way that emphasizes that it is helpful to think about how a story could be told from more than one perspective.

"What I want to suggest is that the story of Paul Revere's ride will be a different story if it is told from the point of view of Paul Revere, or from the point of view of a child of a minuteman—and it will be an even *different* story if it is told from the point of view of a loyalist. To accurately report what happens in your life, a person would need to talk to more than just one person, and get more than one side of the story. Yesterday when you came in from recess, all hot and bothered about the argument over the Frisbee, if I only talked with Sam and only got his side of the story, I don't think that Melissa would feel like I was a very good historian. That's true when writing about yesterday, and even more true when writing about hundreds of years ago."

FIG. 16–2   Rubin optical illusion

If you can't get hold of this picture, you could bypass this portion of the minilesson. It is a nice way to cement your point, but children can grasp the point of the minilesson without the artwork!

There are several of these pictures that can be interpreted as showing utterly different things. Another, for example, shows a picture that when viewed one way looks like an old woman with a scarf on her head, when viewed another, a young woman wearing a hat with a feather. (See Figure 16–3.)

FIG. 16–3   Old or young woman optical illusion

ACTIVE ENGAGEMENT

Suggest ways that students could bring out other sides of the story in their reports, encouraging some to decide to take whatever story they have already written and write it from another perspective.

"There are lots of ways you could bring out various sides of the story in your report. You could simply title one of your chapters, 'The British Side of the Story,' or, if this is about George Washington, 'The Soldier's Side of the Story,' or if it is about the tea party, 'The Ship Owner's Side of the Story.' You can write another chapter, telling another side of the story.

"But another alternative, and one I hope you consider, is that you can take any story you have already written for your book, and write the same story differently, this time telling it from someone else's point of view. That is extremely hard work."

Channel students to discuss, then tell Paul Revere's story from the point of view of loyalists. Coach them to tell about the same events, from a different perspective.

"Let's try it with our Paul Revere story. What sorts of things might you put in a loyalist's side of the story? When we thought about how Paul Revere's story would go, we decided that his major struggle was that he was a silversmith, not a soldier, and he might be afraid he would let people down. What might the conflict or struggle be if we told the story from the point of view of a loyalist? Turn and talk to your partner. What are you thinking?"

As partners talked to each other, I listened in, then after a few moments, I reconvened the class.

"I heard some of you saying that the loyalist might struggle with the fear that war was about to start. She might wish that things could just stay the same, that the colonies were doing just fine with England in charge. I was thinking that the loyalist might feel afraid for the lives of the men in her life who would likely now have to go to war.

"So now I'd like you to try it. I'll get you started, and then one partner should continue, telling the other the story of that morning. I would want to start it with some similar pieces as I included in the Paul Revere story to signal to the reader that the *events are the same but the perspective is different*. It might start something like this":

> "The British are coming! The British are coming!" The call came through Elizabeth's open window and woke her. She listened again, "The British are coming!" She imagined the handsome British soldiers, gathering to protect her and the other Loyalists. Her heart pounded. She knew this man was . . .

I listened in as partners told the story to each other.

Remember to channel students to give the loyalist's point of view on exactly the same events as were chronicled in Grayson's story—not on the war in general.

LINK

Send students off to write, reminding them that historians strive to inclue multiple perspectives. Additionally, reiterate the timeline of the remainder of the unit.

"There's a famous saying among historians, 'History is written by the victors.' That means that people who win the wars are usually the ones who are given the say in how the story of the war is written. Other people say it's not just the winners who have a say. It's also the folks who have the most power. The kings, the presidents, the rich people, for example. And lots of times, the stories that aren't told are the stories of the child's experience of the war, the loser's experience of the war, the slave's experience of the war. Historians go to great lengths to try to find the stories that have been lost, and to bring out the voices that haven't been heard. Would you talk to each other about what you think you could do to make sure that more than one side of your story is told? Turn and talk.

"Writers, although I have tried to teach you today the importance of remembering that there are always many sides to a story, I know that many of you were already engrossed in other work. For some of you, you may just need to tuck today's lesson into the back of your mind to use when the time comes. But there may be some of you who have time today to write another side of your story.

"Remember, today is the last day for drafting the report you'd originally planned to write, although you do have tonight to get more done. We'll devote some time tomorrow to editing.

"For now, size up where you are in your writing process and what the work is that you need to do today. Then get started."

Keeping Engagement and Productivity High

THERE SHOULD BE A SENSE THAT ALL CYLINDERS ARE FIRING, full speed ahead, today. The work that students are doing should be very diverse. Some children will jump right in to the work outlined in the minilesson, writing stories from another perspective. Others will be in the middle of a different kind of chapter, and won't want to be thwarted from their path. Keep in mind that not all writers will be ready for the work described in the minilesson and will do best keeping with the kind of narrative writing they learned in the previous bend. This is perfectly acceptable and typical of a writing workshop, that not every strategy will be suited to every writer. Your work today is to make sure engagement and productivity are high, while also giving your writers the confidence they need to not let fear get in the way of trying something new.

You may want to begin by supporting those children who are actually working on today's lesson about telling stories from more than one perspective, so that you make it more likely that the lessons you just taught are in the room once the minilesson is over. At the end of the link, you might say, "Those of you who will be working to tell a story of an important moment from the revolution from more than one perspective—you should stay on the carpet after the meeting is over." Then you can help those people progress smoothly along—and do that without talking for more than a minute or two!

You probably would want to start by asking them to refer to the chart of strategies you and the class just co-created, suggesting they read this over and do this work, only instead of writing, for now, to first think about the narratives they have included in their second book so far, and to decide whether they are going to write one or two narratives. If they already wrote a chapter with a narrative structure, they can just think about the other side of the story they already told. If some have joined the group who have yet to write a narrative, you may want to channel them to write one version of their event, and then to return once they have done this so that you can help them think through how the other side of the story might go.

MID-WORKSHOP TEACHING
Historical Details Are What Allow Stories into the Genre

"Eyes up here, writers," I said. "For those of you who are writing stories—please don't forget that you need to tuck specific details about that period in history into your stories. Emily has been working on this, and her writing is getting so much more informative—it makes me think some of the rest of you will want to follow her lead. I asked Emily if she had a strategy that she used for doing this, and she told me that our 'Daily Life During the Revolutionary War' chart really helped her. She said that after she drafted for a while, she shifted into some revision work. She reread her writing, and went back through it, replacing details and adding in new historical details. For example, in one part, she had written about money, writing 'The British soldiers owe my master a lot of money.' But then she consulted the chart, and replaced 'a lot of money' with 'one pound and five shillings'! Also, instead of just talking about the British soldiers' red uniforms, she called them *lobsterbacks*.

"Emily's draft now has details from the time period in it to help readers feel as if they are really there, and to teach them what life was like back then. Keep adding to your drafts in the same way; go back to the 'Daily Life' chart if you need some ideas. Back to work!"

When you have your group whittled down to those who have already written a narrative and are ready to think about a story with another perspective, you might begin by helping the writers to select an alternate perspective. Perhaps choose one child's story and ask the group to pitch in, working on that story's alternate perspective first.

(continues)

On this day, I chose Yoshi's story for the group to work on. I asked him to read the first part aloud, which went:

> "Ugg" thought Thomas Jefferson, as he listened to what the other 55 delegates thought of his draft of the Declaration of Independence. "I think it's perfect how it is, and I wish it would be cooler in here." It was the summer of 1776, and it was very hot. All of the delegates were wearing suits.

"So writers," I went on, "Let's think about some of the other perspectives that might be hidden in Yoshi's story, and what they might say if they were telling the story. First, we can ask ourselves, 'Who is telling the story?' In other words, whose voice is heard? Turn and talk to the person sitting beside you."

Right away the students agreed that it was Thomas Jefferson who was telling the story.

"Now writers, talk to each other about how the story goes because of who is telling it." I once again listened in while the writers talked.

Grayson said, "It's all about how hot it is but also that Thomas Jefferson is frustrated because the others are criticizing his draft."

"I agree," I said. "And now, we can ask ourselves, whose voice is not heard here? And how might the story go if that other person was telling it? Turn and talk."

Mirei said, "I think maybe the delegates aren't heard because we don't know what they are thinking. They are probably hot, too."

Jackson agreed. "Yeah, and they are probably thinking that Thomas Jefferson made mistakes, or there are things that could be better. They want to make sure it's right."

"Writers," I said, "You just did some really important work. You took yourselves through a series of questions that writers often ask themselves when considering the hidden perspectives in stories. I imagine Yoshi could write a second version of this story, this time told from the perspective of another one of the delegates, such as Benjamin Franklin. Franklin would still be complaining about the heat, but his version of this moment would be very different. He might be talking about all of the things Jefferson needed to fix, or how he thought Jefferson was being stubborn.

"I'm going to record what you just did on a chart. Since you are some of the first in the class to try this work, would you be responsible for mentoring others? Each of you make it a goal to point out our chart and to talk through what you just did to at least or two other people in the class. That way they'll be able to try this, too."

Questions Writers Ask When Considering Another Perspective

- Who is telling the story?
- How does the story go because of who is telling it?
- Whose voice is not heard here?
- How might the story go if that other person was telling it?

Once all the writers had selected a perspective and had a vision for how their stories could go, I set them up to study the chart of strategies we had created during the minilesson, and to rehearse for writing by storytelling to their partners.

Methods for Writing Powerful History Stories

1. Imagine you are a character, then let the story spin out.

2. Think about a character w/ traits, wants, who encounters trouble that gets worse and worse trying to get those wants.

3. Think of a story as two to three scenes or small moments, glued together with narration.

4. To write a small moment/scene, start w/ a character doing or saying something.

5. Sketch the plot in a story booklet, then touch each page and story-tell the whole story of that page. Make other story booklets to try other sequences.

The Power of Multiple Perspectives

Recruit the class to help one writer improve. Then ask them to consider improving their own work in the same ways.

"Writers, Melissa has been working on writing two sides of a story and she would really love your input." I nodded to Melissa to begin.

Melissa said, "I have started writing about the Boston Massacre from different viewpoints, and I want to know how to make it better." (See Figure 16–4.) I suggested she read one side of her story, and Sam, the other, and I asked the class to listen, thinking, "What's good about what she has done that I could try too? What might I suggest to make this even better?"

Melissa

March 5, 1770

The Sight of the Boston Massacre

     I stood outside my house in Boston near where a bunch of school boys where throwing rocks, sticks, ice, and snow at the guard named Private Hugh White. It was not a bad scene, but not a good scene. I wish I could stop this fighting! I hate it! My mom came outside near me for a few minutes.
     "Don't stand there, you might get hit."
     "OK" I replied. So I moved to a safer place to watch what was going on.

Suddenly, Private Hugh White called out for help! Then all these soldiers came near him to help. A colonist threw a stick and hit a British soldier which made him fall to the ground!!
     "Wow!! That was a scene!" I said to myself.
     "Damn you, fire! Shouted the British soldier that fell to the ground. The British soldiers fired to the crowd of colonists. I saw 3 colonists die right at spot. And one of them included a runaway slave called Crispus Attacks. I heard in my dad's newspaper that 2 other colonists died. And 6 colonists got wounded.

I rushed up the creaking stairs in my house with a candle to tell my mom what happened. My mom and dad were already talking about the Boston Massacre.
     "I know, I saw it outside my window," she said. "Isn't it exciting?
     "It is not that exciting. I don't like to see people fight" , I replied. I rushed down the creaking stairs with my candle and went back outside to see what else was going on.

FIG. 16–4 Melissa's story, version one

"What are you thinking? Turn and talk," I said. After a minute, I suggested Melissa call on people.

"I think it was good the way you showed Hugh White helped you to see the Boston Massacre from the British side. Maybe these soldiers weren't just looking for violence, but were scared and overwhelmed, and were afraid to refuse to follow the order to fire," said Yoshi.

I continued on. "Right now, would you think about ways Melissa could add to her narrative to pop out some of these things even more? What kinds of things could she add to show how afraid Hugh White was, or to show the soldiers felt they had to follow orders to shoot? Turn and talk to your partner."

"She could say more about what he was thinking," said Milo. "Like maybe a part that says, 'Private White thought to himself, "I know I shouldn't shoot at these people, but if my commander just said, 'fire,' I have to do it. Maybe I can shoot but try not to hit anyone. This got out of control too quickly."'"

"Yeah," said Mirei. "And also she could add something about what he was doing, like maybe he is trying to get away, or he is shaking because he is scared."

"I've heard you tell each other so many great ideas for improving this piece of writing! Will you take a moment now and see if any of the suggestions you've made or heard also help your own writing?"

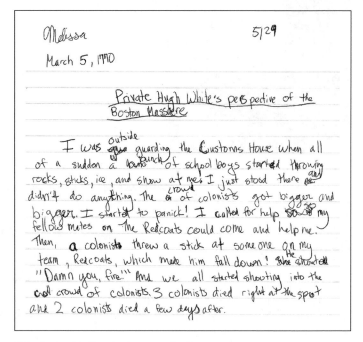

FIG. 16–5   Melissa's story, version two

READING TO ASSESS AND REVISE

Writers, tomorrow is the last day that you have to work on these research reports before we move on to new chapters and a new way of thinking. Our writing workshop time tomorrow will be dedicated to self-assessment and goal-setting. I'd like for you to get a jump start on that work tonight, by reading over all the writing that you have done on your informational books up until now. Tomorrow you'll use the Information Writing Checklists to guide your self-assessment, but for tonight, I'd like you to self-assess more freely. Take a stack of Post-it notes home with you, and as you reread your writing, mark places that you are especially proud of, that you feel show exceptional growth in your life as an informational writer. And of course, as you are rereading, feel free to make any revisions you see as necessary.

Self-Assessment and Goal Setting
Taking on New Challenges

ear Teachers,

You have reached the end of Bend II, and you are soon to help your writers embark on the final leg of the journey that has been this unit. You have taught your students to organize their writing around important information and ideas, and to highlight that structure for their readers. Now is a time to reflect on how far your writers have come since the start of this unit, as the change in their informational writing from then to now. Looking back is important to do because this can help students to see themselves as traveling on a trajectory, and can help them to develop a sense of themselves as people who outgrow themselves.

Although this session supports reflection and goal-setting, it is not the usual end-of-the-bend reflection. Students' writing is not done. So instead of looking back on completed work, students will be looking at chapters that are completed, and anticipating those they will write in the final leg of the unit.

Because your writers will be continuing work on the same piece of writing, this final session does not, then, support a large celebration. But, we do feel it's important to mark the end of the bend in some way, to communicate to your writers that they are wrapping up one kind of work and getting ready to start another kind of work.

In this session, we suggest one way for you to end the bend and to prepare for the more challenging work laid out in Bend III. You may, of course, think of a better way to accomplish this. The most important thing is that you engage your students in some serious self-assessment, using the checklists you introduced at the end of the previous bend. Channel your writers to study their work with both the fourth- and fifth-grade checklists in hand, reflecting on whether they are meeting all of the expectations laid out for fourth-graders, and many of the fifth-grade expectations.

As we have mentioned before, our experience has shown us that the K–5 grades are a powerful time to accelerate students' writing development. It is harder to teach writing well in middle school, when one teacher may have 150 students. Our recommendation, then, is that you do everything in your power to help many of your students enter sixth

COMMON CORE STATE STANDARDS: W.4.2, W.4.5, W.5.5, RFS.4.4, SL.4.1, L.4.1, L.4.2, L.4.3

grade already able to accomplish most of the standards for that grade. This, then, positions them well to meet (or perhaps exceed) expectations for eighth grade.

MINILESSON

You might want to begin by recalling the story of your friend from the earlier session on self-assessment. Tell your writers that you have some exciting news—that your friend finally beat the record for the 200-meter freestyle at his swim club. But, he didn't stop trying to get better as a swimmer once he beat that record. Instead, he looked at what even more advanced swimmers were doing and set a new goal for himself. He decided he wanted to try to beat the countywide record, so he figured out what that was, and he set to work.

Then, transition into your teaching by naming your teaching point. You could say something along the lines of, "When writers are getting ready to take on new, even more challenging work, they reflect on the work they have done, taking stock and setting new goals."

Because writers are already familiar with the process of using the checklists to self-assess, you likely don't need to spend a great deal of time setting them up to do this work. They will probably feel confident jumping right in. Ask them to lay out the following materials: their writing, the list of goals they started in their notebooks, and a copy of the fourth- and fifth-grade checklists. Point out that, at the end of bend, after all of the work they've done, their work should be miles better than when they last assessed their writing.

Suggest that writers look between the two checklists, and, for each item, decide whether they are closer to the goal for fourth-grade informational writers, or whether they are starting to do some of the work set out in the fifth-grade checklist. Be sure to reassure writers that what is important now is that they are doing most, if not all, of the work expected for fourth-grade writers, but that it's important for them to study the fifth-grade checklist so they can push themselves to reach even further.

Give your writers some time to work, moving among them and coaching as they do. You might want to reinforce your writers' work by peeking over their shoulders and asking them to point out particular places in their writing that show they

The Information Writing Checklist, Grades 4 and 5 can be found on the CD-ROM.

Information Writing Checklist

	Grade 4	NOT YET	STARTING TO	YES!	Grade 5	NOT YET	STARTING TO	YES!
	Structure				**Structure**			
Overall	I taught readers different things about a subject. I put facts, details, quotes, and ideas into each part of my writing.	☐	☐	☐	I used different kinds of information to teach about the subject. Sometimes I included little essays, stories, or "how-to" sections in my writing.	☐	☐	☐
Lead	I hooked my readers by explaining why the subject mattered, telling a surprising fact, or giving a big picture. I let readers know that I would teach them different things about a subject.	☐	☐	☐	I wrote an introduction that helped readers get interested in and understand the subject. I let readers know the subtopics I would be developing later as well as the sequence.	☐	☐	☐
Transitions	I used words in each section that help readers understand how one piece of information connected with others. If I wrote the section in sequence, I used words and phrases such as *before, later, next, then,* and *after.* If I organized the section in kinds or parts, I used words such as *another, also,* and *for example.*	☐	☐	☐	When I wrote about results, I used words and phrases like *consequently, as a result,* and *because of this.* When I compared information, I used words and phrases such as *in contrast, by comparison,* and *especially.* In narrative parts, I used phrases that go with stories such as *a little later* and *three hours later.* In the sections that stated an opinion, I used words such as *but the most important reason, for example,* and *consequently.*	☐	☐	☐
Ending	I wrote an ending that reminded readers of my subject and may have suggested a follow-up action or left readers with a final insight. I added my thoughts, feelings, and questions about the subject at the end.	☐	☐	☐	I wrote a conclusion in which I restated the main points and may have offered a final thought or question for readers to consider.	☐	☐	☐
Organization	I grouped information into sections and used paragraphs and sometimes chapters to separate those sections. Each section had information that was mostly about the same thing. I may have used headings and subheadings.	☐	☐	☐	I organized my writing into a sequence of separate sections. I may have used headings and subheadings to highlight the separate sections. I wrote each section according to an organizational plan shaped partly by the genre of the section.	☐	☐	☐

met a certain goal. You might say to one writer, "I noticed you checked off this part of the 'transition words' category: 'When I wrote about things that happened over time, I wrote about the final thing that happened by showing that they were a result of the earlier things that happened. To do so, I used words and phrases like *consequently, as a result, because of this*.' Can you show me a couple of places where you did that?" You might commend the writer, and, depending on how solid you feel the writer's grasp is of the goal, suggest he do it more often before he decides he has fully met the fourth-grade goal, or suggest he aim for the fifth-grade goal.

Before sending your writers off, take a moment to reconvene them to remind them to jot down some of their new goals onto their personal goal sheet. Encourage them to keep those goals in mind as they work today.

CONFERRING AND SMALL-GROUP WORK

You might refer to the letter in Session 8, because much of the coaching you will do on this day will be similar to the coaching you did on that day. You may want to do small-group work around goal-setting to help you reach as many of your writers as you possibly can. One method of small-group work you might do to support goal-setting is to gather writers with the same goal and discuss how they are working to meet this goal. You might choose a portion of your demonstration writing that is lacking in the same area the students identified for themselves. For example, you might choose a part of your demonstration writing in which the elaboration is paltry, or a part that has details that don't really fit with what the section is really about. Next, involve your writers in helping to revise that section of the demonstration text. And finally, channel these writers to return to their own pieces to give the same work a try.

Another way to do a small group around goal-setting is to have partners work together to support each other. You might first ask your writers to study their own work intently, with the checklist in hand. Then, ask them to take notes when they come to parts that could use some revision. In their notes, they should use the rubric to name specifically what they feel they need to work on. Your writers' notes might say things such as: "need a definition of this important word," or "need to put in the name of the source, here." After your writers have marked up their own texts, move on to helping them support each other in partnerships. They can trade pieces and notes with one another, and then proceed to assess each other's work. They'll follow the same process they did in their self-assessment, reading their partner's piece with checklist in hand. After they finish assessing each other's writing, ask them to talk to each other about their pieces and notes, telling each other whether they agree with their partner's notes, and adding in anything additional they notice.

MID-WORKSHOP TEACHING

For today's mid-workshop teaching, you might give writers the opportunity to reflect on how far they've come while also supporting transference. One way to do this is by bringing out the on-demand pieces that writers wrote in the very beginning of the unit and asking them to do a bit of reflection on those pieces, armed with all of their new learning. Many of your writers might greet these on-demand pieces with exclamations of how little they knew back then, and how much their writing has improved. Give them a few moments to think about how they would revise their on-demand pieces based on all that they have learned, and then wrap up by asking writers to share with a partner all the ways they have grown since the unit began.

SHARE

This share session will need to be hefty, as it is one of those that hold dual purposes. You'll want to reserve a portion of it for celebratory reflection, and another part of it to help writers prepare for the road ahead in Bend III. Because your writers will be continuing work on the same books, it will be difficult to have a large-scale celebration. But it will be nice to build in an opportunity for sharing. You might ask students to share the work they did during today's work time with their partners. Coach the partners to comment on how that work affected their reading of the text. You might say, "Historians, I know you've been working hard, not only trying out quotations, but doing all sorts of things to make your pieces better. What I'd like you to do right now is to put three star-shaped Post-it notes on places in your piece where you did some work that you feel especially proud of, that you think made a real difference in how your readers will read your piece. Once you have done that, I'd like Partner 1 to share your work first. Partner 2, your job will be to read with an eye toward, 'How did this work help make this piece better? How did it affect my reading?' Share your thoughts with your partner and then switch roles."

After students have an opportunity to share, shift gears a bit to lay out the work for the upcoming bend. You might tell students how proud you are of the impressive books that they've been working so hard to perfect, highlighting the different strategies that they've been using, such as text features and quotations. Go on to say that you wouldn't be surprised if many of them are thinking, "I'm done! Here's this great book I made. It's finished and I can move on." Explain that when a writer reaches a sense of done-ness, that can actually mean that they're actually ready to begin. Many writers say, "When I'm done, I've only just begun!" That doesn't mean that they plan to start over from the exact same place they did before. It means beginning on a whole new level, opening up their writing to new risks, to brand-new questions and ideas. Congratulate your students on having graduated to a new beginning. Generate some excitement for the work that is to come, perhaps telling them that in the brand-new bend that begins tomorrow, they will have the opportunity to make their writing truly spectacular and take the kinds of risks, ask the kinds of questions, and come up with the kinds of theories that make for truly high-quality writing.

HOMEWORK

For homework you might say, "Writers, tonight continue the celebration of your writing with someone at home. Give your writing to someone to read, maybe Mom or Dad, Grandma, your brother or sister, your babysitter, anyone really. Since the purpose of informational writing is to teach, after they read your writing, ask them to share with you at least three things that they learned about your topic. Hopefully your central ideas and important information will shine through!"

Good luck,

Lucy and Anna

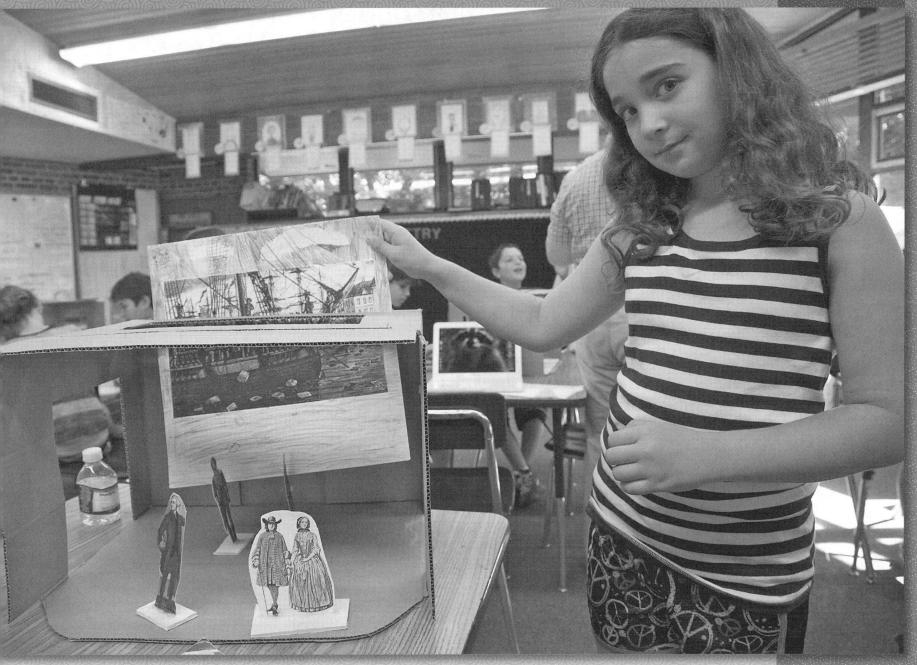

Information Writing Gives Way to Idea Writing

IN THIS SESSION, you'll teach students that history writers write and develop their own ideas about the information that they find as they research.

GETTING READY

✔ An excerpt from *The Revolutionary War* by Josh Gregory, or other source you have been using for research, enlarged for students to see (see Teaching)

✔ Books that students have been using for research (see Active Engagement)

✔ "Ways to Push Our Thinking" chart, from Session 5 (see Link)

✔ "Freewriting" chart, from the *Boxes and Bullets: Personal and Persuasive Essays* unit (see Conferring and Small-Group Work)

COMMON CORE STATE STANDARDS: W.4.1, W.4.2, W.4.8, W.4.10, RI.4.1, RI.4.2, RI.4.3, RI.4.7, RI.4.9, SL.4.1, SL.4.4, L.4.1, L.4.2, L.4.3

D URING THE FIRST BEND OF THE UNIT, when students were writing their first book about the American Revolution, you encouraged them to write on a very general topic. There is some safety in writing about topics such as all about the American Revolution and all about Paul Revere's Ride. When topics have been well documented in multiple books for children on the American Revolution, youngsters writing a chapter on that topic can parrot back information from their sources.

In the second bend, you channeled students to write on more focused subtopics, and meanwhile you also raised the bar. A whole chapter on the consequences of the Boston Massacre? One on the British experience of the Boston Tea Party? You invited more focused topics that meant a more focused research effort. And this time around, your fourth-graders constructed their own plans for their books, determining the format for the chapters they wrote. Their writing was still largely composed of bits of information, mined from other places and cemented together within their unit. But now the writers made choices about the frames within which the information would be set.

Until now, the books that your children have written showcase facts and ideas that can be traced to various research books and sources. By now, though, students have a deeper knowledge base on their topic and no longer need to *rely* on parroting back information they learn elsewhere. This means a new kind of writing can begin: one that allows for greater risks, one that brings in writers' own ideas—the kind of ideas that do not exist in any published book.

Authentic authorship about a historical era relies upon deep knowledge. Your instruction will need to empower children into bringing their own voice, insight and responses—no matter how quirky—to their writing, and you will show them how to formalize these so that they fit the garb of the genre. This may well mean channeling the connections that your students are probably already making between then and now so that they compare and contrast the two eras. This also means taking the questions or confusions they might have about a topic and helping them develop probable hypotheses to answer these.

Information Writing Gives Way to Idea Writing

CONNECTION

Remind students that they grew lots of ideas while reading fiction and suggest that they can do the same while reading history texts.

"Writers, when you read fiction such *Tiger Rising* by Kate DiCamillo or *Stone Fox* by John Gardiner, remember responding to the text? You talked to partners about parts when your stomach would knot up in response to Rob's problems. You talked about the movie you would make in your mind of Willy's one-dog sled racing around a snowy bend and about what you thought might happen next. You weren't just retelling the story to each other, you were growing idea upon idea.

"I'm talking about this because reading *history* isn't all that different from reading *fiction*. I know that when I read about Paul Revere, riding furiously through the night, I have a picture in my mind of hooves against earth, furtive glances left and right, the rider ducking beneath branches, heart pumping—I can hear the furious whisper: 'The Redcoats are coming!'

"As I picture all this. I wonder 'What will happen next? Will people take his warning seriously?'

"But I don't just envision and anticipate what will come next when I read history. I also make personal connections. When I read about the Boston Tea Party, I picture the time I visited Boston Harbor—was the Tea Party in the same place where I had eaten chocolate chip ice cream, watching the sea? When I read about taxation of the colonies, I picture our own taxes, my dad grumbling under his breath as he calculated what we owed. When I read history, I have idea upon idea.

"I know for you, as for me, history reminds you of your own world, your own life. I know that when *you've* been researching for your books, you haven't just been looking at history as a pileup of facts or a chronicle of long-ago events. Some of you have watched your own mental movie of Mohawk Indians dumping tea into the ocean from the edge of a ship. Maybe one Mohawk's headgear fell off to reveal a blond head—Oops! You've also been reminded of other things, you've had questions and thoughts about how times then and times now are the same or different. Like me, when you read history, you have idea upon idea. All these ideas that readers have while researching history are valuable fodder for writing. History writers don't just research, rearrange, and record information about the past."

Recalling work that students did in a reading unit demonstrates to them that the skills they learn in one unit are important always, and also that reading and writing are inextricably linked.

✤ **Name the teaching point.**

"Today, I want to teach you that history writers write and develop their own ideas about the information that they find as they research."

TEACHING

Set the tone for this new bend by suggesting that history writers capture and use ideas that are inspired from researching a topic.

"Writers, readers don't just want to know all the information that writers like you have found. They want to know what you *think* about that information. When I look at the books you've been working on, it is clear to me that you've found lots of information. It is also clear that you've structured your writing well—and used headings and quotes and examples and text features to highlight the most important information. But your readers also want to read *you*. They want to read *your* response to the information. Before you finish your books, before we finish this unit, you'll want to add a chapter or two in which you tell readers *your ideas* about your topic."

Point out that when kids read history, their minds are full of ideas—but too often they record only the facts that are on the pages of the books, not the thoughts that streak across their minds.

"The tip I've given you—that your readers will want to read your ideas about history and not just your information—shouldn't cause you any problems. You have zillions of ideas whenever you read anything about your topic—it is like there is a lightning storm in your mind as insight streak across your thoughts. *But*. But. Here's the problem.

"Although you have a zillion ideas when you read about your topic, for many of you, those good ideas vanish before you have a chance to write a chapter about them.

"So what can you do about this?

"Here is the answer. You need to read *as a writer*. This means that when reading about your topic, you need to be ready to record not just the facts in the article, but almost more importantly, you need to be ready to record *your ideas* when they do streak across your mind. You see, when readers who aren't writers have ideas about what they're reading, those ideas get lost. But readers who are also *writers* are different. They know they have to catch hold of ideas—and they do this by jotting those ideas down quickly, often through marginal notes, so they can then move on to the next bit of text and the next ideas. It often helps those writing-readers to be rereading a text."

Demonstrate how you jot the thoughts that flash across your mind as you read about your topic.

"Watch me as I reread a text that you know, letting thoughts flash across my mind. Notice that I jot my ideas (more, even, than information) in the margins as I read. I jot quickly, briefly, and then move on. I don't linger on any one thought but try to catch a bunch of them."

I opened Josh Gregory's *The Revolutionary War*, and read a bit from it, while meanwhile I displayed an enlarged copy. As I read aloud a chunk of sentences, I jotted a quick response in the margin alongside the text.

In 1774 Parliament began passing a series of laws that became known as the Intolerable Acts.

In the margin, I jotted: "They must have been really awful to be called *intolerable* because that word means people couldn't stand them!"

These acts were designed to punish Massachusetts for destroying millions of dollars worth of property.

I jotted: "One act was Laws to punish the entire state? Seems strict!"

Parliament then ordered Boston Harbor to be closed until the colonists paid for the tea they had destroyed.

I jotted: "That meant that ships couldn't leave or enter either—another punishment."

British general Thomas Gage was named governor of Massachusetts. It became illegal for the colonists to hold town meetings or elect their own officials without permission from the British.

In the column I wrote: "A third punishment. Are British going too far? I bet the Colonist, named them 'intolerable,' not the British."

Debrief what you just did so that students might replicate the process on their own.

"Writers, did you see me talking back to the text? People refer to this as annotating the text. And what I will show you later is that many of those jottings can be thought of as seed ideas and grown into full-blown entries in your writer's notebooks that can be later put into your books. Sometimes these jottings might even turn into whole chapters!"

ACTIVE ENGAGEMENT

Channel students into annotating a historical text.

"Writers, open up a book that you've already read about your topic—it might even be your own book, the one you've written. Read silently to yourself, pencil in hand, jotting any thoughts that come to your mind. Don't judge whether they are important thoughts, and don't linger—just jot and read on."

After about two minutes, I asked them to share one of their ideas with their partner, this time talking as long as they could about that one idea. Meanwhile, I listened in. After giving them a few minutes to share in partnerships, I reconvened the group.

When you shift from the demonstration to debriefing, students should feel the different moves you are making just by the way your intonation and posture changes. After most demonstrations, there will be a time for you to debrief, and that's a time when you are no longer acting like a writer. You are the teacher who has been watching the demonstration and now turns to talk, eye to eye with kids, asking if they noticed this or that during the previous portion of the minilesson.

"Let's listen to some of the ideas that you grew, in just *two minutes* as you read, thought, questioned, wondered. I'm going to be like the conductor of an orchestra. When I point to you, would you share one of the ideas you grew just now?"

I pointed to Kim, who said, "Did Thomas Jefferson want help writing the Declaration? Was he mad that he had to stay behind and write while the others got a break?"

I next pointed to Edward, who said, "I think the Hessians and British might have thought it was unfair that the Continental Army snuck up on them at Christmas."

My imaginary baton next landed on Grayson, who said, "William Dawes never gets mentioned in the Midnight Ride."

LINK

Set writers up to reread their reference texts with a pencil in hand, recording their ideas to turn into future writing.

"Writers, I know this is going to sound unbelievable, but at the start of this unit, when I told you that we are going to be writing about history, I actually heard one of you moan, saying something like: 'History? Awww—boring. It's just names, dates, and facts.' By now, I'm pretty sure there isn't one person in this room who thinks history is boring. It's about secret meetings and people risking everything for fairness, as they see it. It's about newspapers fanning the flames of resentment or of hope. History is about people and what they decide to do when trouble strikes, how they band together or how they turn on one another. It's about lies and truths and perspectives, about midnight rides and unusual partnerships and persistence and grave danger. . . . History is high drama!

"Today, during the first part of writing time, you'll spend a lot of your time rereading and jotting, annotating texts. And once you have written a bunch of jottings, I know you'll want to take one of them, or two that go together, and draft entries in your notebooks in which you think longer about those seed ideas. It might be a good idea to look back at the 'Ways to Push Our Thinking' chart to help you develop a jotting or two into an entry."

Your students will not come up with these exact ideas of course, and if the ones they do come up with are still straight from their books, offer these up as examples for them to learn from.

Ways to Push Our Thinking

In other words . . .

That is . . .

The important thing about this is . . .

As I say this, I'm realizing . . .

This is giving me the idea that . . .

An example of this is . . .

This shows . . .

Another example of this is . . .

This connects to . . .

Using Freewriting to Grow Ideas

YOU MAY BE THINKING AS YOU GO INTO THIS SESSION, "What exactly will the kids' writing look like? This feels like a reading workshop!" And you are right that much of the work of this session is dependent on kids reading. But, tempting though it may be, aim to focus your conferring on just the writing work your students are doing, and to save the reading conferences for later. Your writers will be stopping and jotting about texts, using their annotations to spur notebook entries that will lead to new insights and revelations that they can add to their pieces.

This session is similar to some of the early sessions in the previous essay unit, in which kids were generating ideas in their notebooks. As you confer on this day, you might want to draw on the conferring sections in the first several sessions in the essay unit, as well as on the teaching you did during that portion of the essay unit for inspiration. Aim to support kids on writing with volume as they use their notebooks to grow and explore ideas. Additionally, aim to support them on drawing on a repertoire of strategies from their past experiences with this kind of writing to think on the page.

Some of your writers may be off and running with this work, thinking more deeply about their texts and using their insights to spark writing right away. Others may have a more difficult time getting started. If you notice a group of writers who could use some extra support, you may want to pull them together in a small group for some additional support.

MID-WORKSHOP TEACHING   Historians Grow Ideas by Comparing and Contrasting

"May I have your attention for a minute? Writing one's own ideas about a topic such as the American Revolution can be tricky. Here is one technique that almost always works—compare then to now.

"You are already so good at this work because when you read fiction, you often compare a character in the story to yourself. Just as fiction readers compare a character like Rob or Willy with themselves, historians compare 'then' with 'now.' That is, they compare one part of what happened in history with part of what happens today.

"For example, a person might say, 'The fight for freedom in the colonies is like the fight for freedom that is happening in many Middle Eastern countries today.' Or someone might say, 'The way that George Washington had to turn around the mood at Valley Forge is just what our President needs to do today.' Or perhaps, "The way Paul Revere had to ride through the night to deliver an important message to his friends reminds me of the instant-messaging we do today." I illustrated by wiggling my thumbs as if I were texting on a cell phone.

"Research materials and information books are full of examples of people who have asked, 'How does this or that detail about life in the past connect with a similar aspect of life today?' As you jot your ideas on Post-it notes, then, you might make sure to jot connections such as these.

"One last point—when you do this, you'll find that things are similar—and also that they are different. The word *comparing* is usually said alongside *contrasting* and that really means, thinking about similarities, *and* about differences.

"Again, you'll annotate with Post-it notes—and you'll select a few annotations that are especially provocative, and jot entries about those. The entries you write today may provide you with the material you need for your last chapter or two."

As you gather this group, it might be helpful to start with a quick compliment that reinforces something you noticed they are doing well that you would like them to continue doing. "Writers, I noticed that all of you zoomed in right away on provocative or exciting parts of your texts. You didn't just pick any old part to jot notes about. And that's really important, because when writers are doing this kind of work, the work of annotating the text with ideas, they know that certain parts of books are apt to lead to bigger ideas than others."

Then, shift into your teaching, offering a quick pointer and some brief demonstration. "Writers, I have a tip for you that I think might help you take some of the jottings you've made and use them to grow ideas in your notebooks. The tip is this: When writers land on thought-provoking ideas from texts, they often use a bit of freewriting to grow new and bigger ideas than they had before. Watch me while I take an idea from a text I've been reading, and I use some freewriting to grow this idea into something more.

"When I was researching all about the Boston Massacre for my book, I annotated one of the texts I was reading, just like you are doing. And here is an idea I jotted":

The British soldiers who fired were just following orders. They were scared and confused and didn't know what else to do.

"Then, I took that idea and I wrote it on a new page in my notebook. And to help me write an entry that would lead me to some new ideas, I used the chart we made together in the last unit on qualities of good freewriting. I started by letting any thoughts come out, and then I tried to make my writing better and better as I went. Here is the start of what I wrote":

I think everyone blames these soldiers for killing innocent people, but the truth is they wouldn't have killed anyone if there had never been a fight. And the ones who started the fight were the young men who were throwing sticks and snowballs at the soldiers. Both sides were angry at each other, and in many ways both sides were to blame. So that makes me think that maybe the patriots were just as much at fault for those people dying as the British soldiers were.

After this quick demonstration, ask your writers to try the same, this time coaching in with quick, lean prompts as they write. You might draw on this "Freewriting" chart to help you with your prompting. For example, you might coach one writer to use some comparisons in her writing, and you might coach another to just keep going, without stopping to erase or cross out.

Freewriting

- The writer keeps writing freely, letting any thoughts come out.
- The writer seems to try to make ideas that get better and better as she writes longer.
- The writer sometimes compares things to make you get what she means.
- The writer doesn't cross out.
- The writer sometimes say the big idea over and over (in different ways) as if trying to get it right.
- The writer stays for a long time on one idea.
- The writer goes from big ideas to small examples back to big ideas.

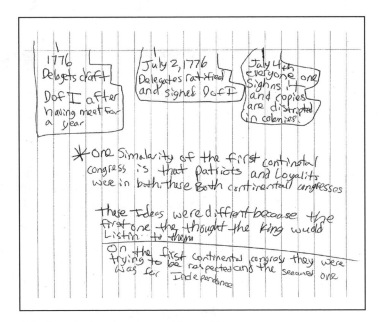

FIG. 18–1   Jackson's notes and freewriting

Discussing Ideas to Rehearse for Writing

Invite students to volunteer an idea that their reading has inspired and set partnerships to help each other say more about their ideas as rehearsal for writing.

"Writers, I know you are dying to talk about the ideas that have been sparked today. Quickly, reread all the ideas you've grown today, and think about one that might lead you and your partner into a real conversation."

I gave the children a minute to reread, select, and think. "Partner 2, why don't you talk to Partner 1 about your ideas? Your goal isn't to tell each other your ideas, but instead, to talk over your ideas. To think for a long time about them."

After a bit, I said, "Listening to your ideas, I realize that you all have some real fodder for writing right there. Partner 2, could you repeat your idea, but this time, write-in-the-air a draft of a chapter on your ideas? Partner 2, begin."

After a bit I said, "Partner 1, you are going to need to do the same work, in your mind's eye. Think about what to say, then say something in the air, then write it."

SESSION 18 HOMEWORK

GRAND CONVERSATIONS ON THE PAGE

Writers, tonight you'll write a different sort of chapter. You'll be writing about an idea you have, or several related ideas. This isn't an easy kind of writing, so I'm going to give you a few final suggestions—and these may or may not work for you.

It might help to make your writing feel like a conversation. You might even put the name of the person you are "talking to" on the top of your page. Fill your mind with that person. Think, as you start, that your goal is to bring that person in on your thoughts. So start by explaining what you have been thinking.

But then—your person is bound to get a little confused. Imagine that your person asks something—what will his or her question be? Clarify your thoughts for your person. For example: "I imagine you might be confused, You might be asking. . . . Those are important questions. The way I think about it is . . ."

Digging Deeper
Interpreting the Life Lessons that History Teaches

IN THIS SESSION, you'll teach students that history writing is not just made from facts but also from ideas. History writers convey larger ideas about a people, a nation, and a time. As they write they ask themselves, "What life lessons might this be teaching?" and write about them.

GETTING READY

✔ "Strategies History Researchers Use to Grow Ideas as They Research" chart (see Connection, Link, and Mid-Workshop Teaching)

✔ An excerpt from *The Revolutionary War* by Josh Gregory, or another source you have been using for research, enlarged for students to see. This should be the same excerpt that you used in Session 18 (see Active Engagement).

✔ Chart paper and marker (see Active Engagement)

SOME STORIES ARE CHOSEN for telling and retelling because they mean something to us. So it isn't by accident that the legend of George Washington owning up to cutting the cherry tree to his father at age six is the stuff of history—or that Revere's ride through the night continues to capture the nation's imagination. These are some of the stories that make up what it means to be an American!

In this session, you will continue to teach your writers to develop their own ideas about history, but this time you'll push them to develop ideas in another way. You'll encourage them to interpret the life lessons hidden in the history that they have chosen to tell. The American Revolution is full of the kind of stories that don't merely document the events that happened at the time, but that also preserve elements of heroism, of building unheard-of alliances, of unforgettable sacrifice, or a willingness to put oneself at risk so as to defend what one sees as right. It is worthwhile for children to explore the ideas behind stories that constitute history. Just as some children may have decided that the novel, *Stone Fox*, was not just a story about a boy who enters a sled race to pay taxes on his grandfather's farm but was also a story about determination, they might interpret the writing of the Declaration of Independence as in fact being a story about the importance of challenging injustices.

When students are interpreting the stories of history, they'll be bringing their own meanings to stories, and also finding meanings that others have brought. Students can be taught to notice that the documented history of any era is made not just from dates, names, definitions, and facts, but from ideas. Some of those ideas will have been advanced by some of the people, living through the event. "Taxation without Representation" represents one such idea, as does, "For the People, by the People." The patriots weren't just a band of people who fought a war, they were a band of people who left a legacy that history has preserved. It is important to enable children to look at that history not just as dates and events, but also as ideas.

COMMON CORE STATE STANDARDS: W.4.1, W.4.8, W.4.10, RI.4.1, RI.4.3, RI.4.7, RI.4.9, RL.4.2, SL.4.1, L.4.1, L.4.2, L.4.3

Digging Deeper

Interpreting the Life Lessons that History Teaches

CONNECTION

Remind writers that we go through life as we go through a novel, interpreting the deeper meanings behind what may seem like mundane events.

"Writers, bring the writing you did last night to the meeting area, and as soon as you get to the meeting area, share that writing with someone. Talk about whether it felt different, writing mostly about your ideas rather than about categories of information, and talk about which strategies you used to grow ideas." I referenced a chart I'd started for the occasion.

> ### Strategies History Researchers Use to Grow Ideas as They Research
>
> • Reread texts, annotating them with ideas, life lessons, and themes you see in them.
> • Connect then and now.

This doesn't seem like a very fancy lead—and it is not. But by creating a little bit of time for students to share the work they did at home last night, you convey that today's minilesson piggybacks on the last one. By asking students to think about what their writing work was like, you sponsor reflection.

The room buzzed as children talked and I listened in. After a minute, I stopped the conversation. "Some of you said that last night's writing was hard and you aren't wild about what you did, and that is okay. It's called a *rough draft*! You may want to work today on fixing up what you wrote last night, but you also may want to collect another entry or two, still about ideas, so you can decide which of your entries is most worth including in your book."

❖ **Name the teaching point.**

"Today, I want to teach you that history is made not just from names, dates, and facts but also from ideas. The stories that are told through the ages survive not just because they are true, but also because they convey larger ideas about a people, a nation, a time. It helps, therefore, to take the stories of history, and to ask, 'What life lessons might this be teaching?' and write about them."

We hope that you are relying on Units of Study for Teaching Reading, Grades 3–5 *as well as on these writing units, as the opportunities for reciprocity between teaching writing and reading will be boundless.*

TEACHING

Remind children that they know how to interpret when reading fiction, asking, "What is this story really about?" Point out that historians, too, interpret.

"You know how to do this kind of interpretation work. During reading time, you've often read fiction and asked, 'What is this story really really about?' Earlier this year, for example, you talked about how *The Tiger Rising*, by Kate DiCamillo (2002) was not just a story of a boy being bullied at school and of a secret tiger he found—that it was really a story about friendship and about opening up your suitcase of emotions. And when we read aloud *Fantastic Mr. Fox*, by Roald Dahl (1970), many of you said that although on the one hand, it was a story about a wily old fox who outwitted the farmers, on the other hand, it was really really about stealing from the rich and feeding the poor, like Robin Hood.

"You need to know that the question 'What is this really really about?' is not just one that scholars apply to stories. It's a question people also apply to life. For example, someone who never notices me suddenly invites me to sit with her at lunch. I think, 'What going on? Is she sidling up to me because she wants help on her math? What is it that is really happening here?' Then again, my best friend snaps at me for no good reason, and I think, 'What is this really really about? Is she upset because her parents had another fight, and taking it out on me, or what?'

"My point to you is that you need to read history like you read novels, and like you read life. You can read about event after event after event, but you aren't really being thoughtful if you don't pause to ask, 'What is this war—this revolution—this hero—really really about? What does the whole Founding Father thing really really stand for?'

"The fact is, history, like all stories and like life itself, is full of much bigger meanings. And as writers of history, it is your job to figure out some of these big meanings and teach them to your reader."

ACTIVE ENGAGEMENT

Invite readers to join you in uncovering bigger ideas and themes in history by asking, "What is this really about?"

"Let's reread the same piece of text that we looked at yesterday, from *The Revolutionary War* by Josh Gregory. This time, though, let's read it with the question, 'What is this event in history really, really about?'" I began reading and thinking aloud:

> In 1774 Parliament began passing a series of laws that became known as the Intolerable Acts. These acts were designed to punish Massachusetts for destroying millions of dollars worth of property. Parliament then ordered Boston Harbor to be closed until the colonists paid for the tea they had destroyed.

Of course, you will want to bring strategies you use when teaching reading over to non-fiction reading, and to history. So, for example, if you are accustomed to asking readers to locate moments that brim with significance, and to think more deeply about those moments, you might suggest they do that when thinking about the story of their historical event. If you are accustomed to thinking, "What objects or phrases play a special role, capturing some of the larger life lessons?" then you might suggest learners do that work when thinking about the event they have chosen to study.

Chin in hand, posturing as if I weighing these lines heavily, I pondered aloud: "What are the Intolerable Acts really really about? True, they are about punishing the patriots—the text already tells us this. Let's unpack this further though. The British didn't just want to punish the patriots. What were they doing—and how did the patriots respond? What is *this* story really about? Hmm, . . . let's read on."

> *On September 5, 1774, representatives from 12 or the 13 colonies met in Philadelphia to decide what should be done in response to the Intolerable Acts. These men called themselves the Continental Congress.*

Again I wondered aloud: "What is the Continental Congress really, really about? Is it only about finding a solution to the Intolerable Acts, or is it the start of something bigger? What are you all thinking these stories are really about? Stop and jot."

Suggest that writers can use these themes as starting points for their own writing.

As students jotted in their notebooks, I looked over their shoulders, and copied bits of what they were saying onto a piece of chart paper. "Writers, I've cobbled together some of your ideas into this entry:

> The British wanted to show the patriots who was boss. They went too far and the patriots responded by saying, "That's it! That's enough." It might look like the Intolerable Acts caused the patriots to form the Continental Congress, but really they were just the last straw. Or maybe the kinds of people who came all the way to America were already the kinds of people who weren't willing to be pushed around.
>
> But the patriots responded by setting up an alternative to Parliament.

LINK

Channel students to write entries today, drawing on their growing repertoire of strategies for writing about ideas.

"Finding and writing about ideas when researching history is a skill that you want to develop, because, as you know, history is made not just from names, dates, and facts but also from ideas. The stories that are told through the ages survive not just because they are true, but also because they convey larger ideas about a people, a nation, a time. It is important, therefore, to take the stories of history, and to ask, 'What life lessons might this teach?' Let's add that strategy for growing ideas while researching history to our chart. Writers, you have just two more days to develop your muscles for finding and developing the ideas in history, and to write a chapter that does this work in your book."

Strategies History Researchers
Use to Grow Ideas as They
Research

- Reread texts, annotating them with ideas, life lessons, and themes you see in them.
- Connect then and now.
- Ask, "What life lessons might this teach?"

Coming Up with Life Lessons

WHEN YOU CONFER WITH YOUR WRITERS ON THIS DAY, you'll want to coach into the entries they are writing and the ideas they are growing about history. Encourage your writers to use elaboration prompts to grow their thinking on the page, and compliment the ways they are using the details of history to inspire lessons they can apply to their own lives.

When I pulled alongside Kathryn, I noticed she was writing about the Sons of Liberty. She had focused on the fact that this group used to tar and feather people. Her entry was a detailed description of the event, along with some commentary about how gross and mean it was to do such a thing.

"Kathryn, how's it going? I noticed the detail about the Sons of Liberty tar and feathering someone really struck you, and you wrote a lot about it. Can you tell me more about the work you're doing in your notebook?"

"I'm just writing about it, how it makes me feel. It's really gross! And I wouldn't want to be around those kinds of people."

"Kathryn, there's something you've done that I think is working really well. You've chosen a detail that stirred a strong emotional response in you, and you've started saying more about it. That is going to lead you to some powerful writing. Can I give you a tip? You just told me that you wouldn't want to be around those kinds of people. That kind of thinking and writing, imagining yourself in the time period and thinking about the choices you would make if you were in the shoes of the people you're reading about, is a launching point to get ready to think about life lessons. Right now, try imagining that you are there, in the time right before the war. What would you say? Or do? What choices would you make? Imagining yourself there helps writers think about the life lessons that can be learned from this part of history. I'll let you work on that, and then I'll come back."

MID-WORKSHOP TEACHING Uncovering Deeper Ideas about Historical Figures by Asking, "What Did This Person Really, Really Stand For?"

I called for students to take a brief pause in their writing. Once I had everyone's attention, I began. "Many of you have been reading stories of the Continental Congress and Valley Forge just as you've read stories of Stuart Little and Willy Wonka. I know, as you've thought about history as a story, you've been thinking about the fact that history, like literature, has its main characters. Quickly, think of three main characters of the American Revolution." Then I said, "One way to grow ideas about history is to think of a historical figure and to ask, 'What can I learn from that person's life story?'

"What can we learn from Benedict Arnold's life story? Ben Franklin's?" Children talked, and then I said, "Of course, the people you are mentioning are not just one way. They are complicated. So one question to ask is: Why has history told the story of that person in just that way? How does the story of that person fit into other life lessons and deeper meanings of other American Revolution stories?

"This is complicated work, so turn and talk about it." After children talked, I pointed out that I would add that new strategy to our chart and channeled students back to work.

When I returned, Kathryn had written the following (see Figure 19–1):

"Kathryn, this is a really important start. You imagined yourself right in the time period, and I noticed you are writing about some of the issues that are emerging for you. You are ready to add on the next part, which is asking yourself what lessons could be

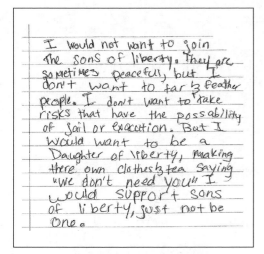

FIG. 19–1 Kathryn's writing about life lessons learned from this period of history

learned from this. You can say to yourself, 'This is important because . . .' or, 'A lesson I learned from this is . . .' and then write some of what you are thinking."

Right away, Kathryn said, "A lesson I could learn is that it's never okay to hurt others and be violent, even if it's for a good reason!"

I nodded and continued, "Kathryn, I'm going to leave you to it; you've got a lot to write, I can tell. Remember, anytime you notice yourself just writing about one little detail and not about bigger ideas or lessons, you can put yourself right into the time period, imagining what it would have been like to be there, and thinking about the choices you would have made. I'll leave you to it."

In addition to the kind of coaching we did with Kathryn, we have some language that we use often when teaching kids to think interpretively while reading. The following questions might be helpful for you to use and offer to your writers on this day as you confer and pull small groups.

- What is this text (or part of a text) *really about*?
- What does this text (or part of a text) say about the world?
- What do I think the author is trying to say?
- Whose story is being told?
- What are the big ideas I have been identifying so far?
- What parts of the text do not fit with those ideas?
- If the author has written his or her point in ten words instead of all these thousands of words, what would it have said?
- What is the lesson from this book that fits not just this story but also lots of other ones? And my life?

Adding Powerful Notebook Writing to Your Drafts

Channel students to reread their notebook entries, boxing out important ideas. Then ask them to reread their informational books, looking for places where these ideas would help their draft.

"Writers, you can stay at your writing spots for this share session, because I want to give you a chance to do some more writing. Over the last few days, you've been collecting some very thoughtful (and thought-provoking) entries in your notebooks. Some of you have started to carry over those ideas into your drafts. I wanted to give all of you a chance to do that, if you haven't already, because those big ideas you are growing, those thoughts you are having about your topics, those are going to make your book uniquely yours, and not just another book of facts all about your topic.

"So right now, look over some of the entries you have written. Box out any ideas that seem to be really powerful or important. Look for any new ideas you grew over the past couple of days that made you say 'Aha!' or 'Yes, that's it!' Then, search in your book for a place where that writing might help you draft. Think about the ways you searched for places where you could add a quote from a famous person or published source. This is kind of like that, only this time, what you are adding is your own thinking. I'll give you the next seven minutes or so to start searching for big ideas that might help your books, and to add those in, so go ahead and get started."

As writers worked, I peeked over their shoulders and offered a tip or two. Grayson was writing the following (see Figure 19–2):

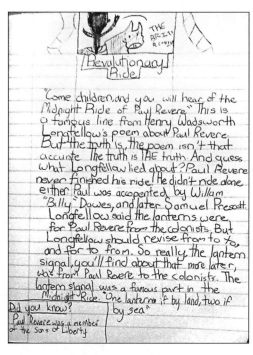

FIG. 19–2 Grayson shares some ideas she grew while reading The Midnight Ride of Paul Revere.

> *"Come children and you will hear of the Midnight Ride of Paul Revere." This is a famous line from Henry Wadsworth Longfellow's poem about Paul Revere. But the truth is, the poem isn't that accurate. The truth is THE truth. And guess what Longfellow lied about? Paul Revere never finished his ride! He didn't ride alone, either.*

After a few more minutes, I called for the class's attention. "Writers, I thought I'd end the share session today by naming what one writer has done that might help others in this class. Grayson is writing about the Midnight Ride of Paul Revere, and she decided to begin a whole new chapter about the true story of the ride because of some of the reading and thinking she is doing. Her chapter begins with a quote from the poem by Henry Wadsworth Longfellow that we all studied. After the line, she tells a bit about the poem, then she shares some of the ideas she grew about it while reading. This is something that might help some of the rest of you, to first include a part from a book or published source (maybe even a direct quote!), then to say a bit about it, then to share your thoughts. I'm going to ask Grayson to read what she wrote so you can hear how she put it all together. It might inspire you to do similar work."

CONTINUE WORK GROWING IDEAS IN NOTEBOOKS

Writers, you have been doing very impressive work throughout this entire unit. Believe it or not, we're nearing the end. Today's work, trying to figure out what these historical events are really about, what the life lesson is, is very important work. Essentially, it's what makes your writing *yours*. *Your* ideas, *your* interpretation of the events. Tonight I want you to continue that work in your writer's notebook. Continue writing off of the annotations in your source materials, growing ideas in your entries. You might use this writing in your draft eventually!

Using Confusions to
Guide Research

IN THIS SESSION, you'll teach students that nonfiction writers don't always start out as experts on the topic they're writing about, but instead work to become short-term experts on their topic. They start with their musings, then turn these into research questions, and then see what they can learn.

GETTING READY

✔ Chart paper and marker (see Teaching and Active Engagement)

COMMON CORE STATE STANDARDS: W.2.b, W.4.8, W.4.9, RI.4.1, RI.4.3, RI.4.7, RI.4.9, SL.4.1, L.4.1, L.4.2, L.4.3

172

THIS BEND HAS OPENED UP A NEW KIND OF WRITING. Children are turning back to the reference books, but this time it isn't information they're gathering. Instead, they're using history books as a springboard for their own thoughts and ideas. All of a sudden, it isn't about what happened in history but about what a student *makes* of those events.

But capturing ideas for writing is neither easy nor straightforward, and so along the way, you'll want to show writers some specific strategies to generate deeper ideas. As part of this, you might teach students the value and power that comes from asking research questions. It is hard to imagine a lesson that could matter more than teaching students that writing well requires a genuine curiosity about a topic and the ability to articulate great questions.

You may have expected an emphasis on asking questions to come at the start of this unit. After all, many traditional methods of teaching suggest that research involves SQR: Survey Question Read. There is truth to that—early on in a research project, one asks questions such as, "What was the Continental Congress anyway?" But it is after a person knows the basics of a topic that he or she can ask questions that can really open up a topic.

In this session, you will teach your writers to welcome the questions that surface as they struggle to understand a topic. After all, chances are good that the questions they find themselves asking will be the questions that others, learning about the same topic, also need answered. You'll encourage your students to stop avoiding the hard questions. You'll teach that confusions—and the questions they inspire—are the valuable fodder from which the best research efforts stem.

Of course, for a question to drive research, it needs to be a researchable question. Scientists have long known that one way to make a question more researchable is to offer one possible hypothesis—and that's true, also, for historians. The thought prompt "Could it be . . ." can help a historian crystallize his or her musings into something that can be researched.

Try it. Ask a simple question. "Why isn't it raining today?" (Usually our questions don't feel researchable until we tinker with them a bit.) Now add, "Could this be because. . . ."

At once you'll come up with one or two theories about why the clouds aren't bursting—"Could this be because the rain clouds were blown away by the wind?" or "Could this be because the clouds are still building up?" At once, you have more concepts to explore. In addition to thinking about *rain*, you can now think also about *cloud*, *wind*, *building up*—all of which can be bread crumbs along the trail of learning.

"It is hard to imagine a lesson that could matter more than teaching students that writing well requires a genuine curiosity about a topic and the ability to articulate great questions."

Researchers, in fact, call this process "narrowing" or "refining" a research question. You'll let youngsters know that a single question leads to related questions. It brings a writer's own ideas out onto the paper. The process of exploring will be full of dead ends, then, but also new trails. It is an exploratory process; that's the life of research.

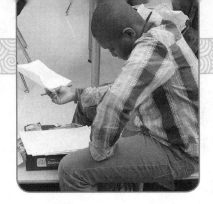

Using Confusions to Guide Research

CONNECTION

Tell the story of a journalist who writes articles on topics—and describes himself not as an expert but as an avid learner, taking crash courses.

"Writers, one of my friends from school became a newspaper journalist, and whenever we bump into each other, we sit together over coffee and talk about writing. He thinks it's cool that I teach writing. I think it's cool that he reports a new story every day.

"'You must know an awful lot about everything,' I said to him the other day. 'In yesterday's paper, you wrote about the problems faced by war veterans, the day before you'd written about camel jockeys in the Middle East, and now you're writing about the current Congressional hearings. How can you be an expert on so many different things?'

"Writers, he laughed and told me something that I knew I'd have to share with you. He said, 'If I had to write only about stuff that I'm an expert on, all I'd ever write about are the Yankees' scores and my mother's pecan pies. *Of course* I don't know everything there is to know about camel jockeys in the Middle East. But if there is a topic I'm writing about, I become what you might call a "short-term expert."' I asked him to explain, and this is what he told me: Short-term experts read up about their topic, you can say they give themselves a crash course."

Explain that you asked the journalist what the secret was to crash courses on a topic, and he said that the key is to pay attention to your questions and confusions.

"When my journalist friend told me this, I knew you'd want to learn from him. I knew you'd want me to ask, 'What's the secret to those crash courses? How do you make them work?' So I asked those questions—and he told me that the really key thing is that a researcher needs to explore what he or she *doesn't* know about a topic; a researcher needs to look for the gray areas. The gray areas, the confusions and the really perplexing questions, actually guide the research.

"Writers, I have to tell you I was confused. I had thought maybe it would be wiser and easier to compile known facts, and to avoid the hard and confusing stuff about a topic. 'No way!' he told me. 'The hard parts are the best parts. Non-fiction writers actually *hunt* the confusions and the complications. That's where the most interesting facts and stories are hidden!'

If you are going to use anecdotes as a way to draw students into your minilessons, it helps if many of those anecdotes reveal to students the life of rich literacy. That is, you could probably have drawn on stories from many realms of life to make the point that researchers value their questions. The fact that this connection humanizes journalists and shows a kinship between their work and the work that students are doing is important.

This is a Small Moment story, and it is given life by the craft moves that are also critical to the stories children write. Notice that the people are speaking and their exact words are quoted. Notice that the story is embedded with details. Also, even though this is a little tiny anecdote, it is shaped as a story, with a problem and a solution.

✤ Name the teaching point.

"You already know that nonfiction writers don't always start out as experts on the topic they're writing about. Writing often involves taking a crash course on the topic. When taking those crash courses, nonfiction writers start with their musings, then turn these into research questions, and then see what they can learn."

TEACHING

Tell the story of when you researched a topic and generated questions but dismissed them to focus only on recording facts. Suggest it was wasteful to dismiss the questions; they could have directed your research.

"Writers, the more I thought about what my journalist friend said, the more I began to see what he meant. I remember when I first read about the Boston Tea Party. I was your age, doing some research on the topic for a paper I had to write. I remember writing down all the facts that the books told me—where and when the Tea Party was, what happened after it.

"But what I really remember is that I was confused over the fact that the books said the tea was grown in East India and brought to Britain, and then *they* shipped it the United States. I remember thinking, 'Why did the tea have to go to Britain anyhow, and why did the Americans pay taxes to the British? Why didn't the Americans just get tea from East India directly and cut the British out of the whole story? Or more to the point—why didn't the Americans just grow their own tea? Or drink coffee?' To me, it seemed like a whole lot of fuss over tea, which no one in *my* house used to drink anyway.

"I remember having those questions, but to do my research, I pushed those questions to the side, I tried to wall them out of my mind, and wrote down the facts. And I definitely skipped right past that whole business about 'Why tea anyway?' and focused on what I knew: where and when the Tea Party was."

"But here is the thing. What I have since learned is that I was really wasteful. I totally wasted those great questions—questions that could have made my writing and my thinking so much better. What I didn't know back then was that unanswered questions are so *valuable*. I should have jotted my musings down and then used them to make research questions."

Teach students how to make researchable questions, starting with musings, crystallizing them into research questions, then speculating on possible answers, which become yet more questions.

"I want to show you how to make and use research questions. You start by wondering, and then try to shape your musings into a question. Sometimes I word the question in a bunch of different ways, because I never know how someone might word the answer."

We believe that the concepts being taught here have the power to make a world of difference. The goal, when teaching research writing, can't just be for students to move information from one place to another. Nor can the goal just be qualities of good writing—powerful action words, rich descriptions, varied sentences. Instead, your teaching needs to aim to support the intellectual work that makes for powerful information writing. Figuring out what that work involves is not easy—we believe this minilesson is one of several in this book that addresses the crux of this. We're aware, of course, that this is challenging work, and that this minilesson will only live up to its potential if you support it carefully in your conferences and small-group work. But we encourage you to do that.

Aloud, I pondered, "Tea went from East India—all the way to Britain—and then all the way to America. . . . Wouldn't it be easier and cheaper to get the tea directly from East India?" On the chart paper, I wrote out the question:

Why didn't Americans buy the tea directly from East India?

"The key is not just to ask a question, and then carry the question around like a magnet, looking for an answer to pop out and stick to it. Instead, what helps is to think about the question. One way to do that is to speculate on possible answers. Try saying 'Could this be because . . . ' In this case, 'Could this be because—they weren't *allowed* to buy this tea?' Then I said, 'Let me rephrase the question.' I wrote a second question that stemmed from the first one.

Could this be because America wasn't allowed to buy tea from India?

Aloud, I answered, "Why not? Who or what could stop them? The British? Did the British make a law that forbade them from getting tea directly? It sounds just like something they'd do . . . " I added another question to the chart.

Could it be that there was a law that said that America couldn't buy tea directly from India?

Debrief in ways that are transferable to another day and another text.

"Writers, do you see what I'm doing? It's the same question; I'm just asking it another way and another way. I'm thinking: 'Could this be because . . . ?' and I then make another question, and another question. Now I have many different ways of looking at my original question."

ACTIVE ENGAGEMENT

Showcase one student's confusion about a topic and elicit the whole class's help in formulating a research question from this.

"Writers, yesterday when I was walking around among you, asking, 'How's it going?' I noticed Willa was glaring at the page before her and not budging. I asked her how her writing was going, and she just shook her head and said she was stuck.

"But then, class, Willa said something else. She said, 'I'm stuck on a big question. I'm trying to just forget it.' And class, you know my feelings about that. I think a good question is too precious to waste, unless we see no way to begin answering it. So anyhow, Willa, tell us the rest of this."

Willa began: "I was planning a chapter about the two sides. 'Cause in a war, there's always two sides. So I wrote British on one side and Colonist Americans on the other. But when I was researching this, I read that some *Americans* were actually on the side of the *British*. These guys were called loyalists. And I don't get why any Americans would want to be

In the mid-workshop teaching, you'll come back to these questions to talk about methods for finding answers to them, so leave the questions in a visible spot.

Teachers, you'll see that the effectiveness of this active engagement requires the support of a student. I used Willa's help to show the class that confusions are real and that the ways out of them are accessible to them all. Of course I did have to speak to Willa before class to get her okay and to help her rehearse our presentation.

Teachers, it would have been simple to tell Willa that some loyalists were actually Northern Anglicans who didn't want a breach with the Church of England—and some loyalists were wealthy merchants who actually benefited from the trade and taxation with the British. But if I were to give her this information outright, I might as well hijack her entire research effort and coauthor her book. Sometimes, although it's the hardest thing to do, a teacher simply has to step back and let the students figure out what to do.

loyalists—how could they be loyal to unfair taxes? It makes no sense. So—that's why I was confused." Willa stopped and began looking at me.

Channel writers to help the student you showcased turn a general question into hypothetical answers that can be researched.

"Writers, you heard her confusion. Right now, I want you to turn to the person next to you and come up with a research question that captures Willa's confusion." After about a minute, I asked students to volunteer various suggestions before writing one down on the chart.

> Why did some Americans become loyalists?

"This is a great research question. Let's add 'Could it be . . .' and come up with a theory of why this might have happened, why some Americans might have become Loyalists. Turn to your partners again and come up with another question that stems from, 'Could it be . . . ?'"

After a while I invited suggestions and wrote a few down:

> Could it be that some Americans were afraid of annoying the British?
>
> Could it be that the loyalists were getting money from the taxes?
>
> Could it be that the loyalists didn't want to go to war with the British?

LINK

Point out to researchers that good questions get to the heart of a topic and often ask "why"?

"Researchers, once you become something of an expert on a topic, you'll find that your questions crystallize—and those questions can lead you into a crash course. The questions we have just studied were all aimed to get at the heart of the matter. They were 'why' questions, and they were central to the whole research topic.

"I'm pretty sure you could come up with silly questions that wouldn't be helpful to your research at all. Right now, think of a really silly question that is tangentially related to your topic." I gave the children a moment to think. "Let's not even breathe those silly questions. Instead, your work today will be to put yourself into a crash course to learn as much as you possibly can, as fast as possible. Be sure that you shift from researching, to writing—and remember that a good question is too precious to waste."

"What Do You Really Want to Know?"
Finding Worthwhile Questions

TODAY, MANY STUDENTS MAY NEED SUPPORT crafting the kinds of questions that yield nuanced, out-of-the-box thinking. When teaching kids to read fiction more deeply, one thing we teach them is to ask questions that do not have an easy or quick answer, but ones that they will need to carry with them for a while as they read on.

To answer questions such as these, readers must collect evidence from more than one place in the book before they begin to formulate a conclusion. On this day, you can teach your writers to do the same thing as they formulate questions about history that are worth thinking more deeply about.

MID-WORKSHOP TEACHING   **No More Needy Rabbits**

Perhaps because I'd encouraged high-level thinking, more than the usual number of students were lining up for help. When the line was especially long, I said to the class, "Writers, can I stop all of you?" I waited until I had everyone's attention. "Would you look at what's following me?" and I gestured to the line of children, each wanting direction. "I feel like the Pied Piper!"

Then I said, "Watch this," and turned to the first student in line. "Why are you here?" I asked.

Paul shifted from one foot to another uneasily. "Well, see, um, I got my notes on Ben Franklin's newspaper, so I wondered if I can write that chapter of my book, or should I go on and get stuff about his later years?"

"What do you think would be a good plan?" I asked.

"To write?" Paul said, his inflection rising to suggest he really wanted an affirmation.

"So it seems like you are able to make that decision all by yourself, aren't you? Being a writer means making decisions—and you are great at that. Next time, you won't need to come to me—just say to yourself, 'I'm a writer, and writers make decisions.'"

Then I turned to the next person in line, and asked, "Why are you here?"

In this way, I channeled students to make decisions. One wanted to know whether he could write two small final chapters, each pursuing a different question rather than one longer one; another wanted to know if it was okay to pursue a question that was more about today than about the Revolutionary War. With each student, I made a great show of asking, "What do you think?" and of saying "So you didn't actually need to come to me after all, did you?"

Then I said to the class, "Do you know that song that goes (and I sang it) 'In a cabin in the woods, a little old man at the window stood. Saw a rabbit hopping by, knocking at his door. Help me, help me! the rabbit cried . . . '" I accentuated the rabbit's needy plea, and threw my arms up in sync with the bunny's cries. Then I stopped singing and said, "Well, sometimes you all remind me of that little bunny. You line up behind me to say (and I squeaked, and threw my arms up in utter neediness) 'Help me, help me.' You guys forget how much you know. Do you need *me* to tell you, 'Better shift from researching to writing?' No way! Do you need *me* to tell you to that you can write two shorter chapters instead of one longer one? No way! Do you need *me* to remind you that you can write your ideas, using words like *perhaps*? No way! So back to work. No more needy rabbits in this classroom."

Olivia, whose topic was Women of the Revolution, had written the following question in her notebook:

How would the soldiers have lived without the women?

I pulled my chair up next to Olivia, and began by prompting her to tell me more. "Olivia, can you say a bit about the question you've just written? Tell me a little about how it came to you and about what you plan to do next."

"Well, I was reading about these battles and I was thinking about all of those men and how they might have missed their families. I was thinking about what they would do without the women, at the camp."

I nodded, and prompted for her to continue.

"I was thinking I could research how the soldiers lived without the women because that would help me to know how much things were different for everyone after the war," she went on.

Before I moved into the teaching portion of my conference, I wanted to show her how close she already was to where I was going to push her next. "Olivia, I think you are getting close to a big idea here, close to something that will really help you as you research. I want to remind you of one thing—researchers often test questions before they start conducting research to make sure those questions are really, really what they want to know about. To me, it sounded like the question you asked and what you were really wanting to know might be two different things. To test this out, you could try answering your own question. See if the possible answers you come up with are the kinds of things you really, really want to know."

Olivia studied her question and said, "I think that without the women the soldiers were probably lonely. And maybe they missed being at home." She paused, thought for a moment, and then said, "But I really want to know how life was different for the women, too. I mean, did they have to take on more chores and work with the men gone?"

"Olivia, I think you are onto something here. Go back to your question. What is it you are really wanting to know?"

Olivia thought and then wrote in her notebook (see Figure 20–1):

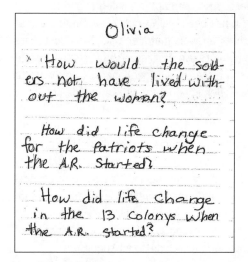

FIG. 20–1   Olivia's questions

She explained, "I think that I really want to know how life was different for the patriots, like the men in the army. But I also want to know about life in the colonies. Like, we read before about the jobs men and women had during Colonial times. I'm wondering how that was different, for women and for people."

I summed up the teaching. "Olivia, keep in mind that anytime you are testing a question to see if it's what you're really really wanting to know, you could try answering it yourself, and checking to see if the answer is what you are really wondering. If not, go back and revise your original question so it gets at what you really want to know."

In addition to channeling kids to ask potent questions, today's minilesson will have raised the stakes on research, and many students will need practical help searching for information. Of course, you can simply remind your writers of the strategies you taught in Bend I when they were initially collecting ideas for their books. But because the searching they are now doing is more specific and, in many cases, more sophisticated, you might need to offer additional support, perhaps in small-group lessons. You might begin by saying something like, "It has been really exciting for me to see that your questions are leading you to search for answers that aren't just lying right there in front of you. A few of you have been trying to use your research questions to guide Internet research, others of you are doing research with book indexes, so I want to give you a quick tip. To look things up, it is often important to use key words, not entire sentence-length questions."

Then for a few minutes you'd want to engage these writers in some shared practice. You might, for example, draw their attention back to one or two especially important words from one of the questions you'd discussed in the minilesson. Perhaps you'd channel the kids to study a question such as, "Could it be that there was a law that said that Americans couldn't buy tea directly from India?" As them to talk to each other briefly about the keywords that might quickly lead to finding this information. Elicit some of their ideas, and work together to test some of the keywords they suggested.

Finally, you'll also want to make sure that your writers are shifting from formulating questions and researching into note-taking. Be sure they are drawing on all they know about good note-taking, and that they are not just jotting down facts, but are taking some time to reflect and write longer notebook entries to begin synthesizing all they are learning.

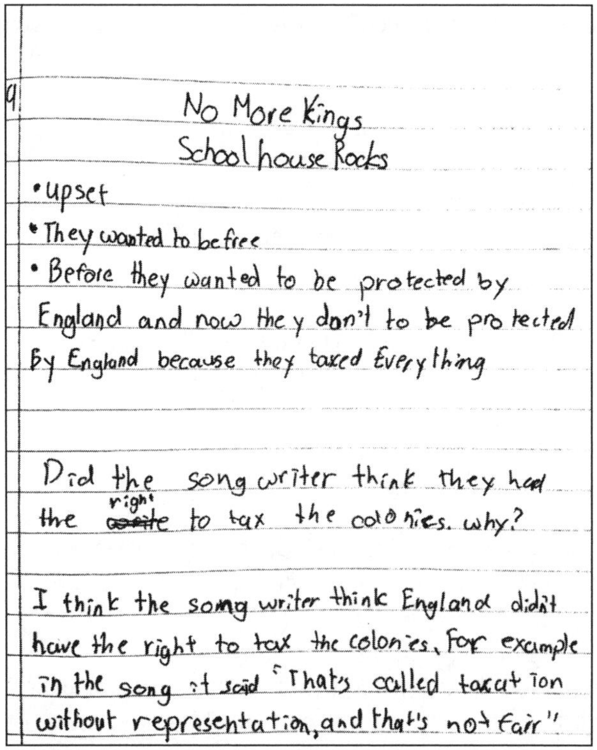
9

No More Kings
School house Rocks

• upset
• They wanted to be free
• Before they wanted to be protected by England and now they don't to be protected By England because they taxed Everything

Did the song writer think they had the right to tax the colonies. why?

I think the song writer think England didn't have the right to tax the colonies. For example in the song it said "That's called taxation without representation, and that's not fair."

FIG. 20–2 Edward's question and hypothesis

Note-Taking

Reflecting, Taking Stock, and Setting New Goals

Ask students to look back at the notes that they have taken over the course of the unit, analyze their note-taking, and share tips with partners.

"Writers, let's gather in the meeting area today. Bring your notebooks, and if you started a new notebook since the time we've started this unit, bring both of your notebooks. As you know, I usually spend all of writing workshop running around, helping as many of you as I can with your writing. Today, I decided to take a couple of minutes to just step back and study the note-taking you were doing. Then, I thought back to the kind of note-taking you were doing at the beginning of this unit. I think sometimes we get so caught up in what we are doing, we forget to reflect and take stock of how far we've come. And you've come so far as note-takers.

"Right now, would you take a moment to look back in your notebook and analyze your note-taking? Think about how far you've come. Tell your partner some of the ways you've grown the most, and be as specific as possible. You might start by saying something like, 'The top three ways I've grown as a note-taker are. . . .'"

I listened in while writers shared with their partners, complimenting ways writers were naming what they were doing in crystal clear, specific ways.

"Writers, can I stop you? I was listening to Jackson and Mirei talk to each other about what they have learned as note-takers. Jackson was saying that he is getting really good at using other kinds of note-taking to make sense of what he is reading. He showed Mirei a flowchart he had done recently on which he didn't just list events and show the order they happened, he also jotted some notes in between each event telling his thoughts about the choices some of the people made that led to the next event on the flowchart. And Mirei was saying that she is getting really good at choosing thought prompts that will help her to write longer.

"So, I started thinking that many of you are really getting good at certain things as note-takers, and you could give each other some really helpful tips. Would you finish our session today by teaching your partner something they could try as a note-taker? You might want to tell him or her step by step what to do, and perhaps show an example from your notes."

REREADING YOUR DRAFT TO COME UP WITH RESEARCHABLE QUESTIONS

Writers, today we talked about how as you learn more about your topic, as you become a short-term expert, you come up with questions and musings, which then guide you toward even *more* researchable questions. And then these *new* questions lead you to more research and note-taking, which then of course, lead you to refining your informational writing. Tonight, I'd like you to take home all of the chapters that you have drafted so far in this bend and reread. Now that you know more about your topic, see if you have more researchable questions that come up as you are rereading what you have already written. Jot these questions down, and then tomorrow you can continue to use these questions to guide your drafting.

Questions without a Ready Answer

F OR THE PAST FEW DAYS, your students have alternated between researching and writing. By today, your students will all be developing idea-based writing, using entries as grist for their writing—and thinking. Some of your students will find it easy to generate thoughtful entries; others will worry about being out on the thin ice of writing about ideas. They may, at times, feel stymied by all that they do not know—and let's face it, your students will still have giant gaps in their knowledge bases. Today's session aims to address those gaps. Your goal will be to help students understand that the fact that they have unresolved questions need not stop them in their tracks.

As a young teacher stepping into a room full of fidgety fourth-graders, I remember thinking with trepidation, "What if they ask me questions for which I don't have answers? Who made me the boss of all these little guys? Am I really knowledgeable enough to be their teacher?" Of course, it wasn't very long before I *was* asked those questions: "If the sun is made of gases, how does it stay in a ball? Why don't Egyptians mummify dead people anymore? What are eyeballs made of?" Much as I aspired to the image of the all-knowing teacher, I had to throw my hands up and admit, "I don't know!"

Something happened in the classroom when I got off my high horse and let my students in on the fact that their questions stumped me. My students and I forged a different sort of partnership. My students listened intently when I told them that for me, following a research question is sometimes like following a deer path in the woods. For a moment you are sure the path is taking you somewhere and then all of a sudden—huh? Did that deer just sprout wings and fly?

In this session, we encourage you to talk to your students about the times when questions remain unanswered. You'll want to tell them that when they can't find answers to a research question, the sheer fact that the answer is hard to find will be interesting to their readers. "Despite my research, this question remains unanswered," you can say, continuing to say, "I *do* have some theories, which are—a, b, and c." Then, of course, you'll provide backing for those theories.

IN THIS SESSION, you'll teach students that historians don't always find answers to every question they have. But they can use all of their research and knowledge to create possible answers to questions for which people can't find ready-made answers.

GETTING READY

✔ Chart paper with hypothetical prompts written out (see Active Engagement)

✔ "Suggestions for Drafting" chart, started in Session 11 (see Link)

✔ The Information Writing Checklist, Grades 4 and 5 (see Conferring and Small Group Work)

COMMON CORE STATE STANDARDS: W.4.2.a,b; W.4.5, W.4.10, RI.4.1, SL.4.1, L.4.1, L.4.2, L.4.3

Questions without a Ready Answer

CONNECTION

Tell the story of a student who asked a question for which there is no answer.

"Writers, a few years ago I had a student who, like you guys, was making a book about history. Except his book was about Ancient Egypt, not the American Revolution. Like you, he was a great asker of questions. So he came up to me one day and said, 'I have a question but I can't find the answer in any old book or encyclopedia.' So I asked him his question. This is what he wanted to know: 'Why did the Egyptians build pyramids instead of cubes?'"

"Cubes? Writers, his question had me totally flummoxed. But he'd been thinking, he said. 'Many buildings in warm climates are in cubes—so that there's more room inside to stand. Why did the Egyptians pick such a strange shape of building? They can't stand in half of it.' My student was stumped. He couldn't find an answer anywhere."

❧ **Name the teaching point.**

"Writers, today I want to teach you that historians don't always find answers to every question they have. But nonfiction writers—particularly historians—use all of their research and knowledge to create possible answers for questions for which people can't find ready-made answers."

TEACHING

Continue the story, showing the student creating possible answers for the unanswerable question.

"Writers, when my student asked me why Egyptians built pyramids, I was a bit speechless. It felt like a question with no answer and I was about to tell him—'You know, we can't rewind time and ask Tutankhamen the answer to that one—why don't you think of another ques . . .'" But he interrupted me. And it's a good thing he did because what he said next was pure brilliance.

◆ COACHING

To formulate an intriguing research question and research the related information and then develop several hypotheses, based on the known facts—this is strenuous intellectual work. It is more challenging than just penning down known facts under various chapter headings. This is the work that will bring students toward the kind of information writing that is central to the work of historians and scientists.

History, like science, is full of questions that writers don't have exact answers to. Who built Stonehenge? Did Cleopatra actually use a snake to commit suicide? Much of history writing involves collecting and sorting and comparing what various researchers know about a period, and then hypothesizing what that means for unanswered questions. Historians write about their confusions as a way to explore and hypothesize plausible answers. Sometimes an unanswered question can actually help create an entire chapter—and that chapter full of questions might very well be the most interesting chapter in a book!

"Maybe . . ." he began, his face full of concentration . . . "maybe they wanted the shape of their building to look like a mountain. Maybe some Pharaoh had traveled west and seen mountains and wanted to change the desert so it had mountains, so it wasn't all flat." I started to say that sounded like it could be true but before I could tell him, he started off again. "Maybe—maybe they thought a pyramid, with its stair-y edges, would help dead people's spirits travel up to the sky. Or . . . "

Step back to explicitly name your point. Stress that students of history will often not have hard-and-fast answers, so they need to become accustomed to fact-based conjecturing.

"Writers, he didn't find an answer, but he had read enough about Ancient Egypt to come up with his own hypotheses! It's true that we can't rewind history to go back to the sources and determine what really did happen. But if we have a question with no ready answer, we can certainly take our best guess based on what we *do* know—and we can write about our best-guess theories."

ACTIVE ENGAGEMENT

Tell the story of one of your students who started to do similar work, and whose efforts can now be extended. Recruit the class to help extend what your student started to do.

"Just the other day, Melissa did some similar work. She'd written this question in her notebook":

> Why did people have secret societies during this time?

"Like Melissa, you all know enough to speculate possible answers. Turn and talk, and try saying," and I flipped over a piece of chart paper where I'd written the phrases:

> "What I know that sort of relates is . . ."

> "So this makes me think that . . ."

After children talked for a few minutes, I intervened. "Listen to what Melissa actually did write, in response to her question," and then Melissa read this (see Figure 21–1):

> I think they had them to sneak up on the British and try to see what they are up to or what they are planning to do. And maybe they might get arrested if they didn't have secret societies.

"That will be an important addition to her report," I said.

When you tell this story, make sure that your "Maybe they wanted the shape of their building . . ." is said in a tentative, wondering sort of a voice. You are trying to demonstrate that writers speculate; they go out on the thin ice of conjecture. And it will be your tentative tone that conveys that ideas were dawning as the student spoke.

You might worry that your students won't understand the term *hypothesis*. In fact, you might wonder if students know the term Pharaoh. We encourage you to use domain-specific terms even if you aren't sure that students will comprehend them because this is how human beings use language. If you want, follow the term with a synonym.

① Why did people have secret societies during this time?
   I think they had them to sneak up on the British and try to see what they are up to or what they are planning to do. And maybe they might get arrested if they didn't have secret societies.

FIG. 21–1   Melissa's notebook entry

LINK

Remind your students of the many alternatives they have for the work they might be doing today, doing so in ways that emphasize that they need to be writing.

"So researchers, I know you are chomping at the bit to get started with today's work. Some of you will spend part of today taking notes to get ready for another chapter—I think asking questions and theorizing about possible answers can be something all of you do when you take notes.

"But others of you will start out immediately writing another chapter, perhaps following our chart. We should add some of our recent ideas to our chart, shouldn't we? Let's look at the chart and think about what we could say—and do—to get questions and theories into our chapters? Will you and your partner think about what you'd add to the chart?"

The children talked, and soon our chart had grown:

Suggestions for Drafting

- Make sure your chapter isn't too broad. Break big topics into several subtopics.
- Start by drafting information you know especially well.
- Think, "What kind of a text will this be?"
- If it's an all-about chapter, make a table of contents for the chapter.
- Start the chapter with a hook, then let readers know how the chapter will go.
- Use words such as <u>first</u> and <u>later</u>.
- Say your plan: "I'll first talk about—then I'll . . ."
- When writing, remember to say more about a subtopic.
- Am I teaching Information (or is my writing full of a lot of hot air, and not that many facts, statistics, quotes, names, dates, stories . . .)?
- Will my writing make sense to a reader or will readers go, "Huh?"
- Is my writing written in my own voice (or did I end up copying from a book)?

"How many of you are in the midst of writing one of the chapters for your information book? You can keep going. How many of you will be rereading your notes and rethinking your research, trying to locate some of the unanswered questions and thinking whether you have hypotheses you could share? You guys can get started, too.

"While you get started, I'm going to admire the way you guys make your own decisions, instead of being needy 'Help me, help me' rabbits."

Nudging Students toward Publication

THE FINAL DAY OF THE UNIT is approaching rapidly, and you want to make sure that all of your writers will have a piece they feel proud of come the day of the celebration. Information writing is a genre for which a stopping point can be difficult to determine. Unlike narrative writing with its clear beginning, middle, and end, or opinion writing, with its boxes-and-bullets structure, in information writing there is always another chapter that can be added, another avenue of thought that can be pursued. Today, you'll want to make sure that your writers are all working productively toward the finish line, and that they spend most of the day revising by adding some of the new thinking they are growing, and even deleting parts of their drafts that don't fit with these new theories.

You may want to convene writers who are lagging far behind, and help them create a task list or some other sort of plan so that they are mostly caught up by the end of today. Don't be afraid to be somewhat heavy-handed with these writers, suggesting they finish drafts of certain chapters and perhaps not others, or that they spend most of the workshop writing fast and furious, leaving some time at the end to check over the new writing they did for possible revisions. Some of these writers might not get to the heady work that others are doing, growing hypotheses based on questions, or perhaps they will try this work but it is not a focus for them. This is perfectly acceptable, as writing workshop is about writers working through the process with growing independence, tackling work that is appropriate for them, not moving lockstep through work that is too difficult for some, too easy for others.

You'll also want to keep in mind some of the most important qualities of informational writing as you confer. You might even want to keep the checklist in hand, using it to remind your writers (and yourself) of the most important goals it outlines. Two of the most critical qualities to keep in mind are organization and elaboration. The Common Core State Standards expect fourth-grade information writers to organize their writing

Information Writing Checklist

	Grade 4	NOT YET	STARTING TO	YES!	Grade 5	NOT YET	STARTING TO	YES!
	Structure				**Structure**			
Overall	I taught readers different things about a subject. I put facts, details, quotes, and ideas into each part of my writing.	☐	☐	☐	I used different kinds of information to teach about the subject. Sometimes I included little essays, stories, or "how-to" sections in my writing.	☐	☐	☐
Lead	I hooked my readers by explaining why the subject mattered, telling a surprising fact, or giving a big picture. I let readers know that I would teach them different things about a subject.	☐	☐	☐	I wrote an introduction that helped readers get interested in and understand the subject. I let readers know the subtopics I would be developing later as well as the sequence.	☐	☐	☐
Transitions	I used words in each section that help readers understand how one piece of information connected with others. If I wrote the section in sequence, I used words and phrases such as *before*, *later*, *next*, *then*, and *after*. If I organized the section in kinds or parts, I used words such as *another*, *also*, and *for example*.	☐	☐	☐	When I wrote about results, I used words and phrases like *consequently*, *as a result*, and *because of this*. When I compared information, I used words and phrases such as *in contrast*, *by comparison*, and *especially*. In narrative parts, I used phrases that go with stories such as *a little later* and *three hours later*. In the sections that stated an opinion, I used words such as *but the most important reason*, *for example*, and *consequently*.	☐	☐	☐
Ending	I wrote an ending that reminded readers of my subject and may have suggested a follow-up action or left readers with a final insight. I added my thoughts, feelings, and questions about the subject at the end.	☐	☐	☐	I wrote a conclusion in which I restated the main points and may have offered a final thought or question for readers to consider.	☐	☐	☐
Organization	I grouped information into sections and used paragraphs and sometimes chapters to separate those sections. Each section had information that was mostly about the same thing. I may have used headings and subheadings.	☐	☐	☐	I organized my writing into a sequence of separate sections. I may have used headings and subheadings to highlight the separate sections. I wrote each section according to an organizational plan shaped partly by the genre of the section.	☐	☐	☐

"Writers, can I stop you for a moment? One of my favorite writers, Antoine de Saint Exupéry, who wrote *The Little Prince*, has a saying about writing. He said, 'Perfection is achieved not when there is nothing more to add, but when there is nothing more to take away.' This really struck me when I read it, because I thought about how so much of the revision work we do is adding more and more. And of course, this is important and valuable work to do, especially since as information writers, we need to say a whole lot to teach others about our topics. But it's also important to study your writing and think, 'Based on the new ideas I'm growing, is there something here I could take away?' As you add new ideas to your writing, think about whether what you had written before all still fits. And if not, you might need to move something to another section, or take it out altogether."

into paragraphs and sections, and to elaborate with a wide variety of kinds of details. For some writers, you may need to reinforce your previous teaching on grouping information according to similarity in content, on making the structure of a chapter or a section clear to readers, and on using transition words to show how parts fit together. Other writers might have organized their writing well but could use extra support rounding out sections with rich information.

Of course, you'll also want to support the teaching you did in the minilesson, coaching writers not just to grow hypotheses about the information they are learning but to incorporate these new ideas into their writing.

I gathered Lucie, Jackson, and Thomas together. I wanted to show them how I took some of the ideas I was growing and integrated them into my writing.

"Writers, I want to show you how I integrated some of the ideas I was growing into my own writing. I went back and reread some of the writing I had done earlier. When I reread my chapter on the aftermath of the Boston Massacre, I wrote this question in my notebook":

> Why did John Adams defend the British soldiers, even though he was a patriot?

"Then, I did a bit of hypothesizing about this. Here is what I wrote":

> What I know that sort of relates is that John Adams was a patriot, and he believed very strongly in fairness and what was right. He believed that government should help people, and that people should be able to vote if they paid taxes. He also believed that everyone should be treated equally. So this makes me think that John Adams thought even British soldiers deserved fair treatment. He believed that being a true patriot doesn't just mean fairness for some, it means fairness for all.

"Writers, now I've got this huge idea that I've settled on. It feels really important. I realized that being a patriot and standing up for fairness doesn't just mean you only support those who are on your side. You have to fight for fair treatment for everyone. Now, I am going to go back to my draft, and see if there is a way I can bring out this important idea."

I then showed them the next section of my draft:

> Another thing that happened after the massacre was the trial of the British soldiers. Everyone knew that John Adams was a patriot, so they were very surprised when he decided to defend the British soldiers in their trial. He said that the soldiers deserved a fair trial, just like everyone else. In the end, two of the soldiers who fired on the crowd, Matthew Kilroy and Hugh Montgomery, were accused of manslaughter. Their punishment was to be branded on the thumb and kicked out of the army.

"Hmm, . . . I'm thinking that I can add something about this in the part where I talk about John Adams defending the soldiers. I'm going to add a line or two with my new idea":

> Another thing that happened after the massacre was the trial of the British soldiers. Everyone knew that John Adams was a patriot, so they were very surprised when he decided to defend the British soldiers in their trial. He said that the soldiers deserved a fair trial, just like everyone else. John Adams's decision shows that for him, being a true patriot means fighting for fairness for all, not

just for the people on your side. In the end, two of the soldiers who fired on the crowd, Matthew Kilroy and Hugh Montgomery, were accused of manslaughter. Their punishment was to be branded on the thumb and kicked out of the army.

"Writers, you know what I just realized when I added this new part? The second part, about what happened to the soldiers, doesn't really go now. I think the first part is all about John Adams defending the soldiers, and I want to highlight that important central idea. So I'm going to make that part be its own paragraph." I quickly added a paragraph symbol before the phrase "In the end."

I debriefed, naming what I had done. Then, I asked the students to get started mining their notebooks for ideas that could be put into their writing. I coached as they worked, aiming to reach each writer twice to support them as they worked through the process.

Sharing Big Ideas
Creating a Living Text

Ask students to find a line in their writing that is an example of a big idea they are proud of. Have students share by creating a living text.

"Writers, let's gather in the meeting area. Because today's workshop was all about growing ideas, I want to celebrate some of the ideas you grew. Right now, would you look through all of the writing you did, either in your notebook as you were growing ideas or in your drafts as you added new ideas to your writing, and would you box or star a sentence or two that captures the idea you're most proud of? In a moment, you're going to create a living text out of all of your ideas, by saying them out one at a time. It will be interesting to see how many of your ideas fit together. Okay, take a moment to find the idea you want to share."

When it seemed most writers had finished, I convened the class. "Writers, I'm going to be silent as you are sharing. Someone can start us off, and when you feel the time is right, go ahead and say out your idea. You don't have to wait for me."

I moved off of my chair and sat off to the side. After a moment, Melissa broke the silence.

She said, "The Boston Massacre is important is because it changed history. For example, it changed history because the Boston Massacre led to more events in history and added to the Revolutionary War."

Lucie was next. "The Boston Massacre was not just the Redcoats' fault. The colonists were using weapons, too."

Then, Willa said, "Some people stayed loyal because they thought government run by rich patriots would be bad. Maybe they thought rich patriots would be just as bad as being ruled by the king."

After everyone in the class had shared, I returned to my chair and said, "Writers, I noticed something about what a lot of you were saying. I noticed that a lot of you are starting to think about the many sides of history. You are noticing that there are other perspectives and points of view to consider besides just the ones in the history books. Your writing is becoming chock-full, not just of facts, but of ideas, too."

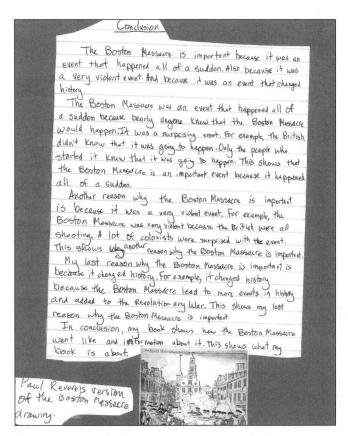

FIG. 21–2   Melissa's writing

FINISHING DRAFTS AND MAKING A SOURCE LIST

Writers, tomorrow will be the final day you have in class to work on your informational books before our writing celebration. Our focus will be on editing and getting pieces ready for publication, so it is important that you take the time to finish your drafts tonight. As with all nonfiction writing, it is also important that you have a list of the research sources that you used. Please come to writing workshop with a list of your source information as well.

Editing

ear Teachers,

You are in the home stretch of this unit, and what a journey it has been! Today is the last day's work session in this unit, meaning it will be the final day for your students to do any of the major work needed in an information writing unit. Prior to today, it will be important for you to do a quick assessment of your writers' work to decide how best to angle your teaching in this session and to make sure you include everything you need to include. Are there any niggling issues your writers are still having, such as lumping facts together that don't really go, or not including text features to elaborate, or perhaps including too many text features?

In this letter, we channel you to use this session to concentrate on punctuation rules that not only are identified by the Common Core as important for fourth-grade writers, but also are important rules for information writing in particular. In addition to some of the fourth-grade Common Core–identified rules, such as "Use commas and quotation marks to mark direct speech and quotations from a text" (CCSS L4.2b), punctuation rules that are key in informational writing are: using commas to offset definitions, using commas in a series (CCSS L5.2a), and using commas in dates. The teaching in this session channels writers to check their work, keeping all of these rules in mind.

At the end of the session, plan to give writers some time to reflect on how far they have come as writers and to take stock of all they have learned. Encourage writers to return to their list of personal goals and to take pride in checking off all of the ones they reached.

MINILESSON

You may want to begin with an anecdote that illustrates the power of punctuation in informational writing. Thomas Jefferson, one of the time period's most prolific writers, was known to use the commas not just because he was correctly following the conventions of grammar, but as a tool to show emphasis and even to give cues to those reading his

COMMON CORE STATE STANDARDS: W.4.2.a,b,c,d,e; W.4.5, RFS.4.4, SL.4.1, L.4.1, L.4.2, L.4.3.a,b; L.4.4.a, L.5.2

writing aloud. In fact, his original documents, many of which can be found by going to the website of the National Archives, are riddled with commas. Scholars today often change some of Jefferson's punctuation to fit with current standard practice. You might tell your writers a version of this story, and then explain that, in information writing, punctuation, in addition to words, is a powerful teaching tool.

As you name your teaching point, be sure to contextualize the purposes for today's work, for example: "Today I want to remind you of the power of the comma in informational writing. Writers often think of the comma as a way to help readers know when to pause. But in informational writing, the comma can also act like a spotlight saying, 'Hey! This information is important!'"

You may want to begin by reminding students of the importance of punctuation. You might say something like, "Writers, as you've been learning since you first learned to write, the tiniest marks on your page pack a lot of power. Those marks, like periods, question marks, and commas, help readers to understand the meaning of your words and to be able to read your writing with ease and expression. One such mark, the comma, is particularly important in informational writing." You could demonstrate this by telling the story of a former student who found that his readers were missing important information in his writing, likely based on poor punctuation. You could enlarge the writing sample, and then ask your students to turn and talk about where the writer went astray in his punctuation.

On April 18 1775 Paul Revere set out on his famous ride from the North End of Boston Massachusetts. He was qualified for this job because he worked as an express rider carrying news messages and copies of resolutions to other cities.

You could then go on to have a discussion about where commas should be placed, and from this discussion, extract the three most common uses for the comma in informational writing: between the day and year in a date, between a city and state in a location, and to separate items in a list.

For the active engagement portion of your minilesson, your students could practice checking for or inserting commas, either in their own writing or in another writing sample that you have enlarged.

Because today is the last session before the celebration, remind your writers that it is a big day! Encourage them to use everything they know as information writers and as teachers, to draw on all they have learned not just today but over the course of the whole unit, and to use all of their energy getting their pieces ready for publication. Get them fired up for writing, reminding them not to let a minute of the workshop go to waste.

CONFERRING AND SMALL-GROUP WORK

Just as many of your writers struggle to let go of their work, wanting to add on here or there, fix this or that, keep tweaking one page or another, it may be difficult for you to wrap up instruction and to shift your teaching toward just supporting your writers with finishing touches. It may be very tempting for you to run around helping your writers to make last-minute improvements and tweaks. But today is not the day for large-scale revision. There won't be time for that. Instead, today is the day for you to adopt less of a coaching stance and more that of a cheerleader. A cheerleader with an agenda, of course!

You might want to focus much of your time on this day to giving sincere and authentic compliments to help your writers feel positive about their pieces and to support transference of all they learned to their next writing experience. These compliments might contain some quick tips, such as: "Willa, I'm noticing that you are looking through your writing with a fine-tooth comb, searching for places where you might need to fix up your editing. To help with this work, you might keep an eye out for the parts of informational writing that are often in need of editing fixes, such as quotations and definitions. This also might be a nice time to check that you gave credit to the source of all the quotes you included, and that you defined all of the important terms a reader would need to know somewhere in your text."

When you do offer teaching points to your writers, aim to limit them to quick tips or enticing suggestions, and to steer away from heftier teaching unless you notice a writer is in serious trouble. In the latter case, concentrate your teaching on just one chapter or section of the writer's work, and channel the writer to just make fixes in that one section, thus making more in-depth revisions more manageable at the last minute.

Of course, in many of your conferences, you'll want to support kids' editing work. You might want to confer with certain rules in mind, and coach writers who need extra support with one rule or another. For example, you might decide to quickly gather writers who need extra support punctuating appositives. Teach these writers that commas are needed around a definition that is embedded in the text, but only if the sentence still makes sense with the definition removed. For example, in the following sentence, the definition requires commas, because the sentence would still make sense if the definition was removed:

The Hessians, German soldiers who were hired to fight against the colonists, were not expecting a surprise attack at the Battle of Trenton.

In the following case the sentence would not be complete if the definition was removed. It would only read "The Hessians were," so a comma isn't needed:

The Hessians were German soldiers who were hired to fight against the colonists.

MID-WORKSHOP TEACHING

Another important and quick tip you can give your writers, in addition to the punctuation rules you taught, is to do a last check that they included all of the words their readers will need, to fully understand their topics.

You might share an anecdote in which you tell about a time that learning the language of experts made you *feel* like an expert. For example, you might say: "I am a huge fan of TED talks, the popular video site that showcases amazing people teaching fascinating topics. When I watch these talks, I immediately feel smarter. After watching a talk about doctors using 3-D images to study the human heart, for example, I sort of felt like an expert. I want to teach you a little of what I learned."

Before continuing, you could make a show of sitting up taller on your chair, and clearing your throat to signal you are about to teach. Then go on to share some of the things you learned by watching the TED talks, using specific expert vocabulary and terminology.

Resume your normal posture as you debrief, noting how using the *language* of experts make you feel and sound like an expert.

Explain to your students that they also are experts on a topic. In this case, they are experts on a time period in history. They, like the scientists, know certain words about their topics that experts know.

Invite them to help you to quickly brainstorm a list of words that experts on the Revolutionary War use. Suggest that they study the texts they brought to the meeting area to get ideas, if needed. With the class's help, quickly construct a chart of commonly used terms for the time period you are studying.

You may decide to take it a step further and teach your students that it simply isn't enough to use an important word once and never again. If a word is crucial to the topic, it should be used over and over, both because it is likely very important and so readers can learn it. You could ask writers to stop, choose a word, and count how may times they used it in the text, other than when they first introduced it. Using an important word only once or twice isn't enough. Give your writers a moment or two to search for other places that the word could be used. If it can only be used in one or two places, perhaps it isn't really all that important to the topic after all.

You might want to end your teaching with a recap of some of the steps writers take when adding a word and its definition to texts:

1. Make a list of the important words you plan to teach.

2. Decide when to introduce the word and definition for the first time.

3. Choose a way to define the word (more → less supportive) for readers.

SHARE

As a way to prepare for your celebration and also celebrate your writers' collective expertise, you could hold a share session in which you channel them to make connections between their topic and the topics of other writers. Tell them that, as a class, you will soon be opening your doors to lots of visitors who will be there to learn about the time period. Each of them will be sharing some important information about their topics in an Expert Fair. You could explain that it might be helpful to visitors if writers were grouped in a way that made sense. For example, as a class, you could decide that everyone writing about the Boston Massacre should be sitting together so that attendees can find the information on that topic easily. Just as information writing has a logical structure, so should your celebration, after all!

The Language of Experts on the Revolutionary War

Instead of	We can use
people who wanted to separate from England	patriots
people who didn't want to separate from England	loyalists
England's government	Parliament
people who were ruled by the King	subjects
people who came to the new land	colonists
someone learning a skill or job	apprentice
groups on the same side in a war	allies
fight	conflict

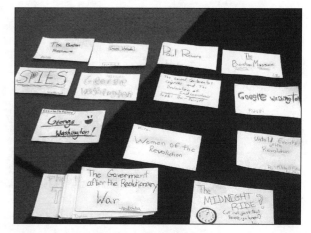

FIG. 22–1   Student's topics on notecards

You might ask writers to all write their topics on a note card, and to place their cards in the center of the meeting area. Then, channel writers to look for connections between topics. You might give your writers a few moments to study the cards, and then give them a few lenses to use to look for connections. Of course, writers with the same topic might go together, but there are other ways topics can be grouped. You might ask your writers to think about topics that go together because of chronology, or because of cause and effect (in other words, one led to the other), or perhaps because they represent contrasting ideas.

After your writers have had a chance to study all of the class topics and to think about patterns, you might get them going in a whole-class conversation to decide how to best organize themselves in groups for the celebration.

HOMEWORK

You might say, "Writers, this is it! The finish line is in sight; the race is almost over. Now is the chance to do the last-minute things you need to do, to be ready for the writing celebration. Since we will be having an Expert Fair that visitors will be strolling through, an attractive display will not only serve to teach visitors about your topic, but also attract them to your station. Use a piece of poster board to create this display. Are there pictures you want to draw? Diagrams or timelines you want to make? Images you want to attach? The choice is yours. But remember, an attractive, informative display will not only teach your visitors but will also draw them to your station."

Good luck!

Lucy & Anna

A Final Celebration

An Expert Fair

ear Teachers,

There were many options we tossed around when we thought about how best to celebrate this unit. One option we were considering was to suggest that you hold a celebration in which you invite younger students into your classroom and ask your students to teach them all they know about informational writing. This option is lovely, and one you might opt for instead of what we describe below. This kind of celebration would showcase all of the hard work and learning your students did and would emphasize the correlation between good information writing and good teaching.

In the end though, we decided on a kind of celebration that lends itself beautifully to informational writing in general and especially well to content-based informational writing. In this letter, we will discuss how you can set up and execute an Expert Fair, in which your writers will have the opportunity to teach others all they have learned about their topics.

Imagine the last expo or informational fair you attended, in which presenters were set up at booths, waiting for attendees to approach so they could begin brief but pointed mini-presentations. The celebration you could orchestrate on this day could be something like this. Your writers would be stationed around the room, ready with a short introduction to their topics, just a few sentences or so that capture the most important ideas from their books. Parents, other classes, and administrators might be in attendance, circling from one writer to the next, soaking up information. These kinds of celebrations are typically lively and informative, and usually are not too taxing to set up or orchestrate.

BEFORE THE CELEBRATION

Give your writers some time to prepare for the teaching they will be doing. It's best if they keep their presentations short and sweet, no more than a minute or two. Remind them of all they know about good teaching, that it helps to give a little introduction in which they tell listeners what they have in store for them.

COMMON CORE STATE STANDARDS: W.4.2, RFS.4.4, SL.4.1, SL.4.4, SL.4.5, SL.4.6, L.4.3

In the interest of time, you might want to have your writers choose just a chapter or two of their actual books to share with attendees, perhaps the ones of which they feel proudest. You'll want to teach your writers to avoid just reading page after page to attendees, because attendees have a lot of stations they need to visit. If you have the time, you might channel your writers to create signs or posters with the titles of their books and perhaps some images or big ideas that they really want to highlight.

Set up your classroom up by moving all of the desks to form a square around the perimeter of the room. Your students will be positioned on the outside of the square, and attendees will mingle in the middle, moving from table to table. Be sure that writers are organizing themselves according to the groupings they discussed in the previous session.

CELEBRATION

Make sure that each group has a place to set up, and give writers time to get their displays ready to present. Each writer will need space to display the pages he or she chose to share, as well as space to display any images he or she created for the purposes of the presentation. Depending on the space in your classroom and the audience you've invited, you might decide to have half of your class present while the other half mingles and attends presentations, switching halfway through.

You might ask writers to leave a blank page at their station with "compliments" written at the top. That way, attendees can jot a compliment or two for each writer (or each group).

As attendees enter, direct them to one of the stations. You'll likely need to spend some time directing attendees and making sure they move from station to station so that they can experience most, if not all, of the stations.

AFTER THE CELEBRATION

After the attendees have left, you might want to gather your class in the meeting area to reflect on a job well done. You may also want to pass out some sparkling juice and snacks, leading your writers in a toast to their hard work and perseverance. You can tell them that reflection with one's colleagues is important, and that after a day of teaching, you and your colleagues often gather in the teachers' lounge and reflect on your days over a cup of tea.

Then shift gears to talk more about what they learned about informational writing that they know they will carry with them, not just throughout the year, but throughout their lives. Celebrate those declarations most of all.

Congratulations, and enjoy!

Lucy & Anna

① The Boston
Massacre

A small battle in the Revolutionary War.

The site of the Boston
massacre today

② Introduction

During the 1760s and the 1770s, there was a lot of fighting between the **colonists** and the British. There was a war between them called the Revolutionary War. The colonists wanted to break away from England because they wanted America to be it's own country. And because they wanted to be independent and didn't want to be ruled by the King. There was a lot of battles between the British and the Colonists. The colonists finally wrote a **Declaration of Independence** and sent it to the King to Declare independence. One event leading up to the Revolutionary War is the colonists not want to pay taxes and wanting **independence** from the King. The **Revolutionary War** mostly took place in the eastern colonies. The colonists wanted America to be it's own country. Would you want to be in the Revolutionary War?

③ The Causes of the Boston Massacre

King George III of England got really mad at the colonists in America. One example that shows why he was mad at them is that they did not want to pay taxes on British goods (ex. lead, paint, glass, wine, tea, etc.). In 1768, King George III sent 4,000 British troops as well with a bunch of warships to the colonies to show them who is charge of them. The colonists got really upset about how they were being treated. King George was acting like he owned the people in the colonies. The Colonists did NOT like the King. The colonists were not even allowed to own their own guns or have a say about their property! The colonists were being treated like they were in jail! If I were a colonist, I would also be irritated.

The colonists were so fed up with this whole situation, that on the evening of March 5, 1770, a bunch of school boys started throwing snowballs, sticks, rocks, etc, and calling the guard names at the Customs House in Boston. The guard was Private Hugh White. The colonists said a lot of complaints about the King.

④ The Beginning of the Boston Massacre:

On the evening of March 5, 1770, Private Hugh White, a British soldier stood on guard duty outside the Custom House on King Street, today known as State Street. A crowd of school boys started throwing ice, snow balls, and rocks at Private Hugh White that was guarding the Custom House on King Street. The crowd around Private Hugh White got bigger & bigger. Church bells were rung which usually meant that there was a fire, which brought more people outside to King Street. Other British soldiers came instead of Private Hugh White to take care of what was going on. A colonist threw a stick at the British soldiers which hit Private Montgomery, one of the British soldiers, that was near Private Hugh White. Private Montgomery fell down to the ground and dropped his **musket** and angrily shouted, "Damn you, fire!" After a few seconds to a few minutes, the British soldiers fired into the crowd of colonists. A bunch of shots were fired which hit eleven men.

⑤ The End of the Boston Massacre

The Boston Massacre did not last more than about 30 minutes. You would think it would last far longer, for about a couple of days, but it didn't. The Boston Massacre did not last long, but it was bloody. During the Boston Massacre, there was 5 deaths and 6 people got wounded. 3 people died right at the spot and 2 people died a few days after. One of three people who died right at the spot was Crispus Attucks. He was the first African-American to be in the Revolutionary War. Crispus Attucks was a free slave. The other people that died are Samuel Gray, Samuel Maverick, James Caldwell, and Patrick Carr. The colonists had come up with the name "The Boston Massacre." The Boston Massacre was a bloody massacre. After the Boston Massacre, the colonists went on with their own lives, and so did the British. The British soldiers stayed in the USA because the Revolutionary War was not over...

⑥ Conclusion

In conclusion I wanted to tell you that the Battle of Trenton is a very important subject. 1 example is that without the Battle of Trenton we would still be under British control. Also it gave confidence to the Americans. You should reaserch the Battle of Trenton. It is a cool subject.

⑦ Glossary

colonists - a group of people who came to America for a new life from England.

independence - to be free from something.

massacre - a fight in which a lot of people on one side die.

musket - a gun with a long barrel used in hunting and battles.

Declaration of Independence - A letter to the King from the colonists to declare independence.

King George III - the king of England during the Revolutionary War.

Revolutionary War - A war between the colonists and the British.

FIG. 23-1 Melissa's book

①

The Battle of Trenton

By: Edward

Hessians Attacked! after their christmas feast

②

Intro

It's the Revolutionary War and colonists starts war because of British taxes like on tea, glass and all paper. Colonists lost so many battles, they are so poor and desprete for a win On the other hand British stood strong and suplied very well. Would Americans arm this next Battle called "The Battle of Trenton"?

The Battle of Trenton

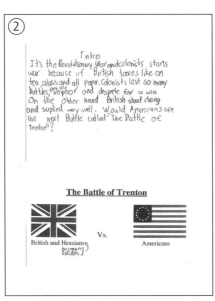

British and Hessians (German soldiers)   Vs.   Americans

③

Before the Battle

Before the battle there was a spy named John Honeyman He was a butcher from New Jersey. Americans thought he was for the British but really he was a spy for the Americans. He told the Americans that the Hessians were taking a break and having a christmas celebration so they were not ready to attack.

The strength on both sides were very different. The Hessians were very strong and supplied by the British. Also they were paid. On the other hand Americans were poorly fed, low on artillery

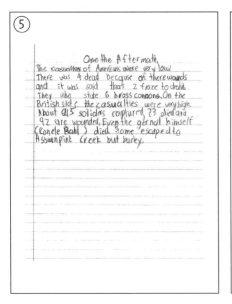

④

Crossing

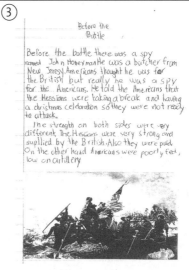

Did you know that this picture is very inaccurate. One reason why it is inaccurate because the flag wasn't established yet, Another reason why it is inaccurate is because that Washington wouldn't stand up on such dangerous river

Do you know why this picture is so famous? This picture is famous because it represented the turning point in the war

Going to Attack was not easy for the Americans. The christmas night was good for one side but not the other.

⑤

One the After math,

The casualties of Americans where very low. There was 4 dead because of there wounds and it was said that 2 froze to death. They also stole 6 brass cannons. On the British side the casualties were very high. About 915 soldiers captured, 23 died and 92 are wounded. Even the gernal himself (Conele Rahl) died. Some escaped to Assunpint Creek but barley.

⑥

Conclusion

In conclusion I wanted to tell you that the Battle of Trenton is a very important subject. I example is that without the Battle of Trenton we would still be under British control. Also it gave confidence to the Americans. You should reaserch the Battle of Trenton. It is a cool subject.

⑦

Glossary

Hessians- German soilders who were paid by the British.
inaccurate- Not quite right.
casualties- Any thing damget

⑧

FIG. 23–2   Edward's book

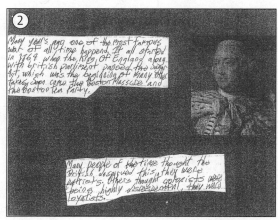

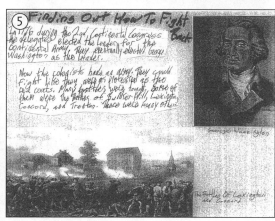

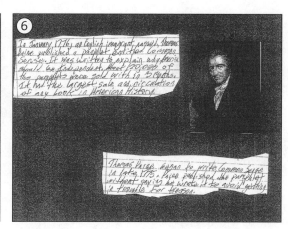

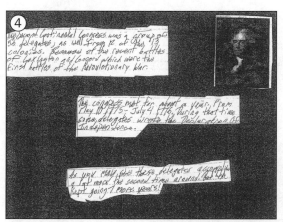

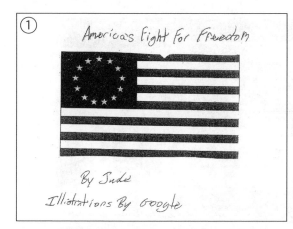

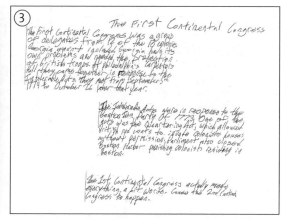

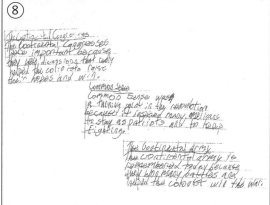

FIG. 23–3   Jude's book

① The Gove ment aft r the Rev lutiona y War

By: Natasha

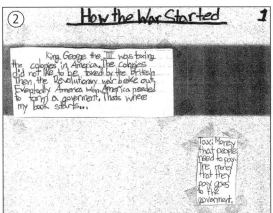

How the War Started 1

King George the III was taxing the colonies in America. The colonies did not like to be taxed by the British. Then, the Revolutionary war broke out. Eventually America won. America needed to form a government. That's where my book starts...

Tax: Money that people need to pay. The money that they pay goes to the government.

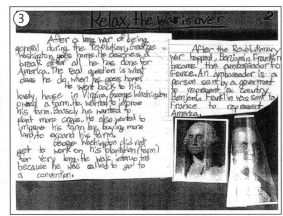

Relax, the war is over 2

After a long war of being general during the Revolution, George Washington goes home. He deserves a break after all he has done for America. The real question is what does he do when he goes home? He went back to his lovely house in Virginia. George Washington owned a farm. He wanted to improve his farm. Basicly he wanted to plant more crops. He also wanted to improve his farm by buying more land to expand his farm.

George Washington did not get to work on his plantation (farm) for very long. He was interrupted because he was called to go to a convention.

After the Revolutionary war happened, Benjamin Franklin became the ambassador to France. An ambassador is a person sent by a government to represent a country. Benjamin Franklin was sent to France to represent America.

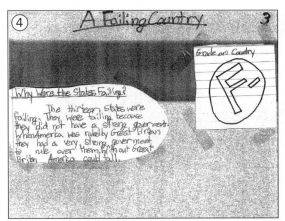

A Failing Country 3

Grade on Country

F

Why Were the States Failing?

The thirteen states were failing. They were failing because they did not have a strong government. When America was ruled by Great Britan they had a very strong government to rule over them. Without great Britan America could fall.

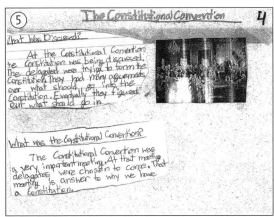

The Constitutional Convention 4

What Was Discused?

At the Constitutional Convention the Constitution was being discussed. The delegates were trying to form the Constitution. They had many arguments over what should go into the Constitution. Eventually they figured out what should go in.

What was the Constitutional Convention?

The Constitutional Convention was a very important meeting. At that meeting delegates were chosen to come. That meeting is answer to why we have a constitution.

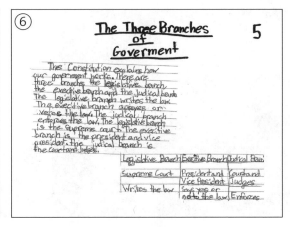

The Three Branches of Goverment 5

The Constitution explains how our government works. There are three branches the legislative branch, the executive branch, and the judicial branch. The legislative branch writes the law. The executive branch approves or vetoes the law. The judicial branch enforces the law. The legislative branch is the Supreme court. The executive branch is the president and vice president. The judicial branch is the court and judges.

Legislative Branch	Executive Branch	Judical Bran
Supreme Court	President and Vice President	Court and Judges
Writes the law	Says yes or no to the law.	Enforces

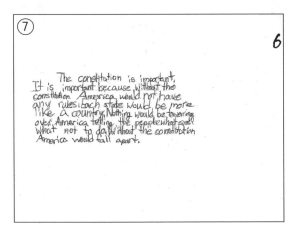

6

The constitution is important. It is important because without the constitution America would not have any rules. Each state would be more like a country. Nothing would be towering over America telling the people what and what not to do. Without the constitution America would fall apart.

FIG. 23–4 Natasha's book

1. THE Midnight Ride! Of Paul Revere

By Grayson

2. THE BIG PICTURE

In the 1770's, a lot was going on. Taxes, taxes, and taxes! King George III & Parliament were slaping out taxes! But after the Boston Massacre, an event where colonists were shot at by British soilders on March 5, 1770, all taxes are removed except the tax on tea. The tea tax was raised in 1773, and that lead to the Boston Tea Party, that led up to the Intolerable Acts. This caused the first Conteintal Congress. In 1775, they had a Second Conteintal Congress that lasted from 1775-1781. Then came the story of ye Midnight Ride.

Word Section
Parliament- a government like the US Congress
tax- a extra price that goes to the government.
ye- old-school word for "the"

3. THE RIDE

Word Section
Sam Adams- leader of Sons of Liberty
John Hancock- president of Conteintal Congress

Paul Revere might have been working when Joseph Warren told him the British were marching to Lexington & Concord to capture Sam Adams and John Hancock and steal American supplies! Him and William Dawes, a patriot, went off. Revere got on a boat to the vilages. A fellow Patriot saw his lantern signal and got him a horse. Have you ever heard of one if by land, two if by sea" It's about Revere's lantern signal, one lantern if the British were attacking by land, two if, you know. So Paul got to Lexington, and saved Adams and Hancock. William came minutes later. They continued on when Samuel Prescott joined. Minutes later, the British got them and Prescott and Dawes escaped. Revere did not. He walked and the British let him go. But they took his horse. As Revere walked back to Lexington, Samuel Prescott saved the supplies in Concord. The Midnight Ride ends.

4. Lost Voices

These men are usually forgotten in the story of the Midnight Ride. The men are Joseph Warren, Willam Dawes, and Samuel Prescott. Joseph Warren started the Midnight Ride. He did not ride. Dr. Warren died on June 17, 1775. Willam Dawes was the second rider. He didn't finish his ride. He died on Feb. 25, 1779. Samuel Prescott was the third rider and the only one who made it to Concord. No one knows when he died.

Don't forget me please!

5. And then what?

So that's not the end of the story! The next morning the Revolutionary War had begun. The colonists fired at the British and those were the Battles of Lexington & Concord. In 1860, Henry Wadsworth Longfellow wrote "Paul Revere's ride." It was unaccurate but still became popular among the public. He knew the real story, but wanted to spice it up. The End. Oh, one last question. Would you change the Midnight Ride?

6. Would you? ANSWER ME!

FIG. 23–5   Grayson's book